A Decisive Decade

A DECISIVE DECADE

AN INSIDER'S VIEW OF THE CHICAGO CIVIL RIGHTS MOVEMENT DURING THE 1960s

Robert B. McKersie

With a Foreword by James R. Ralph Jr.

Southern Illinois University Press
Carbondale

16 15 14 13   4 3 2 1

Publication was partially supported by a grant from the
MIT Sloan School of Management.

Library of Congress Cataloging-in-Publication Data
McKersie, Robert B.
A decisive decade : an insider's view of the Chicago civil
rights movement during the 1960s / Robert B. McKersie ;
with a foreword by James R. Ralph Jr.
    pages   cm
Includes bibliographical references and index.
ISBN 978-0-8093-3244-1 (cloth : alk. paper) — ISBN
0-8093-3244-2 (cloth : alk. paper) — ISBN 978-0-8093-
3245-8 (ebook) (print) — ISBN 0-8093-3245-0 (ebook)
1. McKersie, Robert B. 2. African American civil rights
workers—Illinois—Chicago—Biography 3. African Americans—Civil rights—Illinois—Chicago—History—20th
century. 4. Civil rights movements—Illinois—Chicago—
History—20th century. 5. Civil rights workers—Illinois—
Chicago—Biography 6. Chicago (Ill.)—Race relations.
I. Title.
F548.9.N4M34 2013
323.092—dc23
[B]   2012040463

Printed on recycled paper. ♻
The paper used in this publication meets the minimum
requirements of American National Standard for Information Sciences—Permanence of Paper for Printed Library
Materials, ANSI Z39.48-1992. ♾

To the memory of two ministers who were not
afraid to march and in so doing made their mark:
Rev. Jack Kent and Rev. W. Alvin Pitcher

Contents

Contents

Illustrations

Foreword

James R. Ralph Jr.

Robert McKersie's book *A Decisive Decade: An Insider's View of the Chicago Civil Rights Movement during the 1960s* tells an important story.

It is important for three principal reasons. First, it makes a significant contribution to the burgeoning literature on the black freedom struggle in the North, especially in Chicago, arguably the most important site in that sprawling battleground. Second, it offers an in-depth, firsthand account of how a white professional of conscience became engaged in the fight for racial justice during the 1960s. Third, it is more than a narrative account, for even though McKersie focuses on telling the story of his involvement in a broader struggle, he could not then—nor today—resist asking searching questions about the efficacy of various strategies and tactics in promoting social change.

Recently, the Organization of American Historians' *Magazine of History* devoted an entire issue to the black freedom struggle outside the South.[1] And on the front cover was a picture of Martin Luther King Jr. being struck by a rock in Chicago's Marquette Park during a demonstration in early August 1966. The magazine lined up many of the leading interpreters of the civil rights activism in the North—Thomas Sugrue, Jeanne Theoharis, Lisa Levenstein, and Patrick D. Jones, to name a few. In his overview, Jones stated that while "insightful new work on civil rights struggles outside of the South appears each year, we are still in . . . the 'archeological stage' of this overarching intellectual project, with much terrain yet to be excavated."[2]

McKersie's book reveals that much more can be said about the contours of civil rights in the North, even in one of America's most closely studied cities.[3] And yet McKersie is, in some respects, a surprising author of such a study.

At the start of the 1960s, McKersie was an untenured faculty member of the Industrial Relations Group in the Graduate School of Business at the

University of Chicago, located in Hyde Park on Chicago's South Side. At that point, he did not have a deep history of progressive activism, although his personal convictions and experience primed him to be drawn into the struggle for racial justice. Over the next few years, even as he tended to his growing family and his promising career, he found himself more deeply immersed in the Chicago civil rights movement. But, as he readily concurs, he was never one of its leaders or principal protagonists. Rather, he was one of the many thousands of Chicagoans who participated in the diverse actions of that movement. Over time, his involvement might have been best characterized as contributing to an extraordinary upsurge in activism by ordinary, independent citizens. McKersie, however, possessed both a penchant for keeping files and records and a good memory. And, thus, roughly fifty years after his involvement in the Chicago civil rights movement, he has prepared this timely and insightful book.

McKersie's study deepens our understanding of the fight for racial justice in Chicago. It reminds us that the Chicago Freedom Movement, the remarkable alliance that ran from 1965 to 1967 between the Coordinating Council of Community Organizations (CCCO), a coalition of local civil rights groups, and the Southern Christian Leadership Conference (SCLC), Martin Luther King's organization, was just the most well-known chapter in a much longer and variegated story to advance racial equality.

McKersie's book nicely complements Alan Anderson and George Pickering's *Confronting the Color Line: The Broken Promise of the Civil Rights Movement in Chicago*, which covers in detail the CCCO, the central actor in the Chicago civil rights drama.[4] As the 1960s wore on, McKersie served as a delegate to the CCCO, and he was present at many of its most important meetings and demonstrations. His account evokes the feeling and the flavor of the debates inside the CCCO's meetings and its protests, but he also enlarges our understanding of the Chicago civil rights movement by covering relatively unknown episodes, such as the efforts of the Chicago Negro American Labor Council(NALC) to open up jobs at Motorola, the actual running of a freedom school during a school boycott, and Dick Gregory's marches on Bridgeport in the summer of 1965.

McKersie recognizes that the CCCO did not encapsulate the full range of civil rights efforts in Chicago. That is why his chapter on the work of the NALC in the early 1960s is so important, and toward the end of his study, he features his involvement with Operation Breadbasket, an organization that emerged out of the Chicago Freedom Movement, the alliance between the CCCO and SCLC. Founded in 1966, Operation Breadbasket became the focus of Jesse Jackson's work. And while the CCCO disintegrated in the aftermath of the open-housing marches in the summer of 1966, Operation Breadbasket, under Jackson's dynamic leadership, emerged as the central engine in the fight for racial justice in the Windy City.[5]

McKersie's emphasis on the various streams within the Chicago civil rights struggle aligns his study with one of the most significant developments in recent scholarship on the northern front in the fight for racial equality. As Jeanne Theoharis has argued in *Freedom North: Black Freedom Struggles outside the South, 1940–1980,* "tens of thousands of people were active in freedom movements of varying ideologies" in the North during the middle decades of the twentieth century.[6] McKersie, it is true, does not attempt a full inventory of protest currents in Chicago, and while he does mention the influence of more radical black leaders like Lawrence Landry, he does not link the civil rights battles of the first half of the 1960s with the later agenda of the Black Panther Party or probe the relationship of civil rights activism to the rise of Black Power, as many recent books do, including Komozi Woodard's *A Nation within a Nation: Amiri Baraka (LeRoi Jones) and Black Power Politics* and Matthew Countryman's *Up South: Civil Rights and Black Power in Philadelphia.*[7]

McKersie's attention to the multiple issues that activists engaged also conforms to a recent trend in civil rights historiography. The multiplicity of targets of northern activists was stressed in a pioneering study in 1973 by August Meier and Elliot Rudwick, *CORE: A Study in the Civil Rights Movement.*[8] In 2008, Thomas Sugrue organized his seminal history of the northern battleground, *Sweet Land of Liberty: The Forgotten Struggle for Civil Rights in the North,* around this theme.[9] McKersie features the assaults on discrimination in public education and then in the housing market, the most well-known targets of Chicago insurgents during the 1960s, but he also shows how access to quality jobs and economic opportunity was an ongoing concern.[10]

The recent surge in scholarship on the northern freedom movement has seen books explore developments in Philadelphia, Milwaukee, St. Louis, Wichita, Seattle, and elsewhere.[11] These studies have greatly extended our appreciation for the geographical extent of northern activism and also for the extent of local variation. Perhaps not surprisingly, in some quarters the Chicago story has been viewed as something of an aberration, even a distortion, of the general trends in northern insurgency.[12] No doubt this reading is in large part a response to the fact that Chicago was, unlike these other cities, a place where the southern and northern movements fully merged. The Chicago Freedom Movement was the product of that merging, and, as a result, developments in Chicago from 1965 to 1967 have been closely investigated by scholars.[13]

Not only in this foreword but in other venues as well, I have strenuously made the case for the significance of the Chicago Freedom Movement.[14] Robert McKersie also recognizes the importance of the alliance of the CCCO and SCLC, although unfortunately he was away on sabbatical leave during most of the formative period of the Chicago Freedom Movement. He does, however, leave us with a riveting, firsthand account of participating in an open-housing march on Chicago's Southwest Side in late July 1966.

But the most important message from McKersie's study is that it was not just on account of whim that Martin Luther King and the SCLC selected Chicago as the site for their first nonviolent, direct-action campaign in the North. They were persuaded to come to Chicago because it had—as McKersie documents—arguably the most vibrant indigenous movement outside of the South.

A Decisive Decade, as McKersie himself describes it, is a hybrid. It is, he writes, "[the] fusion of a participant's journal and an analysis of the civil rights movement as it unfolded during the 1960s in Chicago." Civil rights studies have been greatly enriched by a wealth of memoirs and autobiographies that have been published. Here I think of the accounts by leaders in the SCLC (Ralph Abernathy and Andrew Young), in the Student Nonviolent Coordinating Committee (John Lewis, Stokely Carmichael, James Forman, Cleveland Sellers, and Mary King, to name a few), and in the Congress of Racial Equality (James Farmer).[15] But this nice run of firsthand accounts has largely focused on southern developments. There is a need for more memoirs and autobiographies of activists primarily based in the North.[16]

Published accounts by participants in the Chicago freedom struggle are rare. The Reverend Arthur M. Brazier offered in 1969 an assessment of the early years of the Woodlawn Organization, an organization that, along with Saul Alinsky, he helped to found.[17] Dempsey Travis later wrote two notable books about black Chicago, which incorporated recollections of his involvement with the Chicago NAACP in the 1950s and 1960s.[18] The most comparable book to McKersie's is Don Benedict's *Born Again Radical*.[19] Like McKersie's study, it offers a progressive white man's perspective on the struggle for racial equality in Chicago. Benedict's memoir tells the story of a life that was fully intertwined with the struggle for social justice starting with his work in inner-city parishes in Harlem and Cleveland in the 1940s and with the Chicago City Missionary Society in the 1960s, before he became involved in the Chicago civil rights struggle. Benedict was not as involved as McKersie in activities associated with the CCCO.

We do not have memoirs for the three most prominent whites in the Chicago civil rights movement—John McDermott of the Catholic Interracial

Council, Kale Williams of the American Friends Service Committee, and Al Pitcher, McKersie's friend. Unlike McKersie, McDermott and Williams played leadership roles in the CCCO because they headed well-established local activist groups and served on the Agenda Committee of the Chicago Freedom Movement, which gave them access to the inside stories of some of the most important decisions in civil rights circles in Chicago during the 1960s. Pitcher was the other white person who figured very prominently in the Chicago civil rights story. And while this University of Chicago Divinity School professor who became an indispensable assistant to Al Raby, the convener of the CCCO, wrote reflective essays on the Chicago Freedom Movement, he did not write a memoir.[20] Pitcher's influence has often been noted, but McKersie's portrait of Pitcher and of his contribution to Chicago activism is the most revealing in print to date.

The role of white liberals in the struggle for racial equality has been commented on and debated for decades. Martin Luther King Jr. sought to build as broad a "coalition of conscience" as possible.[21] But by the middle of the 1960s, black militants were regularly denouncing the cancerous influence of white liberals.[22] McKersie does not exhaustively engage this debate, but he nicely illuminates how a young academic, with a growing family, could be drawn, step-by-step, into one of the most compelling causes of the day. McKersie is neither a romantic nor preoccupied by self-introspection. His account of his journey is refreshingly straightforward, direct, and candid.

Like many white progressives, McKersie was propelled into activism by his church.[23] To be sure, his academic preoccupations—he was at the time a professor of industrial relations and mediation—made him sensitive to inequalities in the workplace, but it was the growing moral concerns about racial injustice pulsating through the First Unitarian Church of Chicago that fired his activist spirit.

The First Unitarian Church, located in Hyde Park, hosted an Adult Discussion Group before its weekly services. With the escalating evidence of injustices in America, the Adult Discussion Group grew in size and its sessions became more intense. McKersie was later named the convener of this group. And he also was active in the Social Action Committee of the church, its direct interface with the civil rights movement.

McKersie's moral discomfort with racial discrimination was reinforced by growing friendships with black Chicagoans. The extent to which most white people and black people lived separate lives—reinforced by housing, school, and economic segregation—is well established in the middle decades of the twentieth century, but McKersie reveals how friendships across the racial divide could heighten awareness of the shaping role of race in America.[24]

McKersie became friends with two of the most extraordinary black Chi-cagoans of the second half of the twentieth century—Timuel Black and Alex Poinsett. The First Unitarian Church was the space that gave rise to these interracial friendships. McKersie's friendship with Black quickly became tied to activism. By 1960, Black had become the head of the Chicago Negro American Labor Council, a new group founded by the famed civil rights leader A. Philip Randolph, who was seeking a new vehicle to promote em-ployment opportunities for African Americans. Black was a teacher by day in Hyde Park High School, but he threw himself into the work of the NALC in his own thoughtful, low-key way. Black possessed a special concern about the lack of access for African Americans into the skilled trades, and that concern resonated with McKersie's own research into the dynamics of in-dustrial relations in America.

Poinsett was a native Chicagoan who grew up in poverty; a veteran of World War II; and by the 1960s, a leading writer for *Ebony*, one of the most important black publications in the country. McKersie and Poinsett engaged in a decade-long dialogue about current affairs, especially race relations.

The lengthy, intense exchanges between McKersie and Poinsett point to another important—perhaps the most important—characteristic of *A Decisive Decade*. McKersie is now—and was then—very reflective about the strategies and tactics employed by civil rights activists. Without question, this tendency resulted from his profession, with its premium on analysis. And it also certainly flowed from his step-by-step evolution into activism, conditioned by the heady seminars of the First Unitarian Church's Adult Discussion Group. Indeed, in the midst of debates over the wisdom of the sec-ond school boycott called by the CCCO in February 1964, McKersie offered a stirring defense of the call for black parents to keep their children out of the public schools in protest of an unresponsive school administration. But, on the whole, McKersie was inclined to ask questions about the efficacy of direct action. He did so after the Good Friday demonstration against School Super-intendent Benjamin Willis in the spring of 1965; he did so again during the downtown marches against Willis in the summer of 1965; and he questioned Dick Gregory's decision later that summer to march to Bridgeport, the home of Mayor Richard J. Daley. At one point, he asks if all of the person-hours allotted to demonstrating could have been better spent on other kinds of initiatives. (Interestingly, McKersie frequently participated in such marches as a sign of solidarity even if he possessed reservations.) At the end of his study, he offers a thought-provoking assessment of the various approaches employed by civil rights groups, including boycotts, demonstrations, and community mobilization. The question of the best strategy was certainly on the minds of leaders in the black freedom struggle. Martin Luther King Jr.'s *Where Do We Go from Here* and Stokely Carmichael's *Black Power* were just two of the most famous treatises in the debate over what approaches would work best. What is distinctive about McKersie's reflections and analysis is that they are directed to decisions about local, Chicago tactics, albeit with implications elsewhere.[25]

A Decisive Decade tells us that there is much still to be learned about, and learned from, the Chicago civil rights movement. That movement was part of a broader struggle unfolding across the country during the 1960s. But it also had immense consequences, shaping the election of Harold Washington, Chicago's first black mayor, in 1983, and then the two historic runs for the Democratic nomination for president by Jesse Jackson in 1984 and 1988. All of this ferment in Chicago attracted a young Columbia graduate to this midwestern metropolis. It is inconceivable that Barack Obama would have been elected president in 2008 had he not chosen to come to Chicago. The reverberations of events in Chicago in the 1960s have not yet faded.[26]

Preface

At the outset, I would like to offer a few words of explanation for this fusion of a participant's journal and an academic's analysis of the civil rights movement as it unfolded during the 1960s in Chicago.

Upon retiring from full-time work as a faculty member at MIT, and finding time to start "putting my papers in order," I turned to my 1960s files, recordings, notes, and "fugitive" materials gleaned while I participated in the civil rights movement. Initially, I envisioned a project of short duration—basically assembling the pieces that had been written during the fall of 1965 while on sabbatical leave at the London School of Economics—with the objective of placing them in some appropriate historical archives.

However, as I reviewed the materials, I reached the conclusion that they contained stories and insights that could be of interest to a wider audience. I am familiar with the literature, now quite voluminous, about the surge in civil rights activities during the 1960s, and I felt my observations could add some new data and perspectives. Among other things, I wanted to describe the uncertain path that white liberals traveled during the 1960s in attempting to bridge the racial divide. My initial thought was to write a novel as a way of dramatizing the events and the personalities, while at the same time protecting relationships. But I am too deeply engaged in the nonfiction accounts of a social science researcher for that to be a serious option.

So I decided to develop a chronicle of the civil rights movement of Chicago, largely from the perspective of a participant-observer—a participant, as defined by my activist role during the 1960s in the civil rights movement of Chicago, and at the same time an observer, as defined by my penchant for analysis and reflection. So this story is a product of the feet (marching), of the heart (commitment), and of the head (commentary).

Unless otherwise noted, the story of how the civil rights movement in Chicago unfolded during the 1960s that I tell relies on my notes dictated during the 1960s. In addition, I have referred to minutes from the many meetings I attended and other documents that I archived. In a number of instances I have conducted follow-up interviews, and these augmenting perspectives are so identified.

The timeline of this memoir begins with the early 1960s and finishes with the end of that decade. For many reasons, this time period can be thought of as a defining era politically and socially—highlighted by the Vietnam War with its accompanying domestic turmoil and the demographics that saw postwar "baby boomers" coming of age.

I believe the case can also be made that the decade of the 1960s was also a defining era for race relations. While the drumbeat for racial equality had started before 1960 (e.g., the Montgomery bus boycott, December 1955 to November 1956; and the integration of Little Rock High School, September 1957), what came to be called the civil rights movement or "revolution" assumed prominence with the lunch counter sit-ins that began in February 1960,[1] freedom rides on buses in May 1961, the jailing of Martin Luther King Jr. in Birmingham, Alabama in April 1963, and the march on Washington of August 1963.

Consequently, the years between 1960, when President John F. Kennedy took office, and 1968, when Rev. Martin Luther King Jr. was killed, can be seen as a fundamentally different period of time in the tenor and history of race relations than our country has experienced either before or since. The major developments for what I call the "decisive decade" at both the national and Chicago levels are captured in a timeline found in Appendix C.

Until recently, accounts of the civil rights movement, and indeed, the way most Americans viewed the racial struggles of the 1960s, situated the story in the South, illustrated by the geographical locale of the events just mentioned. However, recently a number of scholars have sought to correct this impression with documentation of the activism that occurred in the North.

Foremost in this collection is the monumental study by Thomas Sugrue, *Sweet Land of Liberty: The Forgotten Struggle for Civil Rights in the North*,[2] a comprehensive treatment of the civil rights movement in the major urban centers of the North, including New York City, Detroit, Philadelphia, and Chicago. His coverage begins in the 1920s and documents the unfolding story of the struggle for racial equality through the years, right up to the beginning of the twenty-first century.

Another publication joining the effort to document the history of the civil rights movement in the North is *Freedom North: Black Freedom Struggles outside the South, 1940–1980* by Jeanne Theoharis and Kozomi Woodard.[3] Separate chapters address developments in New York City, Detroit, Oakland,

Newark, and Chicago. The focus of the section on Chicago is on the Black Panther organization.

Other scholars have produced important histories of the civil rights movement in key cities. Martha Biondi, in her book *To Stand and Fight: The Struggle for Civil Rights in Post-War New York City*, chronicles the development of the movement in this major metropolis. Although set in New York City, this story has interesting connections to developments in Chicago. In 1964, Rev. Milton Galamison, following a similar event in Chicago, "led the biggest act of civil disobedience of the decade when thousands of parents heeded his call to boycott the racially segregated public schools."[4]

In his book *Up South: Civil Rights and Black Power in Philadelphia*, Matthew Countryman[5] describes black activism, with special attention to the pioneering work of Rev. Leon Sullivan. One of Sullivan's key strategies, selective patronage, inspired Jesse Jackson to launch Operation Breadbasket in Chicago, and this organization plays a central role in the story of the civil rights movement in Chicago during the 1960s and beyond.

Patrick Jones, with an engagingly titled book, *The Selma of the North: Civil Rights Insurgency in Milwaukee*,[6] presents the high drama and the special role of a Catholic priest, Father James Groppi, in the civil rights movement in that city.

For the most part, these chronicles of the civil rights movement in several northern cities describe the main events, but they do not fully capture the moods and feelings of the participants. Such a vantage point has been vividly presented in the personal story of Mary King and in the interviews conducted by Doug McAdam. However, these observations and perspectives are anchored in the events that transpired in the South.[7]

Turning to Chicago, it is not surprising that a city with the second-largest African American population in the country and the setting for a series of dramatic events in the 1960s has prompted several studies. James Ralph, *Northern Protests: Martin Luther King Jr., Chicago, and the Civil Rights Movement*,[8] focuses on the campaign to achieve open housing during the summer of 1966. In *Confronting the Color Line: The Broken Promise of the Civil Rights Movement in Chicago*, Alan Anderson and George Pickering[9] tracked the activities of the Coordinating Council of Community Organizations and the Chicago Freedom Movement, culminating in the protest marches led by Rev. Martin Luther King Jr. during the summer of 1966.

The question then could be asked: Why another study of the Chicago civil rights movement? The answer rests with the firsthand perspective that I was afforded on major episodes and activist organizations that showcased this important decade. I now turn to outlining these vantage points.

• Early on, I focus on the subject of *employment*, especially efforts by the Negro American Labor Council (NALC)[10] to expand hiring and advancement opportunities for African Americans at the Motorola Corporation. Specifically, I helped plan a direct-action program that forced Motorola to enter into negotiations with NALC, and I participated in those talks. Several years later, when Motorola challenged a decision of the Illinois Fair Employment Practices Commission (FEPC), I criticized the company publicly. In the process, I strained relations between Motorola and my employer, the Graduate School of Business at the University of Chicago.

• Then the story shifts to *education* and the campaign waged by the Coordinating Council of Community Organizations (CCCO) to unseat Benjamin Willis, the superintendent of the Chicago school system. As one of two delegates from the Unitarian-Universalist Churches of Chicago to the CCCO, I participated in decisions regarding school boycotts, marches, and demonstrations aimed at forcing the ouster of Willis. As a result, I was able to observe at close range the leadership of this nerve center of the civil rights movement in Chicago. Between 1963 to 1966, when the campaign was in high gear, I often found myself in a more activist position than the majority of the church congregation I represented, yet at the same time becoming increasingly uneasy about the escalating tactics of the CCCO, especially the decision to conduct nightly marches during the summer of 1965 into Bridgeport, the home neighborhood of Mayor Daley.

• With the arrival of Martin Luther King Jr. and his Southern Christian Leadership Conference (SCLC) in the summer of 1966, the chronicle shifts to *housing* and the marches that were held in various parts of the city aimed at dramatizing the pervasiveness of residential segregation. Being an activist in the North during the 1960s normally did not carry with it the same risks of bodily harm as was the case in the South. However, in one instance when I joined an open housing march on the Southwest Side of Chicago during July 1966, the scene quickly turned violent as the crowd pelted us with rocks and bottles and set fire to our parked automobiles. To say the least, I was frightened and saddened by this episode.

• Upon returning from a sabbatical leave in June 1966 and capitalizing on my role as professor of business, I joined Operation Breadbasket, participated in the membership committee that screened applications from fledgling businesses, conducted seminars with the help of MBA students, and developed an appreciation for the leadership talents of Rev. Jesse Jackson. The Breadbasket story is framed within the larger theme of *minority business development.*

My vantage point over the decade of the 1960s varied, as the agenda of the civil rights movement unfolded in Chicago. My involvement took shape as a result of my membership in the First Unitarian Church of Chicago, and throughout the book the deliberations of the church's board of trustees, its Social Action Committee, and the congregation are presented to illustrate the tensions and dilemmas that the strategy and tactics of the civil rights movement created for "religious liberals." Black consciousness took hold toward the end of the decade, creating tough choices and numerous dilemmas for members of the congregation.

The other end of my life was the university. As a junior faculty member "bucking for tenure," my involvement in the civil rights movement carried with it both pull (the excitement of working for an important cause) and push back ("McKersie, remember your priorities to publish in refereed journals").

Because the university is such a large institutional presence on the South Side of Chicago,[11] I was regularly asked by activists, "How can the university be persuaded to help?" Given its location, Hyde Park, and given the urban challenges facing adjoining communities like Woodlawn, the university needed to, and did, find ways to get involved; specifically, by providing staff support to the Woodlawn Organization (TWO) in developing its Model Cities proposal and launching the Black MBA Scholars program.

Today (2012), the South Side of Chicago has bragging rights that were not available to it at the time of the civil rights movement in the 1960s. Two African Americans who have lived in or near Hyde Park during formative periods of their lives have risen to unprecedented heights in the political world: Deval Patrick, governor of Massachusetts; and Barack Obama, president of the United States.

Four individuals appear and reappear throughout the book. Tim Black introduced me to the civil rights movement, and his thoughtful leadership inspired me to help his organization (NALC) design and implement several direct-action programs. Rev. Al Pitcher (now deceased) was probably the most influential white leader in the movement at the Chicago level. He played key roles in the CCCO and Operation Breadbasket. He came to live with us one summer, and having him close at hand deepened my understanding and involvement in the civil rights movement. Throughout the story, I include material from my many conversations with Alex Poinsett, a talented writer with whom I have engaged in friendly sparring over the past forty years. The fourth individual is Rev. Jesse Jackson who, early in the development of Operation Breadbasket, challenged me as a professor from a business school to apply my energies and those of my students in behalf of black economic development. These four "heroes" demonstrate the possibilities of working for social change on a multiracial basis.

Before ending this memoir, I have an obligation to answer a few questions: What difference did the civil rights movement of the 1960s make? Why did some activist organizations have more staying power? Should the civil rights movement of Chicago be viewed as a failure?

Finally, working across and within the racial divide is fraught with many dilemmas and choices, and I will present in the final chapter some thoughts about this important subject which is a work in progress for our country.

Acknowledgments

The events portrayed in this book occurred almost half a century ago. Given the fact that this chronicle attempts to present an eyewitness account of the civil rights movement in Chicago during the 1960s, the question could be asked: what took you so long to get this story into print? Well, it took extensive reflection to bring these dramatic events into focus. At the same time, many individuals have helped shape my understanding as this account moved through many stages of development. So, fundamentally, this book is really an acknowledgment, writ large, to the many friends and associates who helped tell the story.

I could stop here and say "thank you" to all of those who appear in this memoir, and in this sense, I would be a drummer boy for the larger parade of individuals involved in the civil rights movement during that decisive decade. At the same time, however, there is a back story that begins with individuals who first typed my notes and others who provided diligent and careful work, organizing and correcting the many rounds of revision. They include Barbara Newbury, Ossadell Lambert, Cherie Potts, Pat Steffens, and Keira Horowitz.

Colleagues and former students willingly agreed to read the manuscript and offered helpful comments. They include Thomas Kochan, Rick Locke, Kirsten Wever, Mary Rowe, and Gerd Korman. In the same vein, I would like to thank two readers who provided incredibly helpful commentary: James Ralph and Aldon Morris.

Seth Patner knows Chicago and its diverse neighborhoods, and he contributed invaluable information to my understanding of the shifting makeup of racial neighborhoods (embodied in appendix B, "Chicago Geography").

Terry McKiernan, Holly Menino Bailey, and John Wilson applied their editing talents to what has been an extended work in progress.

Librarians are often the unrecognized members of the support team, and in this regard, I would like to thank Anita Perkins of MIT, as well as her colleagues at several other universities, all of whom have been extremely helpful in searching their archives for images that bring the civil rights movement alive: the University of Illinois, Urbana and Chicago campuses; Wayne State University; and the University of Chicago. Anyone interested in reviewing documentation from the 1960s will find a rich resource in the Urban League Collection at the University of Illinois at Chicago Library.

William LaCapra, a freelance video professional, also provided invaluable assistance in assembling images for this book, and Jill Manca created the two maps that locate the major events I describe.

Finally, I thank my wife, Nancy C. McKersie, for her support and for allowing me to create and occupy office space on all four floors of our home.

A Decisive Decade

Prologue: Starting an Academic Career

When I finished my graduate studies at Harvard Business School in the spring of 1959, our parents hoped that Nancy and I would locate somewhere on the East Coast. My parents lived in New Jersey, as had their parents; Nancy's parents and ancestors had always lived in New England, primarily in western Massachusetts. When we announced that we would be going west—almost a thousand miles away to Chicago—they accepted the decision with good spirit. After all, this was the expected pattern for the first generation to graduate from college: seize the best opportunities, even if that meant a long-distance move.

Selecting the University of Chicago as my first academic employer was easy. Finding an academic position in the 1950s did not involve the careful search and candidacy procedures that characterize today's academic job market. My supervising professor, E. Robert Livernash, knew George Shultz (they had taught together at MIT), so Robert picked up the phone and called George who, just a few years before, had been recruited to establish an Industrial Relations Group at the Graduate School of Business at the University of Chicago. "George, you should take a look at my student, Bob McKersie. He has been doing research for his dissertation right there in Chicago [at International Harvester] and he would be a good addition to your team." So I spent a day meeting faculty at the Graduate School of Business. The new leadership team outlined their plans to put the business school "on the map" with a first-rate program emphasizing coursework in the underlying disciplines of economics, quantitative methods, and organizational behavior. I wondered whether my bent for the case method and lack of formal coursework in many of the key subject areas would be a handicap. "No," they answered. "We need some individuals like you with your practical interests to balance our more theoretically oriented faculty." So I agreed to join the faculty, starting in September 1959.

Nancy had not accompanied me on my recruiting trip to the university the preceding spring. So we did not have housing lined up, and we felt like gypsies as we headed west. And to add to the suspense, Nancy was close to term with our first youngster, due sometime in early October. We were driving an Oldsmobile station wagon with no air conditioning, making our drive in early September quite uncomfortable. Between the roar of the powerful engine and the flow of air through the open windows, we felt like pioneers of some sort, heading for new beginnings.

When we arrived, Hyde Park was in the throes of urban renewal, with many buildings coming down—and their replacements not yet constructed. As a result, the housing market was extremely tight. Fortunately, Nancy met a building superintendent who took a liking to her and felt inclined to help this expectant mother find space for her family. He lined up a third-floor walkup for us, about a mile from campus.

As was the case for many faculty members, our decision to live in Hyde Park rather than in the suburbs brought with it regular and intense exposure to most aspects of race relations. Nancy and I saw this as a plus. While many of our friends back East wondered about the wisdom of living on the "dangerous South Side" of Chicago, we considered living in Hyde Park an adventure.

At the office, space was also tight. The renaissance that the school was experiencing translated into many new faculty hires, and I was asked if I would mind sharing an office with an economist. Not at all, especially since economics dominated the pecking order of disciplines at the Graduate School of Business. While the Chicago School of Economics had not yet garnered national recognition, luminaries such as Milton Friedman and George Stigler were very much on the scene.

My immediate reference group consisted of labor economists, including Greg Lewis and Albert Rees from the economics department, and George Shultz and Arnie Weber from the business school. Joel Seidman, a sociologist, completed the group. Since I did not have a PhD in economics, but rather a doctorate in business administration with a behavioral concentration, I found Joel a kindred spirit.

In terms of their political leanings, most members of the faculty were decidedly Republican. I can remember being invited to the home of George Shultz in November 1960 to watch the election returns for the presidential race between Kennedy and Nixon, and learning that the only other Democrat in the room was Al Rees. Later Al became provost of Princeton University and thereafter president of the Sloan Foundation.

When I started at the university in October 1959, I plunged immediately into teaching two sections of a collective bargaining course. Students in the collective bargaining course were required to complete a term paper, and one of my students, Monty Brown, who was enrolled in the personnel and industrial relations concentration of the MBA program, asked for approval to study an organizing drive at a nearby facility with the hard-to-believe name of the "Home for Incurables" and a larger teaching hospital named Mt. Sinai. Of course, I approved the proposal. What could be more suitable for his course project than studying organizing strikes initiated by the local district of the American Federation of State, County, and Municipal Employees (AFSCME) after management at these two institutions refused to recognize the union, even though a majority of workers had signed authorization cards? Most of the nonprofessional workers, who were striking for recognition at the Home for Incurables, were what would be classified today as minorities: a few Hispanic and the vast majority, African American.

In 1959, hospitals were not covered by the National Labor Relations Act (NLRA) nor were any State of Illinois statutes applicable, so the union could not avail itself of any statutory procedure, such as a representative election, that could lead to certification. Consequently, it did what unions have long done (before the NLRA): it initiated a strike, hoping that management would be forced to recognize the union. Instead, management hired replacements.

The director of the organizing campaign was a young leader, Victor Gotbaum, not long out of college—he had studied psychology at City College in New York City. I could not help wondering what Gotbaum was thinking in seeking to organize the nonprofessional workers at these two healthcare institutions, Mt. Sinai and the Home for Incurables. Was he onto something that would represent a breakthrough in organizing hospital workers, especially in the occupations where blacks were heavily represented? Quite possibly, if the nonprofessional workers at these two institutions could be organized, then other organizing victories across the growing sector of health care might be successful.

Gotbaum knew the campaign would be difficult. Many observers asked the question: Why would these workers have any interest in joining the union that Gotbaum represented, or for that matter, any union? Both positive and negative forces were at work. As of the early 1960s, the percentages of blacks and whites in unions were reasonably comparable, falling in the range of 30–35 percent.[1] Given the fact that unionization occurred primarily among the semi-skilled and unskilled workers—where the preponderance of African Americans worked—it was a puzzle that their membership in unions was not higher than that.

To this paradox, Julius Jacobson observed: "The Negro masses today, on the whole, have an attitude that covers the narrow range from indifference to pronounced hostility towards the American trade union movement."°¡° What were some of the historical reasons for this attitude? As will be noted in a subsequent discussion of efforts to bring blacks into apprenticeship programs, most craft unions had excluded blacks. History also had played a role: during the 1920s and 1930s, many black workers had been recruited by the steel and meatpacking industries in Chicago as replacements for striking white workers, thus placing black workers in direct conflict with the organizing efforts of the unions in those industries. Given all these background factors, the prospects for organizing the workers at Mt. Sinai and the Home for Incurables could be seen at best as very uncertain.

The campaigns at the Home for Incurables and Mt. Sinai represented, in a way, a type of baptism for Gotbaum. The strikers referred to him as their "white Moses" with the expectation that he would deliver them out of the "bondage" of their low salaries and poor working conditions. He divided his time between the picket lines at the Home and at Mt. Sinai. Often he napped in his old station wagon, a necessity given the long hours spent supporting the strikers with food and words of encouragement.

Gotbaum's lieutenant was Lillian Roberts, an African American and chief steward at the nearby University of Chicago Hospital, where a collective bargaining relationship existed. She found the task of maintaining the morale of the strikers especially important and challenging. Like Gotbaum, she never left the picket line. As she put it, "You had people who got a little bit down and I wanted to be there for them. And if they didn't

tell me, others would tell me that I needed to talk to one of them and keep us cohesive." Roberts observed that many of the strikers did not have the necessities, "milk and stuff like that. And I could help them with that."[3]

Both strikes dragged on through the fall of 1959 without success. Out of economic necessity, many workers returned to work. Gotbaum and his staff kept close track of the "stalwarts" who stayed with the organizing

Lillian Roberts and Victor Gotbaum, who led organizing drives in Chicago at Mt. Sinai Hospital and the Home for Incurables, fall 1959. Courtesy AFSCME, District Council 37 Photographs Collection, Robert F. Wagner Labor Archives/Tamiment Library, New York University.

campaigns to the very end when the drives were finally terminated in January 1960. Roberts and Gotbaum contacted other unions and attempted to find jobs for all the strikers. As Roberts noted, "The workers wanted a union and went on strike for this. We could not let them down."

After the organizing effort at the two hospitals ended, Gotbaum returned to New York City to head the large local of the AFSCME, District Council 37, representing a wide range of municipal workers. Roberts accompanied him, serving the union in a variety of roles. Roberts subsequently capped her career by becoming the industrial commissioner for the State of New York during the 1980s. In 2005, she came out of retirement to be elected executive director of District Council 37. After retiring from the labor movement, Gotbaum held a chair at City University of New York for many years.

While these organizing drives and accompanying strikes were not successful, they set the stage for others that occurred later during the 1960s. Specifically, when Martin Luther King brought his SCLC organization to Chicago in late 1965, a coalition involving AFSCME and several civil rights organizations was formed, launching organizing drives at several hospitals, especially on the West Side of Chicago.

My student, Monty Brown, and I were able to collect information about who struck, who returned to work, and who remained on the picket line until the bitter end. At this early stage in my career, my interests concerning the economic position of blacks were primarily academic. Neither Monty nor I carried picket signs or wrote letters to the management of the two institutions protesting their refusal to recognize the union; rather we saw our role as observing, collecting data, and answering research questions.[4]

However, as I think back to that first year on the faculty at the University of Chicago, I can see that at some unconscious level, observing the commitment and dedication of labor leaders like Victor Gotbaum and Lillian Roberts clearly had set the stage for my own involvement in what was emerging across the country: a major civil rights movement, or what some termed a civil rights revolution. In Lillian Roberts, I saw a talented worker who was willing to take a big risk by joining the campaign to organize low-paid hospital workers. In Victor Gotbaum, I saw an idealistic young leader who sacrificed traditional comforts by sleeping in a station wagon as the only way to stay in touch with those on the picket lines.

While I subscribed to the highly analytical approach of my colleagues in the business school and economics department and felt fortunate to be on the faculty at the university, at the same time, I felt uneasy about remaining on the sidelines as an observer. Both Nancy and I shared deep concerns about the social and economic position of blacks, and we were looking for ways to take constructive action. Balancing or reconciling these two values—the objective stance of the academic and the passion of the activist seeking social change—would characterize and dominate my life throughout the 1960s and beyond.

1. The First Unitarian Church of Chicago: My Gateway to the Civil Rights Movement and to Alex Poinsett

There have been many unsung heroes of the civil rights movement who were Unitarian Universalists.

—Amanda Smith, High Street Unitarian
Universalist Church, Macon, Georgia

I became part of the civil rights movement in Chicago as a result of my membership in the First Unitarian Church of Chicago.

While an undergraduate at the University of Pennsylvania, I had been active in the university's Christian Association and came to know Bob and Wanda VanGoor. Bob and I had served as counselors at University Camp (more about this experience later), and I kept in close touch with the Van-Goors while I was in the navy, visiting them several times in New Haven where Bob studied for a bachelor of divinity degree. Upon graduating from Yale, Bob decided that rather than work as a minister he could better serve society by getting involved in the then-nascent concept of health maintenance organizations. He took a position as executive director for the Group Health Foundation in Chicago.

While doing fieldwork for my dissertation at Harvard Business School, I visited and sometimes stayed with the VanGoors, who had decided to live in Hyde Park. As a result, I became acquainted with the community. Wanda was active in the Hyde Park–Kenwood Neighborhood Association and several other service organizations, and I came to appreciate the activism of the community's many residents.

When we decided to move to Chicago, the opportunity to live in Hyde Park—an interracial community with some of the same characteristics (due to its location near the university) as I had experienced in Cambridge, Massachusetts—was appealing. Soon after moving to Hyde Park in the fall of 1959, Nancy and I decided to check out the Unitarian Church where Bob and Wanda were active members. We joined the church, and our first two children, Bill and Liz, were dedicated there.

I welcomed this opportunity to be a part of the community at the Unitarian church. I saw it as a good balance to my work at the university. The latter, with its emphasis on research and rigorous analysis, and to some extent embodying a fairly conservative approach to social problems, often left me with the feeling that my "glass was half empty." The folks at the Unitarian church, while not rabid and emotional (as subsequent chapters will demonstrate)—indeed, they tended to intellectualize—reasoned from a liberal perspective, one that I found quite congenial and supportive of the emerging civil rights movement.

Soon after joining the church, I began attending the Adult Discussion Group, which met an hour before the regular church service, and before long, I agreed to facilitate the weekly meetings.

My role in chairing the Adult Discussion Group required gathering background materials, setting the agenda, and keeping a firm hand on discussions that generated wide-ranging opinions and perspectives. When I first joined the group, it numbered about ten or twelve participants. However, as the galvanizing events of the early 1960s unfolded, attendance grew, and fairly soon the group numbered thirty to forty individuals. Two sisters traveled from Evanston each Sunday, and they remarked that the spirited give-and-take of the discussion group "made their week worthwhile."

Two black individuals, Alex Poinsett and Tim Black, were both very active in the group. They became close friends, were instrumental in shaping my thinking and motivating me to get involved in the unfolding civil rights movement in Chicago. Alex spoke eloquently and passionately, capsuling the thinking of the black community. His eloquence was illustrated in a sermon he delivered as part of the service conducted by the Adult Discussion Group on Layman's Sunday. He stood in the pulpit, his dark skin complemented by the walnut woodwork. After a few quips about being an NAU (Negro American Unitarian), in which he differentiated himself from WASU (White Anglo Saxon Unitarian), he delivered a stunning talk about what Unitarianism meant to him.

Alex existed in two worlds. His feet were certainly in the African American community. He grew up with five sisters in Depression-era Chicago. His family was so poor, he reflected at one point, that some days they had only sugar sandwiches to eat. In 1944, he was drafted into the U.S. Navy, where he experienced the same segregation he found in housing and education in Chicago, replicating what he called "America's top-down, border-to-border racism."

The G.I. Bill funded his BS in journalism and MA in philosophy at the University of Illinois. But jobs were hard to come by. The publisher of *Ebony*

Alex Poinsett in Gary, Indiana, at an October 1970 event honoring the publication of his book *Black Power, Gary Style: The Making of Mayor Richard Gordon Hacker.* Courtesy Alex Poinsett.

and *Jet* magazines finally gave him a job as a file clerk in the print morgue. Within two months, however, Poinsett became a *Jet* editor. Seven years later, he was promoted to the *Ebony* staff.

Even though his accomplishments definitely placed him in the professional class, he and his wife, Norma, a schoolteacher, lived in the all-black neighborhood, Chatham. Their attractive home was well landscaped, and Alex's careful dress and polished speech also attested to his middle-class status. Unlike some blacks on the way up, Alex did not forget his background. In fact, he was proud of his ghetto origins. The problems of poverty, discrimination, and poor education for blacks captured his compassion and imagination.

Years later at a conference sponsored by Starr King School for the Ministry, in California, Alex reflected on the events that had shaped his thinking. In that talk, he acknowledged that he had been radicalized by the almost daily lynching of blacks in the "land of the free and the home of the brave," angered by the "Jim Crow" navy he had served in, and traumatized by all sorts of insults at the University of Illinois, including a "nigger-in-the-woodpile" joke told by a professor to about one hundred students that included only one African American—Alex. He noted that his master's degree in philosophy only qualified him for a $40-a-week job as a spray painter in a "pigsty" factory. It disgusted him that too many black and white liberals were so "mortgaged to the establishment" that they were unwilling to challenge it seriously. Most important, he had been radicalized by the mass beatings and jailings of black students in the South who staged lunch counter sit-ins and freedom rides, risking their lives for "integrated education" and voter registration. In his remarks, Alex concluded, "Given these circumstances, scraping across the national consciousness like a fingernail across glass, I no longer could relax in the relative ease and comfort of my politically liberal but guilt-ridden middle-classness. No longer could I float in a psychological space capsule above the social and economic suffering of most of my black brothers and sisters."[1]

Returning to the agenda and activities of the Adult Discussion Group, in January 1962, a group of students and adults from the Congress of Racial Equality (CORE) occupied the waiting room of the chancellor's office at the University of Chicago, as well as the university's realty office. Before engaging in the sit-ins, members of CORE had dispatched teams to apply for housing in the Hyde Park area owned by the university and had documented serious discrimination against blacks seeking housing. Since this action brought to light practices of my employer that were very questionable, I was happy when members of the Adult Discussion Group urged that this matter be discussed at the next meeting.

Sit-in by student members of CORE at administration offices of the University of Chicago protesting racial exclusion in the university's housing policies and practices. Courtesy Special Collections Research Center, University of Chicago, Political Activities, CORE Sit-in, 1963-3, series IV.

It was clear that civil rights protests, which up to this point had been occurring only in the South, were now very much in our neighborhood. But many members of the Hyde Park community asked, "Why the sit-in in *our* community?" In an open meeting, Alderman Leon Despres observed that Chicago was residentially the most segregated large city in the United States. His statement was supported by the findings of the U.S. Commission on Civil Rights in 1959—and since that time, Chicago's housing segregation had only grown worse, becoming in his words a "monstrous social cancer," with 825,000 African American Chicagoans living in a single continuous area that stretched north from the Indiana state line to the near North Side, and west from downtown almost to the city limits.

Despres added that outside of Hyde Park–Kenwood and Lake Meadows, other neighborhoods had in effect said, "No matter how urbane you may be, no matter how educated, no matter how good your record, no matter how successful you have been professionally or financially, no matter what you have achieved or how honorable you are, you must remain inside the segregated area."

Despres noted that housing segregation was the number one enemy of urban progress, not only because it blocked urban renewal, but because it fostered urban decay at a rate that outpaced urban renewal. It was against such evils that CORE was protesting.

Finally, Despres turned to the question on everyone's mind: Why did CORE choose to sit-in in Hyde Park? Why did it select the University of

Fifth Ward alderman Leon Despres in conversation with Martha Fried-
berg, Hyde Park resident and poet. Courtesy Special Collections Research
Center, University of Chicago, Exhibitions, Feb. 1978–7, series III: Events.

Chicago's real estate office as the symbol of housing segregation? Why did
it not go, for example, to the community of Bridgeport, which not only practiced housing segregation but where a mob recently had driven out families—
black victims of a fire—for whom the American Red Cross was providing
brief sanctuary in the local Holy Cross Church? Despres replied that deeply
committed protesters could not always go only to the most "sinful" person.
He pointed out that protest occurs when feelings are so strong they boil
over. "We have to accept the fact that here in this community, university
students, filled with admiration for the scientific, intellectual, and academic
achievements of the university, became indignant that the university real
estate office should practice housing segregation."[2]

The housing policy of the University of Chicago could be traced back
to the era of its famous president, Robert Maynard Hutchins, who in 1937
said that an examination of the university's record would convince any fair-
minded person that "neither the Trustees nor the administrative officers are
activated by race prejudice." He went on to say that the university needed to
stabilize its neighborhood as an area in which its students and faculty would
be content to live, and however unsatisfactory and restrictive the covenants
might be, they were legal instruments, and Hyde Park's residents had the
right to invoke and defend them.[3]

Against this background, the Adult Discussion Group tackled a series of questions:

- *Was CORE really a noncoercive group?*
  Many felt that a sit-in should not be viewed as passive. It was designed to embarrass, to inconvenience, and to be coercive—and refusing to leave the realty office at closing hour was clearly disruptive. Moreover, several demonstrators who were sent to jail had refused to leave when their sentences were commuted.
  Most members of the Adult Discussion Group endorsed the CORE guidelines: "We will meet the anger of any individual or group in the spirit of good will and creative reconciliation. We will submit to assault and will not retaliate in kind, either by act or word."

- *Were the tactics used by CORE legal?*
  Some wondered about the legality of sitting in at the chancellor's office and the realty office of the university. Could a distinction be made between sitting-in at a lunch counter in the South (i.e., a public facility) versus sitting-in at the university and its realty office? Some in the discussion group cited a recent faculty report that used the word "manufacture" to describe the rationale for the sit-ins.

- *What was CORE's constituency?*
  Others questioned the propriety of CORE seeking to negotiate with the university, envisioning some type of agreement that would change the way the university operated its real estate offices. "Shouldn't there be a process for establishing legitimate representation from the community, rather than self-appointed leaders seizing the initiative?"

After considerable intense debate, the group concluded that the sit-ins by CORE at the university represented a legitimate campaign. Without the sit-ins, the university's policy of restrictive covenants would have continued unnoticed. (It is interesting to note that the CORE sit-ins of early 1962 were a harbinger of what was to become a major commitment of the civil rights movement of Chicago and the SCLC during the summer of 1966 (over four years later) to secure open housing throughout Chicago.)

Throughout the remainder of 1962 and into 1963, the Adult Discussion Group continued to meet, and I served as its convener. Our discussions were not exclusively devoted to civil rights, but this subject certainly generated the most interest and probing discussions. I remember one Sunday in particular when the very moving "Letter from Birmingham Jail," written by Martin Luther King Jr. in April 1963, served as the springboard for discussion. I first encountered this letter in the magazine *Christian Century* and was persuaded by the rationale that King presented in support of civil disobedience. The letter was written as an answer to a group of clergymen who called his involvement in direct action "unwise and untimely." Several sections of the letter captured for me the power of King's argument:

> You may well ask, "Why direct action? Why sit-ins, marches, etc.? Isn't negotiation a better path?" I have earnestly opposed violent tension, but there is a type of constructive, nonviolent tension that is necessary for growth. . . .
>
> If one recognizes this vital urge that has engulfed the Negro community, one should readily understand why public demonstrations are taking place. The Negro has many pent-up resentments and latent frustrations, and he must release them. So let him march; let him make prayer pilgrimages to the city hall; let him go on freedom rides—and try to understand why he must do so. If his repressed emotions are not released in nonviolent ways, they will seek expression through violence; this is not a threat but a fact of history. So I have not said to my people: "Get rid of your discontent." Rather, I have tried to say that this normal and healthy discontent can be channeled into the creative outlet of nonviolent direct action.[4]

As a camper, I had often sung the refrain, "Send me a letter, send it by mail, and send it in care of the Birmingham Jail." King's vigorous defense of the need to march and demonstrate provided much to talk about over several Sundays and reversed the image. This was not a letter "to" but "from" the Birmingham Jail, and there was nothing light or humorous about its content. The subject of civil disobedience in the spirit of Gandhi, and the circumstances under which breaking the law could be justified—these were profound issues and questions that required careful thought and reflection.

Then in 1963, when the civil rights movement in Chicago turned its attention to the city's school system discussions within the Adult Discussion Group turned in the same direction. The group concluded that the isolation resulting from segregated schools perpetuated a bad situation: the deprived students ultimately became parents who lacked awareness and motivation to help their children move into the mainstream of society, thereby prolonging a disheartening and dysfunctional cycle. Disagreement centered instead on tactics, especially boycotting classes.

One Sunday morning at the Adult Discussion Group, Bob Moore, a black post office worker, spoke heatedly about the issues he saw for his children. He wanted the civil rights movement to emphasize the need to improve the quality of education, regardless of a school's racial makeup. He asserted that placing too much emphasis on integration was a patronizing approach to the problem. If the predominantly Negro schools were inferior, then they should be improved. He felt strongly that "gerrymandering" the enrollment (via transfers and busing) was not going to solve the problem, and there was nothing inherently wrong in the neighborhood school concept. This issue of whether good education could be achieved for blacks—short of integration—would reappear frequently in the years to follow.

As my involvement in the civil rights movement deepened, I worked closely with Tim Black and staffed several campaigns organized by Tim in conjunction with the Chicago chapter of the Negro American Labor Council (NALC); at the same time, Alex Poinsett and I continued to discuss and debate the important issues of the day. I remained active in the Unitarian Church and served on the Social Action Committee during the years when it deliberated over the church's involvement in school boycotts and the extent of its support for the protest actions of the civil rights movement.

The church served as a base, a "home away from home," for many of us who became active in the civil rights movement. For me, the Unitarian Church provided the gateway to the movement and to several activist organizations, especially the Coordinating Council of Community Organizations (CCCO). More important, the church served as a multiracial community within which individuals could discuss and debate the moral issues involved in the various tactics and programs being advanced by the civil rights movement.

2. Campaigns on the Employment Front

In Chicago, the racial division of the labor market, resulting
from discrimination and segregation in the labor market, has
created serious problems for both Negroes and whites.

—Harold Brown and Bennett Hymer, "The Negro

Worker in the Chicago Labor Market," 1968

Throughout my career, the employment relationship between labor and management has been the central focus for research, teaching, and practice. Initially, my exposure to race relations in employment was very much academic. For example, my study (earlier described) of the unsuccessful effort by the labor movement to organize the nonprofessional workers (mostly black) at two hospitals in Chicago was undertaken as a traditional research project. I crossed the threshold and became active in the developing civil rights movement as a result of meeting Tim Black, also a member of the Unitarian Church.

By day, Timuel Black was an inspired teacher at Hyde Park High School. He invariably found creative ways to motivate his students to move over the barriers that existed for black people in the labor market. Often he recruited alumni to speak to his classes; in a powerful way, they served as role models to challenge his promising students.

Born in Birmingham Alabama and raised in Chicago, Tim was very active in the local Chicago chapter of the American Federation of Teachers. But by far his most important extracurricular work was with the Chicago chapter of the Negro American Labor Council (NALC). This organization was founded by A. Philip Randolph, president of the Sleeping Car Porters Union—which was, important to note, the only all-black-led union in the AFL-CIO. At the national AFL-CIO convention in 1960, Randolph observed that, although there were some black members in the railroad industry (primarily porters and waiters in the union that he headed), very few blacks enjoyed the opportunity to work as skilled craftsmen. George Meany, president of the AFL-CIO, who had come out of the skilled trades, responded by asking, "Who the hell chose you to be spokesman for the Negro people?" This response created a stir, not only among the black trade union representatives attending the convention but also among the more liberal whites.[1] As a result of this rebuff, Randolph called for an organizing conference in Detroit, and the NALC was formed, with Randolph as its first president. The stated mission was to create jobs in industry and government and to equalize opportunities for people of color. Tim Black became the first president of the Chicago chapter when Willoughby Abner, an official with the United Auto Workers (UAW), nominated him for this position.

Some wondered whether it was wise for Randolph and other black leaders to form a separate organization. Whether it was wise or not, the move was certainly necessary to focus attention on the labor market conditions facing blacks. While some labor leaders (such as Walter Reuther, president of the UAW, and Ralph Helstein, president of the United Packinghouse Workers) were very outspoken on the subject of civil rights and the need to improve the economic position of blacks, in general the labor movement was indifferent or negative (as illustrated by Meany's reaction to Randolph's request for special action). While the AFL-CIO had taken action against several unions for being Communist-dominated or corrupt, resulting in these unions' being expelled from the house of labor, no such action had been taken against unions that were known to be excluding blacks from membership, especially the craft unions.[2]

Lack of leadership in behalf of the "Negro issue" at the top of the AFL-CIO was very disheartening to Tim and the

A. Philip Randolph, president of the Sleeping Car Porters Union and national president of NALC. LBJ Library, photo by Yoichi Yakamoto, file #A1070–14a.

other leaders of the NALC. Leaders taking a stand could make a critical difference, as had been illustrated in the 1940s by the integration of conductors and motormen working for the Chicago Transit Authority.

Blacks in Chicago had long resented being unable to obtain jobs for which they were qualified in the transit industry. While large numbers of blacks used the transportation system as passengers, very few if any served as motormen or conductors. In August 1943, black action groups staged a series of meetings and demonstrations with banners demanding "Jobs for Negroes on the Streetcars."

At meetings involving the Chicago branch office of President Roosevelt's Committee on Fair Employment Practices, top officials from the transit system agreed to hire a black conductor. Subsequently, several white union members voiced opposition to the action, but when the issue was brought up at a union meeting, the president refused to discuss the matter, saying, "Everyone has the right to work regardless of his color and this right is not a debatable issue in the Amalgamated union." He went on to say that trouble was bound to result when union leadership was weak or indefinite on such an issue.[3]

Tim came across as thoughtful and soft-spoken, yet at the same time intently focused on making a difference. His pockets bulged with newspaper clippings, and throughout my association with him he was always alert to what the press was saying and the need to maintain a good relationship with the media. At the time, I noted that while many black leaders, including Tim Black, felt alienated from many aspects of white-dominated society, they depended on newspaper, radio, and television media run by white people to get the attention of the public and to have their voices heard. And that depended in large part on tapping these communication channels and learning to use them skillfully.

Early in our association, Tim shared a paper he had written—"Jobs: The Crisis of Chicago"—which described the poor employment situation facing blacks in many industries. The heart of the paper dealt with the building trades and the role of Washburne Trade School in preparing individuals for the construction industry.

Tim's position paper set the stage for a series of direct-action moves that would follow in the early 1960s. On the basis of the data contained in his report, the NALC organized protests outside the offices of the Chicago Board of Education to protest the exclusion of blacks from Washburne.

Back in the Adult Discussion Group, Tim's work served as an excellent springboard for discussing the issue of employment of blacks in the skilled trades. Tim described the factual situation that only a small number of blacks held journeymen cards. The most disturbing statistic was that, as of June 1962, out of a school enrollment of 2,600 students at Washburne, only 36 were black.

Nationally, the numbers were just as bad. Ray Marshall estimated that, as of 1964, only 1.3 percent of all apprentices were black.[4] George Strauss, in 1965, estimated the percentage at 3.3 percent.[5] Whatever the exact number was, black enrollment was very low given the fact that in the early 1960s blacks represented approximately 13 percent of the workforce in Chicago.

While examining other data (submitted by employers to the Equal Employment Opportunity Commission in 1966), I noted that black participation in the craft occupations stood at 6.6 percent.[6] To be at parity with whites, their participation should have been at least double that number. Moreover, to the extent that blacks had gained membership in the crafts, they were concentrated in the "brush and trowel" trades, that is, painting and masonry. While some of the underrepresentation for blacks could be rationalized in terms of limited information within the community, poor training, and lack of qualifications, the low numbers implied that something else was taking place: discrimination.

Historically, unions had played a key role in the design and administration of apprenticeship programs, especially in selecting entrants, designing course offerings, and certifying successful completion. Apprenticeship had served as a gateway for young people who did not desire to enter one of the major professions (or perhaps were unable to go to college) but aspired to the middle-class status and income. Such opportunities existed in the skilled trades, especially in the construction industry.

The determination of who would be selected to become apprentices at Washburne was in the hands of the unions, which maintained long waiting lists and more often than not selected brothers, sisters, and other close relatives of existing members. As the data from Washburne showed, few blacks were enrolled in its programs. No doubt much of the exclusion was due to discrimination, but the discrimination was not just against blacks but also against anyone who was not connected or did not have a relative already in the system. Over the years, fathers (historically, apprentices were almost 100 percent male) wanted to pass the "tools of their trade" on to the next generation, their sons. As Strauss and Ingerman pointed out, "Building tradesmen believe that the right to work in a trade is a property right that a man should be able to pass on to his children as part of his estate."[7] Consequently, if a segment of society (in this case, the black community) was not already participating in the system, then it was unlikely that they would have an easy time gaining entry. The need, then, was for black pathbreakers and role models, for fathers and uncles who had gone the route and could counsel young men, urging the next generation to enter apprenticeship programs as an important pathway to economic well-being.

The Washburne School was financed with funds from the Chicago Board of Education. Actually, most of the funds came from a national mandate; federal legislation had been passed in 1919 to support training and apprenticeships in the skilled trades. Tim appeared before the board but got nowhere. Later, in an interview, he elaborated on what had happened. One of the strongest, most vocal persons on the board was a union person. Tim noted this handicapped him. But more important, the board also had among its members an African American woman always referred to as "Mrs. Green." At one meeting of the board, Tim said, Mrs. Wendell Green took him on verbally when he challenged the board's policy that perpetuated the exclusion of minorities while at the same time using public funds.[8]

The Washburne project continued to be a high priority for Tim Black and the NALC. Tim went to Washington with Al Raby, leader of the Coordinating Council of Community Organizations (CCCO), to appear before the House Education Committee, chaired by Adam Clayton Powell. Tim remembered that witnesses, both black and white, who had been sent to Washington by the Chicago Board of Education, attacked him fiercely. Tim felt that Adam Clayton Powell was not fooled by what was going on. Tim also recounted how amusing and insensitive it was for Congressman Roman Pucinski to instruct Tim on how freedom had been won. After the session was over, Pucinski took Tim on a tour of the Washington Monument and the Lincoln Memorial. Tim thought all of this was quite bizarre.

Early in my association with Tim Black, I urged him to target an employer near the University of Chicago, and I volunteered to do the staff work. Employed as I was at the University of Chicago, located on the South Side of Chicago, and surrounded by black residential communities, I had been noting the racial makeup of employment at different institutions in the area. At the University of Chicago, many blacks were on the payroll, usually working as secretaries.

Several office complexes were located across the Midway Plaisance (a large park-like tract that had been the site of the 1893 Colombian Exposition) that served as a separation boundary for the University of Chicago from the adjoining community of Woodlawn. One of these, the Industrial Relations Center, provided study space for faculty in industrial relations and I shared an office with a research associate. Located nearby was the national headquarters of the American Bar Association (ABA). The idea occurred to me that if the ABA were not employing blacks, then it would make a fine target for an NALC campaign. Moreover, the ABA planned to hold its annual national meeting that June (1963) in Chicago, and as part of the convention, meetings would be held at its headquarters on East 60th Street. This gathering of key leaders would afford a good opportunity to put pressure on the ABA to expand black employment.

Tim agreed, and in early May 1963 I found a spot outside the ABA entrance and positioned myself to count the number and racial makeup of the ABA workforce. I took up my station about 4:30 P.M., and by 5:30 I felt numbness settling into my lower left side. Sitting cross-legged on the grass for at least an hour had begun to affect my circulation. But the task would soon be finished, and within a few minutes I would be back in my study at the university.

As the discomfort increased, I was forced to confront the question: "Why in the Sam Hill am I engaged in this wild venture?" As a college professor, I had pursued the traditional path of teaching classes, meeting students, writing research papers, attending seminars, and so forth. Conducting a racial census was a new experience—exciting but also somewhat risky to my professional reputation.

Afraid of being discovered, I had taken a few books and a notepad to the observation post on the Midway. If anyone recognized me (and frequently I saw acquaintances, both students and colleagues, who crossed the Midway en route to the main campus), I would explain that I was just "enjoying the day in the cool shade of an elm tree." Actually, no one happened along and the only issue was the physical discomfort that made my lower regions feel like they had become part of the ground on which I was sitting.

Before getting up to return to my office, I reflected on what had pulled or pushed me into this activist role. Why was I so primed? Several early experiences surfaced.

During the summer of 1959, between completing my graduate studies at Harvard Business School and commencing my academic career at the business school of the University of Chicago, Nancy and I spent two months at the University Camp for Boys in Green Lane, Pennsylvania. The camp was operated as a joint venture between the Christian Association of the University of Pennsylvania and a group of social service agencies serving inner-city areas of Philadelphia. Previously, I had spent portions of several summers at the camp during my undergraduate years, usually after the termination of my navy cruises. Nancy and I had also worked at the camp the first summer after we were married (1956). These stints deepened our respect and affection for the pioneering work of the camp director, Dana How, and his wife, Thelma.

Campers from the author's cabin, University Camp for Boys, operated by the Christian Association, University of Pennsylvania, summer 1949. Author's collection.

These two Quakers (one by birth, the other by confirmation) pursued a vision that provided youngsters from both the black and the white sections of inner-city Philadelphia a positive experience in race relations. Starting in the late 1940s and into the 1950s, they proceeded, in a natural and quiet way, to integrate all sessions of the camp. The changeover progressed from reserving the first two weeks for campers from white sections of the city that were hostile to any social contact with blacks, to a completely interracial camp. Working with kids and counselors of both races for those summers exerted a profound influence on my values. For a while I even contemplated switching careers and assuming a leadership position for the camp when Dana and Thelma retired. Having declined this offer, I knew that working to improve race relations would always remain, for me, a priority in one way or another.

Probing a bit deeper to explain my predisposition involved "peeling back the onion" several more layers. When I was a young boy growing up in Haledon, New Jersey, Della Pinder came for a visit each summer. Della was a tall, quiet, stately black woman who raised my mother when my mother's mother died suddenly and left her, then age five, and a younger brother, age three, without a caregiver. My grandfather had many business interests and traveled frequently. On one of these trips while he was in Philadelphia, he recruited Della to come live with the family, which she did for many years. Even though my grandfather remarried, and my mother found herself in a family with a stepmother, in thinking back on her childhood (which she frequently did), my mother always observed, "Della raised me, and I think of her as my second mother."

Family picture, summer 1933. *Left to right*: Marion McKersie (mother), Robert (author), Alan (brother), Fran Whittaker (step-grandmother), and Della Pinder (caregiver). Author's collection.

When Della visited us, she didn't just sit and talk, she went to work as she had done for decades in my grandfather's household. She gave my brother and me baths on a regular basis, and took care of us for the week or two she was with us. I wonder how many white boys at our young age had been bathed by an African American, but it seemed quite natural, and it generated a deep feeling of affinity for people of different skin color than my own.

Returning to the census story—the count at the ABA headquarters confirmed my suspicion that the workforce was "lily white." Over 80 women had emerged from the building between 4:30 and 5:30, many of them heading toward the Illinois Central station to take trains home to the suburbs (which convinced me that ABA was hiring outside of the immediate neighborhood to maintain an all-white workforce). Some of the women were young, but many were middle-aged. Most of them were well dressed. Their attire was not the type found on Chicago's South Side, particularly near the University of Chicago.

As the stream of high heels stopped, I gathered up my papers and started to leave. But just then a side door in the building opened and another secretary emerged. "Damn," I said to myself. Here was a fair-skinned black woman. She moved quickly across the street and before I caught a good glimpse of her, she disappeared into a waiting car. For the first time I noticed the driver of this car, who probably had been waiting for some time. He too was black. I mused about how often working black women were chauffeured around. I recalled seeing black men, at all hours of the day on the streets near the university, waiting for their girlfriends and spouses to quit work. My study at the Industrial Relations Center looked out over the Conference Center, and I had often seen cars waiting to pick up passengers at 2:00 in the afternoon when the waitresses, many of whom were black, stopped work.

The sight of Miss X walking out of the ABA building unnerved me. I had been thinking about the slogans that would make good signage: "ABA is lily white" and "Start integrating and stop debating." The last was a reference to their annual meeting soon to be held in Chicago. A group of liberal lawyers had placed on the agenda a resolution condoning civil disobedience. A floor fight was certain to occur. It was precisely because of the convention and the prospect of the civil rights discussion that I had been able to persuade Tim Black and the NALC that ABA would be a good target.

However, things were quite different now that the ABA had one black employee on its payroll. We couldn't say that management was totally antiblack. While it was true that other offices along the Midway employed many more blacks (20 to 50 percent of the workforce), the ABA could not be characterized with stark adjectives. When it came to arousing emotions, it was always better to have a "black and white" rather than a gray picture. So I reasoned.

I recoiled from the emotion of being upset at the black secretary. I caught myself thinking, "Why did she have to show up?" At a more reasoned level, I knew that our aim was to create more jobs for blacks, so why should I begrudge this individual a job at the ABA? Still, I felt conflicted as I left the Midway and headed back to my office.

The next morning, I returned to the ABA. This time a research assistant accompanied me from the business school where I worked. Ours was only a nodding acquaintance at school until we saw one another at a civil rights rally. We were both pleasantly surprised when we realized we were "comrades in arms." As it turned out, he was not the only research assistant from the business school who was active in the civil rights movement. The highly professionalized, formalized, and even compartmentalized organization of the school tended to obscure the outside-of-work interests of its staff and faculty members.

As we climbed the front steps of the ABA, we discussed a plan for surveying the workforce. First, we would walk past the receptionist as if we knew where we were headed. Second, we would scout the individual offices by slowly walking down each hallway.The plan worked perfectly. No one so much as inquired about our business. As we traversed the various hallways and glanced into each office, I marveled at the composure of my partner (since my stomach was churning). Back at school, he appeared quiet and efficient. His work as a computer expert shielded his passion for the civil rights movement.

Finally, we reached the office of Miss X. It was at the end of a hallway and obviously a part of the executive director's complex. How typical, I thought, for the black to be working for the boss! The thought crossed my mind that we should talk to Miss X. It would be helpful to get her answers to a few questions: Are you the only black working here? How were you hired? Are you treated fairly? However, we kept walking. I decided not to risk being thrown out. And besides, since she held a job in this elegant office, how could she be expected to answer our questions, let alone identify with the civil rights movement? I concluded that in a situation of conflict between her role as a black person and as an employee she would probably defer to her job interests.

With the information in hand that the ABA employed only one black secretary, I drafted a letter to the ABA over the signature of Tim Black. The letter made the following points:

- NALC has conducted a survey of employment at ABA and is disappointed to learn that only one black secretary is employed.

- NALC would like to meet with ABA to discuss ways in which employment for blacks can be expanded.

- NALC is contemplating a demonstration to alert conferees at the upcoming ABA annual meeting that the home office of ABA is very exclusionary with respect to employing blacks.

- NALC has no intention of disrupting the meeting, but it does want to express its concern about the employment situation and will do so with a demonstration.

The NALC never received a reply from the ABA. When the day arrived for the large convocation that opened the ABA meetings (scheduled to be held at the university's Rockefeller Chapel, with conferees walking back and forth across the Midway between ABA headquarters and the main campus), hundreds of policemen were in evidence. Certainly, the officers of ABA had taken the letter seriously and alerted the police that there might be a demonstration. Since at that point the NALC was preoccupied with another project, the upcoming Motorola campaign, no demonstration took place.

I can remember observing the scene and feeling a sense of power because our research work, followed by the letter, had generated such a big response.

While I initially experienced considerable discomfort and unease in moving into an activist role, nevertheless this episode illustrated a core principle of negotiation theory (one of my research interests); namely, that a threatened demonstration can be a very powerful tactic and indeed, often more effective than the actual event itself. Of course, to be effective any threat must possess sufficient plausibility. Given other serious demonstrations that the NALC had announced for the summer of 1963, as well as the many demonstrations in the South that had been growing in intensity, culminating in the jailing of Martin Luther King in Birmingham in April 1963, the letter to ABA obviously had been taken seriously—a development I should have anticipated and not been surprised at.

So how did I feel about the ABA campaign? We did provoke the assembling of a large police detail (and I recognize that this came out of some budget; "nothing is free"). However, in our defense, we never received an answer to our demand for a meeting, which could have given us the opportunity to cancel our "intended" protest. Also, and to our discredit, we never made contact with the ABA to determine what impact, if any, our "campaign" had made on their hiring practices.

3. Tim Black and the Motorola Campaign

Timuel Black is walking history.

—Curtis Lawrence, 2003

During the spring of 1963, Tim Black spoke with the leadership of the Coordinating Council of Community Organizations (CCCO) about the possibility of targeting Motorola's employment policies. In making his proposal for a direct-action program, he was supported by the co-conveners, Rev. Arthur Brazier and Al Raby. However, Bill Berry, executive director of the Chicago Urban League, opposed the plan to target Motorola. Years later, Tim reflected on this split in support for the Motorola campaign. Tim acknowledged that many people had a high regard for Bill Berry and were consequently unwilling to support the Motorola project. On the other side, those who supported the proposal, such as Nahez Rogers, were seen in the general community as radicals, especially those who were affiliated with SNCC and CORE. As Tim summed up the situation: "We were considered rabble-rousers."[1]

Before turning to the details of the campaign against Motorola, it is useful to step back for some perspective on the employment of black people by large corporations during the 1960s. For purposes of setting this context, several statistics are relevant. First, the unemployment rate among the black population was then (and has persisted to this date) to be twice that for the white population. As noted earlier, blacks only had limited access to apprenticeship programs, and in general they were not represented proportionately compared to whites in other desirable occupations.

Turning to Motorola, what was the participation rate for blacks in the electrical equipment industry (within which Motorola fell)? Interestingly, it

Timuel Black Jr. speaking in front of three signs: "Dump Daley"; "Blacks Together, Vice Lords, P. Stones, Disciples"; and "Black Community Black Control." Courtesy Chicago Urban League records, University of Illinois at Chicago Library, Special Collections.

was 12 percent for black males and 14 percent for black females—very close to their presence in the Chicago labor market—13 percent. Indeed, based on regression analysis of companies reporting EEO-1 data, large companies in the electrical equipment sector employed a higher percentage of blacks than would have been expected.

However, when I analyzed relative occupational positions, those held by black males stood at only 86 percent of those held by whites, while black women held such positions at 97 percent of the rate of their white counterparts.[2] The fact that black and white females were almost at parity was explained by the fact that in the 1960s discrimination against *all* females was a reality, with white females segregated into clerical occupations and black females segregated into manual jobs in the factory—both being classified as semi-skilled.

The leadership of NALC reasoned that a large corporation like Motorola should be targeted because that was where the good jobs were located. Also, a large corporation held the prospect of career advancement, which added to the attractiveness of Motorola as a target.

Large corporations such as Motorola were not unmindful of the need to address disparities in employment of minorities. As far back as 1941, the government had established a business committee to foster, on a voluntary basis, the hiring and upgrading of black workers. This initiative in part resulted from the efforts of A. Philip Randolph, who just prior to the onset of World War II called for a march on Washington to draw attention to the plight of African Americans. He was persuaded to call off the march when President Roosevelt issued an executive order establishing a committee on fair employment practices. In 1961, President Kennedy issued a subsequent executive order and then established a new group called the President's Committee on Equal Employment Opportunity. And in 1962 President Kennedy also established an advisory council to an industry-initiated program labeled Plans for Progress.[3]

The leaders of the NALC were aware of these programs, but they judged these efforts for the most part as amounting to nothing more than public relations gestures. Targeting Motorola would focus attention on the need to hire more blacks into skilled occupations and hold this corporation accountable for the slow progress it had shown in the 1940s and the 1950s.

But why was Motorola chosen and not some other large employer in Chicago? Several factors were involved in this decision. Motorola was a government contractor, so it would be embarrassing, especially with the interest that President Kennedy and his administration had shown in the subject of enhancing black employment, for a large supplier of military equipment to be the focus of a civil rights campaign. In addition to its military production, Motorola produced many consumer products under a well-established brand name, and the company would be sensitive to any adverse publicity.

Tim and other members of NALC had done their homework. During the summer of 1963, college students (most of them white) had been posted as observers at all Motorola factory gates. These observations confirmed that Motorola had hired very few African Americans. Tim presented these findings at a meeting sponsored by the Woodlawn Organization (TWO). At the end of his talk, Tim mentioned that, in addition to the "gate census," information received from the Urban League indicated that in a factory that employed over 10,000, fewer than 50 were African Americans.

When Tim sat down, a well-dressed gentleman stood up and identified himself as the program director of the Urban League. He said, "I am embarrassed by what Tim has just said. This information was given to the NALC on a confidential basis and should not have been disclosed. We have been working with Motorola for several years in an attempt to integrate their work force."

Another person in the room asked, "How can we be sure that Motorola is really discriminating?" Tim then called on a member of his taskforce who described several incidents. Invariably, when the white applicants applied for employment they were accepted, and the black applicants were turned away. Then he told about a group of blacks that had just completed a Manpower Development and Training Administration (MDTA) training program in soldering. Even though they had passed this approved government course, they were refused employment. All these individuals intended to file complaints with the Illinois Fair Employment Practices Commission. One of these was Leon Myart, soon to be the focus of a major controversy.

A motion was made at the meeting to conduct a demonstration at the company's showroom in the Chicago Loop. The motion passed overwhelmingly, and sign-up sheets were passed, asking for volunteers and financial support.

At the meeting, I noticed a familiar face, someone who had been working part-time at the university's Industrial Relations Center where I had a study and spent considerable time. On the Monday following the meeting he and I talked about the Motorola program. As it turned out, he had done extensive investigative work and had taken on the role of field captain, handling all the logistics for the upcoming demonstration. He showed me a copy of a letter that had been sent to Motorola, which stated, in part: "With regard to your plants in Chicago, we demand that you employ 1,000 Negroes by August 1, 1964 and at least 100 Negroes by October 1, 1963. A policy statement by you indicating compliance with these demands would be an important first step." I remember my reaction at the time: "Wow! This letter really lays it on the line."

A few days later, Motorola released a statement denying discrimination and claiming compliance with all government procedures:

> Our program for integration is reviewable by the Federal Government, and we are reviewed annually and have been found in compliance every year. We have Negroes on the payrolls who have been with us for many years and who share in the same benefits as other employees.
>
> To meet the objectives of the President's program, we have accelerated the hiring of Negroes, such talent as Negro engineers, college-degree accountants, technicians, office and clerical employees, and hourly workers.[4]

The company never responded to the NALC. The field captain for the campaign referred to Motorola as "those SOBs" when he read their press release. "They are liars. I know they are discriminating."

As the day for the demonstration at the company's showroom in downtown Chicago drew near, Tim's staff worked feverishly lining up buses, recruiting trade union participants and other interested groups and, most important, raising money. The "battle plan" covered a week of intensive activities, including five days of leaflet distribution and picketing.

Then CCCO held an emergency meeting in response to a request by the Urban League that the campaign be postponed. Tim and several other representatives from the NALC attended this stormy meeting, and under pressure from the other member organizations of CCCO, he agreed to a one-week delay on the grounds that "the rest of the civil rights movement wanted to participate and we must give them a chance to join forces with us." Within the NALC ranks, many criticized this decision. The field captain, in particular, was dismayed at the problems posed by putting on hold all of the logistical arrangements.

During the following week, I attended a meeting on the Motorola project held at the offices of the Packinghouse Workers Union on South Wabash. The building also housed the offices of NALC and several other civil rights groups. The union, under the leadership of its president, Ralph Helstein, had donated space in keeping with its strong commitment to progressive causes. While some people thought that the Packinghouse Workers were communist-dominated, whatever their political orientation, they were one of the few trade unions that supported NALC and the other civil rights groups engaged in direct action. While the leadership of the Packinghouse Workers might have been "left leaning," it had not been ejected from the CIO in the late 1940s, as was the case with the United Electrical Workers, another union that was heavily involved in supporting the civil rights movement in Chicago.

Several University of Chicago undergraduates and key members of NALC attended the meeting. One of the NALC members was Nahez Rogers, a militant trade unionist who recently had traveled through Africa. He sat quietly and pensively during the meeting. He seemed to tolerate the students since they were helpers; they did the chores and menial jobs for the civil rights movement. However, I felt that he looked with suspicion on my presence. I reasoned that he wanted all the decision making to rest with black leadership, but because of my friendship with Tim and my outspoken manner, I might be seen as exerting undue influence on strategic decisions.

At the meeting, Tim reviewed the state of affairs for the Motorola project. The budget amounted to $1,300, mostly for hiring buses for getting demonstrators from the South Side to the Loop. Few civil rights groups had donated any money, and he expressed considerable disappointment: "They asked us to postpone the demonstration and now none of them are giving us support.

Looks like it was nothing more than a diversionary tactic on the part of the Urban League to maintain their own inside track with Motorola."

When Tim announced that he had just received a telegram from the company expressing willingness to sit down and discuss race relations, the group groaned. The field captain, in particular, reacted vigorously. "Now I have to call off the demonstration a second time. Those SOBS; they wait until the last minute to tell us that they will meet with us." Clearly, Motorola's overture created a dilemma for the NALC. The demonstration was scheduled for two days hence, and this was the first communication that the NALC had received from the company after repeated letters and telegrams.

Most of the group wanted to go forward with the demonstration, but Tim argued that since the company had expressed a willingness to meet, the demonstration would have to be suspended, "at least for the present." As we drove home, I suggested to Tim that we get together at some point during the next week to plan our strategy for the forthcoming talks with the company.

The group making the decision whether to go forward with the demonstration was unaware that several days earlier Tim Black had been invited to a meeting by the president of the Chicago chapter of the NAACP, Theodore Jones. Tim reported to me that as soon as he entered the room, he realized he had walked into a trap, even though he had considered the president of the NAACP "an honest, friendly guy." At the meeting were the president of Motorola, Bob Galvin, and the head of the Urban League, Bill Berry. Tim felt very uncomfortable because he knew that many in his group would condemn him for meeting with Galvin and Berry. Tim said to them, "If my people know that I'm here, I'd get fired" (from his nonpaying job). During the meeting, Tim noted that several of the Motorola officers present were former FBI agents, and at a certain point one of them implied that the FBI might have information about him. Tim responded by saying, "I'm a member of the Unitarian Church and the Democratic Party." He felt that must have confirmed their most serious suspicions! Galvin told him that the company would be willing to meet with him if the pending demonstration were cancelled. Tim responded that if the company made a formal request to engage in discussions, he would take the matter up with his team.

The next Sunday afternoon, Tim and another member of the executive committee of the NALC came to my home in Hyde Park, and we sat in the back yard in the summer sunshine and fashioned a plan for conducting the first negotiating session with the company.

We wondered what had finally brought Motorola to the negotiating table. The Urban League had not recruited participants for the demonstrations against Motorola, and it was clear that behind the scenes they had been advising the company, in effect saying, "The direct-action people mean business; you had better deal with them." Surprisingly, in the earlier strategy sessions, the representative from the Urban League had urged the NALC to take a *hard* line with the company and, more important, he said he would prefer *not* to be at the opening session for negotiations with Motorola.

The first session was held in the offices of a law firm in the Loop, and the only person present from Motorola was Ken Piper, vice president of human relations. He went to great lengths to explain why Motorola had not communicated earlier or met with the representatives sooner. As he explained: "At first we thought this was a union organizing campaign disguised as a civil rights drive. When it became clear to us that you were focused on civil rights, we decided it was proper to meet with you."

Piper complimented Tim Black and the other leaders present at the meeting, saying, "I've always gotten along fine with Negro leaders; I'm counting on you people to help me solve my problem in recruiting more Negroes." He also emphasized that it would take time to "prepare my organization for the necessary changes."

For its part, the NALC delegation pressed its demands, emphasizing that the demonstration had not been cancelled but was being held in abeyance, and the company must quickly hire many more African Americans. Tim Black, in his role as spokesperson, asked for the establishment of an employment office in the black section of Chicago, the placement of want ads in the black press, a public statement that discussions were taking place, and a policy commitment that the company recognized its responsibility to hire without respect to color.

In response, Piper said he would consider the idea of an employment office on the South Side.[5] While the company did agree to institute a program of advertising in the black press, it did not agree to issue press releases that might create the impression that it was giving in to pressure from the civil rights movement.

On the question of expanding employment opportunities for African Americans in the short run, the parties remained far apart. Tim wanted to be able to report back to "my people" that something concrete was coming out of the sessions. Piper said that he could not make any commitment to numbers or a timetable, again returning to the premise that he needed time to prepare "his people" for change.

At one point during the meeting, Piper—with a chuckle—asked an unusual question: "Why have you turned your attention only on Motorola? There are many other companies in Chicago that have *not* done well in employing Negroes. Have you thought about targeting Bell & Howell?" The significance of this comment would only become clear later: a former executive of Bell & Howell, Charles Gray, was chairing the Fair Employment Practices Commission for Illinois, and when the commission subsequently held Motorola guilty of discrimination, another stage of the Motorola saga unfolded.

During the latter half of August, the Motorola project marked time as Tim Black's attention turned to organizing a large turnout from Chicago for the upcoming March on Washington to be held on August 28, 1963. Since A. Philip Randolph served as national chair for the march, he used his NALC network to rally participants across the country. Tim, as chair of the Chicago chapter, was the logical point person.

Interestingly, Randolph had planned just such a march many years earlier (in 1940, before World War II started), and, as mentioned earlier, was persuaded at the last minute to call it off when President Roosevelt agreed to meet with him and address the issue of how black men were being treated in the armed services. Now, twenty-three years later, Tim found himself dealing with a mountain of details. Most people planned to travel to Washington by train or bus, making it necessary to find places to stay the night before the big rally. I learned through my contacts with the labor movement that the UAW was planning to charter a plane to take people into Washington early the morning of the march and return that same day. This seemed like a great way to participate—if only I could find a seat on the plane. I got in touch with Herb Rebham, who was coordinating activities for the UAW, and he responded that there might be an extra seat and to stay in touch.

Before everything fell in place, George Shultz, dean of the business school where I worked, returned for a brief visit to his home in Hyde Park. It was his pattern to spend the summer breaks with his family in Massachusetts at his farm in Swift River, and Nancy and I and our three young children, who had been living in a third-floor walkup apartment, welcomed the invitation to shift to the Shultz residence. I can remember our conversation about my plans to go to Washington. "Bob, from my contacts with Ralph Helstein [president of the United Packinghouse Workers] and others who are close to the civil rights movement, there is considerable concern that there may be violence. I wonder whether it really is a good idea for you to be participating in the march."

While I valued George's perspective, my desire to be part of what was developing as a major milestone for the movement dominated my mentor's advice, and I continued to stay in touch with Rebham. A few days before the march, Rebham reported that there was indeed a seat, and I traveled out to O'Hare early the morning of August 28.

And then what seemed like a neat way to travel to the march turned into a big disappointment. United Airlines, which was providing the charter, told us as we arrived at the airport that a "mechanical problem" had developed on the plane and it was not clear when we would be able to take off for Washington. After a rather long delay, the flight was cancelled, and there was no alternative at that point for getting to Washington in time for the march. So I traveled back home to Hyde Park and listened to the rally on radio and over television while over 2,000 other Chicagoans witnessed this historic event firsthand.

Soon after the highly successful march on Washington, during which King delivered his famous "I Have a Dream" speech, I sent a letter to Tim Black, as we prepared for a second meeting with Ken Piper. First, I expressed my admiration for his success in assembling a large Chicago delegation and for the impact of the march. Then I outlined some ideas to be presented to Motorola at the meeting scheduled for September 9—a program for enhancing the skills and job opportunities for the unemployed:

- Private industry contributes large sums of money for social causes—some of this money could be devoted to the training of the unskilled.

- Private industry does the best job with training (by Piper's own admission, the MDTA program for soldering and wiring was quite inadequate).

- Considerable precedence exists for a company-sponsored program, for example, the Carson Pirie Scott program, the Yellow Cab program, and the Shell Oil Company program.

- By aiming the program at the unemployed, both whites and blacks would be helped, although the latter group would benefit more since they make up the greater proportion of the unemployed.

- The company would not be obligated to hire every trainee; only those who qualified by the company's normal hiring standards.

- The Urban League would be asked to help formulate and execute such a plan.

The second meeting was held several weeks later in September, and Tim Black asked Hampton McKinney of the Urban League to plan and chair the meeting.

McKinney was very skillful at running the meeting; he facilitated a calm and deliberative discussion. At a critical point, he squelched one of the militants who was challenging some of Ken Piper's statements. McKinney also vetoed the idea of releasing a joint press statement. During this second session, the company reported that it was experiencing difficulty attracting qualified African Americans. The civil rights advocates countered by saying that the company was putting too much emphasis on experience and not giving enough attention to potential and the ability to learn. The meeting ended on a reasonably cordial note, with NALC representatives agreeing to inform the community, especially churches and social agencies, about the willingness of Motorola to hire African Americans. The activists wanted to pin Piper down regarding a date for a follow-up meeting, but McKinney left this open, wanting to see how much progress would take place.

Ultimately, a third meeting was held at which time the company presented a new test procedure aimed at identifying applicants who, without experience but with good IQ scores, could, with training, become qualified employees. The negotiations quickly moved beyond a discussion of numbers and timetable to a process where the leaders of the civil rights community were asked to be, in effect, an extended arm for the recruitment and referral process that Motorola needed, if it were going to find qualified African Americans for employment.

Between meetings, Piper spent time developing a working relationship with many civil rights leaders; I estimated that he maintained one-on-one contacts with at least thirty different civil rights leaders in Chicago. These leaders were asked to help Motorola recruit qualified applicants, and Piper personally checked on each referral and provided feedback. I felt Piper showed considerable good faith and commitment in dealing with the NALC.

After the third session, no further meetings—at least with the NALC—were scheduled. Tim presumed that the Urban League was working closely with Motorola. The NALC had served the useful function of motivating Piper and Motorola to move more aggressively with programs that the Urban League had been quietly promoting with Motorola behind the scenes. But another chapter of the Motorola story was still to unfold, a major confrontation between big business and government, with repercussions that reached the floor of the U.S. Senate (with much behind-the-scenes maneuvering) and destroyed the career of a hard-working and conscientious official, Charles Gray, chair of the Illinois Fair Employment Practices Commission (FEPC).

This controversy started during the summer of 1963 when Leon Myart, who had completed a MDTA course in soldering and was rejected for employment by Motorola, filed a charge of discrimination with the Illinois FEPC. After several months of investigation, the trial examiner at FEPC concluded that Motorola had discriminated against Myart and observed that the selection test, which Myart had failed, was culturally biased against African Americans and should be dropped by Motorola. The decision attracted nationwide attention. During the discussion of the Civil Rights bill considered by Congress during the winter and spring of 1964, the Motorola case was cited in support of an amendment that companies should not be allowed to use psychological tests for selection.

In response to the Illinois FEPC action, Motorola quickly went on the offensive and demanded that the Myart case be heard in a formal open proceeding. Under the Illinois FEPC provisions, an appeal normally would have proceeded to off-the-record conciliation. However, Motorola refused this option and pressed to have the case heard in a courtroom setting. The company demanded that stenographers be present and the record be released to the press. Again, such a request was at variance with the operating procedures of the commission, which did not adhere to the formalities of the courtroom.

The full commission did not rule on the Motorola case until after the presidential elections in November 1964. Motorola charged that this delay was politically motivated. Charles Gray, the commission chairman, responded that the period of review was no longer than that taken for other cases. Nevertheless, reports in the media intrigued the public with the fact that previously Gray had served as vice president of industrial relations at Bell & Howell, whose ex-chairman, Charles Percy, was running for governor of Illinois in the November elections. To complete the circle of significant linkages, Robert Galvin, president and CEO of Motorola, was serving as finance chairman for Percy's campaign. Years later, George Yoxall, a retired executive from Inland Steel, provided a perspective on these connections. He noted that both Bell & Howell and Inland Steel had lobbied actively for the establishment of the Fair Employment legislation in Illinois. Specifically, the chairman of Inland, Joe Block, succeeded in getting the Chicago Association of Commerce and Industry to publicly support the pioneering legislation. Indeed, it was the first time in the United States that a Chamber of Commerce had come out in favor of Fair Employment legislation.[6]

The decision by the full commission exonerated Motorola on the issue of the test but supported the trial examiner's position that the company had discriminated against Myart. Accordingly, the commission instructed Motorola to pay $1,000 to Myart for damages suffered as a result of being denied employment.

The response of the company was quick and vehement. Ken Piper blasted the commission, called for the resignation of all its members, and offered to provide help to any company engaged in a similar proceeding before the commission. Yoxall held a different view: "Any objective observer would have to say that Charlie Gray was conscientious and fair-minded in his approach to the Myart case."

From that point on, matters heated up considerably. Motorola solicited the help of several large corporations and developed plans for bringing about the defeat of Charles Gray should his name be placed before the state senate for reconfirmation during 1965. Because of the furor occasioned by the Myart case, Gray decided to step aside and not serve a second term as commission chairman. However, many political leaders felt that such a course of action would be admitting error, and they urged Gray to allow his name to be placed in consideration for renomination. Gray reluctantly agreed to be renominated.

I was genuinely concerned about these developments, and I contacted Tim Black and suggested we sit down and discuss what course of action the NALC could take to deal with Motorola's efforts to defeat Gray. Both of us realized that as a result of the earlier negotiations, we possessed special knowledge about Motorola, and both of us felt that we had an obligation to go public. We recalled the discussions with Motorola during the summer of 1963 and the suggestion advanced by Piper that the NALC should also target Bell & Howell (Gray's former employer). So I drafted a letter for Tim to sign, and it was sent to Kenneth Piper.

As I review the letter almost five decades later, I am embarrassed at the choice of such words as *self-righteous, peevishness, inept, intemperate, impugn,* and *undermine.* I attribute the strident tone of the letter to the rashness of youth and also to the fact that I could stay in the background and not be identified by name. If I had it to do over again, I would have confined my letter to just these points (that did appear in the letter):

> We feel compelled to break our silence and to report another side of Motorola that has not thus far been reported in the press. We refer to the series of discussions that took place between your company and representatives of our organization and other civil rights groups over the sad state of race relations at Motorola. On several occasions you admitted how slow and inept you were in introducing Negroes into employment.
>
> Had you been following the dictates of good human relations, you would have recognized the advantages of the conciliation stage provided in the FEP statutes. On the contrary, you insisted that no conciliation take place, and that everything be conducted publicly with a court stenographer present. This is not the essence of good human relations!

Indeed, another of your statements takes on sharper meaning. At one point you suggested that the Civil Rights movement might want to turn its attention to Bell & Howell—all of us being mindful that the FEPC chairman is a key official at that company. At the time, the suggestion seemed quite innocuous, but in retrospect it has become clear that it was part of a campaign instituted by you to discredit the effective operation of the FEPC in this state.

My "blast" produced no reaction from Motorola. A press release incorporating the most hard-hitting portions was released by the NALC but no newspaper carried the story. Copies of the letter were also sent to all the state legislators and key officials. Again, nothing happened. No doubt, the material was too "hot," and the reputation of NALC too "activist" for others to show interest or support.

However, I began to feel increasingly uneasy about remaining in the background, so I decided to take an open stand against what Motorola was doing. The first opportunity for this came at a meeting of the Social Action Committee of the Unitarian Church. With Tim's help, I introduced a resolution on the Motorola question. It passed, and the chairman asked me to develop a letter to be mailed to the congregation. This time I signed my name and, not surprisingly, the letter struck a more temperate tone. Given my professional work in the field of human resources, I focused on the issue of tests.

An important issue relates to testing. The Commission was right in allowing the principle of testing to stand. It is desirable for companies to use tests in their selection procedures. In fact, one of the beneficial results of the civil rights revolution has been to force employers to put their selection operation on a much more rational and systematic basis. One way of doing this is through the use of tests.

Of course, tests have to be designed to select without bias and psychologists have found it very difficult to design tests that are "culture free." The point is that the principle of testing is sound but the particular application may be faulty.

It is for this reason that individuals and groups concerned about the rights of minority members have to be on guard to challenge the results of a particular selection decision that involves testing. On the basis of other considerations, such as experience, education, and the like, the individual may be qualified, but on the basis of tests he or she fails. In these circumstances more weight must be given to other qualifications for employment.

About this time, I received a call from George Yoxall. He was calling all his friends, urging them to write letters to members of the Illinois Senate in support of Charles Gray. Numerous companies had appeared in Springfield and criticized the chairman for his handling of the Myart case. Yoxall reported that Inland was the only company to speak in support of Gray. Just as Gray was about to speak, Chuck Percy entered the room and whispered to him, "Let me know if I can be of help." Then he proceeded to "glad-hand" the politicians. It was obvious that the deck was stacked against Gray and that the legislators were overtly hostile.

The next day, the *Chicago Tribune* had a front-page story about the FEPC hearing in Springfield. Yoxall was appalled when he read the article. There was very little correspondence between what actually happened at the hearing and the way it was described in the *Tribune*. Yoxall summed it up by saying, "Those were the days when Colonel McCormick's *Tribune* editorialized about what were supposed to be news stories."

I drafted a letter to the chairman of the Executive Committee for the Illinois Senate expressing my high regard for Gray and noting a "corporate campaign" underway to defeat his renomination.

Early in April the crucial vote was taken. Voting along party lines, the Senate rejected Gray's renomination by the governor. I talked with Yoxall on the phone, and we shared our dismay at the decision. Yoxall said he was upset enough to be motivated to locate someone who could draw together the strands of the Motorola story. It was something that needed to be publicized. At a subsequent lunch, he indicated that he had been in touch with the chief of staff for FEPC and a writer from a nearby university to lay the groundwork for a fully documented story about Motorola's actions. Yoxall also cited another example of the lengths to which Motorola had gone in its campaign to oust Gray. During the initial hearing of the Myart case before the commission, Inland Steel had sent its staff psychologist to observe. He was in attendance primarily as a representative of the Illinois branch of the American Psychological Association. Soon thereafter, Bill Caples, vice president of industrial relations for Inland, received a complaint about the presence of the Inland psychologist from the lawyer representing Motorola. Caples, a no-nonsense type of executive, told the Motorola lawyer to "hang up." When I heard this, things began to fall into place. It was in the offices of this very lawyer that the discussions between the NALC and Motorola had taken place two years earlier.

A psychologist from Science Research Associates (SRA) reported a similar experience. The commission, lacking sufficient professional help on the matter of tests, had approached SRA and asked for the services of one of its staff psychologists. Shortly thereafter someone at IBM (SRA was a subsidiary of IBM) received a call from Motorola questioning the company's action in sending a psychologist to the hearings. When the SRA psychologist who had been asked to handle the assignment heard about the Motorola maneuver, he commented: "At first I wasn't sure whether to take this case; after this pressure, my only course of action now is to handle the assignment."

For my part, I drafted a letter to the *Daily News*. Some of the material came from the earlier press release I had composed for the NALC. However, I dropped the charge that Piper had sought to induce NALC to target Bell & Howell. I sent the letter to the paper, but several days went by and nothing appeared. Then the *Daily News* published three letters on the subject, one of which was mine. Here is the final paragraph:

> The campaign by Motorola to discredit Gray after it was found guilty of discrimination in the Myart case represents the worst kind of company citizenship. It will be hard to find a successor to Gray in a setting where as soon as a large company is criticized, that same company takes the initiative to discredit the commission and the individuals involved. This is akin to firing a judge because he has ruled against you. The actions of Motorola and the other companies that have been induced to join the attack have gone a long way to undermine the confidence of people in this state in the operation of an FEPC.

I was not aware the letter had been published until a colleague at school asked me: "Have you been receiving any threatening phone calls?" Since no one else said anything about the matter, I concluded the letter had not made any "waves." However, such was not the case. The first indication came from a phone call from Yoxall inviting me to lunch. At lunch, I learned the full impact of my letter.

Yoxall told me that in a conversation with Charles Gray, he learned that shortly after my letter appeared in the *Chicago Daily News*, an official from Motorola called my employer, the Graduate School of Business, indicating that their executives would not continue to be students in the management programs if I remained on the faculty.

At no point did Dean George Shultz or the director of the executive programs ever say anything about this to me. However, reports of pressure from Motorola persisted, and I heard about it on several occasions. Several students from the executive program stopped me one day in the hall and asked, "How are you and Motorola doing?" I had taught in the executive program the previous fall, and four of the students were from Motorola. In fact, one of them had selected the Myart case for his term paper. Fearing a conflict of interest, I alerted the student to my involvement and adversary relationship with Motorola. The student acknowledged the point and said he wanted to write about the Myart case anyway, and he took a strong pro-company position in his report. Then on a trip to Boston, while I was talking with some faculty members from MIT, one of them said, "I hear the school is under the gun from Motorola." Apparently news of the event had moved along the academic grapevine.

At the final social event of the year for the executive program, I did not interact with any of the Motorola students, but during the student skit the announcer quipped: "And we're happy to announce that Motorola has endowed a chair in race relations for Professor Robert McKersie."

Two tables away, George Shultz and his wife laughed a bit nervously at the joke. While Shultz had never spoken to me about the matter, he had been heard to remark that Charles Gray got what was coming to him because he had chosen a poor lawyer to handle his renomination case. While I admired Shultz's honoring of academic freedom, I was bothered by his silence on the Gray matter, which I attributed to the school's need to maintain a close relationship with the Chicago business community. In this sense, a faculty member was free and a dean was not. Charles Gray wrote a letter saying he appreciated my expression of support and that this was the best justification he had seen for "tenure and academic freedom."

In personal correspondence many years later, Shultz reflected on the episode: "I do not remember much about the Motorola or the Charles Gray issue, but I certainly felt free to speak or act as I chose, even when I was Dean. Of course, that does not mean I would sound off on any issue that came along, particularly when I was not involved or particularly knowledgeable."[7]

The Motorola saga continued to unfold. In September 1965, one of Mike Royko's columns in the *Daily News* carried the headline: "A Mystery Man Buys Up All Issues of a Magazine Here." The article, in *Focus-Midwest,* titled "Press Swallows Motorola Hoax," was about Motorola and its battle with the Illinois FEPC. Royko reported that someone was trying to buy up all the copies of this issue of *Focus-Midwest.* Motorola denied taking any part in taking the magazine off the stands. I concluded that this indeed was the article by the writer Yoxall had recruited.

In the fall election of 1966, Charles Percy, with Robert Galvin of Motorola serving as his campaign chair, defeated incumbent Paul Douglas for his seat in the U.S. Senate. (Percy's earlier 1964 bid to become governor of Illinois had failed.)

Years later (August 2002), I caught up with George Yoxall. I was traveling regularly to Chicago to attend meetings of the board of directors of Inland Steel, having been tapped for this union-nominated position by the United Steelworkers of America, and by this time, Yoxall had retired. We met for lunch, and he provided an update and perspective on the Motorola episode. He said that some years after the events I have described, he and another Inland executive, Frank Cassell, had dinner with Charles Gray in San Francisco where Gray was working as an executive in a department store chain. Gray was extremely bitter about the lack of support he had received from Charles Percy, especially in view of the fact that Percy had urged him to take the chairmanship of the FEPC. Gray felt that Percy was more interested in maintaining support from Galvin and Motorola than supporting him (Gray).

Yoxall summed it up by saying, "The misleading Motorola attack on the FEPC and Charles Gray was a sad chapter in the struggle for fair employment practices. Motorola's current leadership would probably deny that the company ever engaged in these deceptive practices, but those of us who were close to the scene know the true story."

We reflected on the insights that the saga provided about George Shultz's leadership. In a quiet and decisive way, he took the heat from a corporate sponsor. In effect, the buck stopped in his office, thereby protecting academic freedom without any fanfare. His low-key style, backed by a highly analytical and principled mind, served our country well in his cabinet appointments in several Republican administrations, finally culminating in service as President Reagan's secretary of state.

In a fundamental way, the Motorola case put academic freedom to the test and, thanks to the school's leadership, this hallmark of university life remained unaffected; indeed, it was probably strengthened as a result of this episode. Helping the civil rights movement target employers and pressure them to expand job opportunities for blacks brought together, if not integrated, my professional interests and personal commitments. One reason that academics sometimes want to take an active role in the domain they study is to test in practice propositions they are developing in their emergent theories. Doing so may involve risks. The task of academic leaders, as George Shultz so ably demonstrated without fanfare, is to support and stand behind faculty who do so.

During the same time period that Tim Black and the NALC were confronting Motorola, many similar engagements between other activist organizations in the civil rights movement and the corporate community were occurring around the country. One of the more publicized encounters pitted a

Rochester-based arm of Saul Alinsky's organization called Fight, and the Kodak Company. It is instructive to compare how Ken Piper responded to the NALC, versus how Kodak responded to the campaign by Fight.[8]

To summarize briefly the sequence in Rochester: a representative from Kodak met with Fight and agreed to a very comprehensive program of working with the organization to hire many more African Americans. A number of other measures involving community development initiatives were also included in the agreement. What happened next gained nationwide attention. Top management repudiated the actions of the Kodak representative, and discussions between Kodak and Fight were terminated.

In contrast, Ken Piper was able to keep his discussions "off the record," and he never entered into any formal agreement. Thus, while the interactions between Kodak and Fight veered between cooperation and something approaching a very adversarial relationship, Piper kept his process on a low-key, problem-solving pathway. If the story had ended in 1963, Motorola would have been seen as responsive and a "good" company.

To be fair, after the three face-to-face meetings, contact between Motorola and the NALC ended, and Tim Black never learned how much Ken Piper had delivered on his promise of increased employment for blacks. There was the possibility that Piper was only going through the motions, that is, listening to and developing a personal relationship with the leaders of the NALC and others in the African American community as a way to cool the discontent—in today's vernacular, "lots of talk but not walking the talk." However, taking at face value the current information that appears on the company's website, I must conclude that what may have been Motorola's slow start along the road of hiring minorities has today evolved into inclusion and diversity.

What took the Motorola saga in a very different direction was the company's reaction to having been found guilty of discrimination by the Illinois State FEPC. Piper was willing to meet "behind the scenes" with the NALC, but once Motorola had been challenged publicly with a decision by a state agency, he became very combative and adversarial. It was one thing to be put on the spot by a civil rights organization, and Piper had found ways to accommodate this reality. It was another to be told by the government that a particular personnel decision was wrong, and to have this decision publicized widely.

A number of insights emerge from reflecting on the negotiation process that took place between Motorola and the NALC. Foremost is confirmation of the premise that parties only enter into discussions when they perceive that the cost of maintaining the status quo would be higher than entering negotiations (with the possible outcome that hiring practices may need to be changed).

Motorola characterized these meetings as discussions—"we are always willing to listen." But regardless of the label that Piper used to describe his approach, he was acting out of self-interest: Motorola wanted to avoid the negative effects of the expected publicity that would accompany the direct action programs being planned by NALC. Once Piper agreed to meet, Tim Black, for his side of the table, suspended but—significantly—did not cancel the planned demonstrations. In other words, he kept alive the possibility that this source of power would be used.

The Motorola saga also confirmed a long-held tenet that internal negotiations are often as difficult as those across the table. Tim Black certainly experienced this phenomenon in full measure when the militants on his side of the table objected to postponing the demonstrations. Tim also faced tough challenges in reaching an accord with moderates, namely, with representatives from the Urban League who favored a more conciliatory approach to Motorola.

Participating in the Motorola episode also provided grist for understanding contrasting strategic choices in negotiations: forcing versus fostering.[9] The NALC adopted a forcing strategy; and Motorola a fostering strategy. The NALC kept its forcing restrained by focusing on the objective of more jobs, by not personalizing the conflict, and by being willing to call off the demonstrations planned for outside the company's showrooms once the company agreed to negotiate.

On the Motorola side, Ken Piper clearly followed a fostering strategy. He emphasized his commitment to the cause of more employment opportunities for African Americans; he sought to establish rapport by empathizing with the "black condition"; and he personally followed up on every referral made by members of the NALC. By appearing alone and using the offices of Motorola's legal counsel, he sought to create a pleasant setting devoid of any dissonant notes that might have come forth from the presence of other members of Motorola management.

How does one put the various NALC campaigns in perspective? Were the employment situations involving Washburne School (apprenticeships), the American Bar Association, and Motorola representative of what was facing African Americans in the Chicago labor market more generally—and for that matter, across the country? I believe so. Washburne illustrated the systematic exclusion of blacks from better jobs as a result of tradition and policies that had become embedded in unions and educational institutions.

The American Bar Association, with less than one hundred employees, and Motorola with thousands of employees, spanned the range of organizations operating in the Chicago labor market, especially with respect to size and type of business. These cases illustrated the reality that an office adjacent to black residential areas and a large manufacturing firm were systematically excluding blacks from employment and were symptomatic of what existed throughout Chicago and the rest of the country. Thanks to the exposé function of the civil rights movement, Congress passed and in July 1964 President Johnson signed the Civil Rights Act, which outlawed discrimination in employment and established the Equal Employment Opportunity Commission to ensure federal oversight.

4. Campaigns on the Education Front

Separate educational facilities are inherently unequal.

—*Brown v. Board of Education*, May 17, 1954

While the Motorola campaign was taking place during the spring and summer of 1963, another saga was unfolding. The Chicago civil rights movement, writ large, selected for its first campaign the removal of Superintendent of Education Benjamin Willis. To this end, it sponsored two citywide school boycotts and mounted a prolonged series of demonstrations.

To understand the coalescing of energies in Chicago during this time period, it is helpful to note what had been taking place on the national scene as the civil rights revolution gained momentum and presence in all parts of the country. Initially, most of the activity was in the South: lunch counter sit-ins in 1960; freedom rides during the summer of 1961; and dramatic attention to the admission of James Meredith to the University of Mississippi in 1962.

All of these developments served as a powerful backdrop to the growing awareness that the time was ripe for direct action in the North as well as in the South. In addition to activist organizations such as CORE and the NALC, religious groups and especially community organizations were meeting to discuss how they might work for racial equality now that "the time had come."

The antecedents of this campaign to unseat Willis can be traced back to the catalytic role of the Temporary Woodlawn Organization (TWO). Formed during the early 1960s and affiliated with Saul Alinsky's Industrial Areas Foundation, TWO focused on problems in the immediate community and mobilized residents at the grass-roots level to get involved in protests and demonstrations. As the organization solidified (rather quickly), the name was changed to the Woodlawn Organization.

During the early 1960s, it was difficult to tell in what direction TWO was going because it entertained so many diffuse objectives. It did not want anyone displaced from Woodlawn, yet it demanded that certain buildings be torn down to improve the community. Regardless of its stance on specific issues, it provided a cohesive force in the Woodlawn community. It gathered together a range of constituencies: clergy, businessmen, and rank-and-file citizenry. Whether it would carry out Alinsky's hope of acting as a strong bargaining force remained to be seen. Alinsky's point of view was that the urban community could only be saved when community groups developed and bargained for "satisfactory arrangements." Satisfactory arrangements that involved racial quotas—in this case, he envisioned TWO bargaining with white community groups; and satisfactory arrangements for the use of community resources—in this case he envisioned TWO bargaining with the University of Chicago over its South Campus plan, which had been announced in July 1960.

While the objectives might have been diffuse, the tactics were not. TWO believed in direct action. For example, in dealing with landlords in Woodlawn, the leaders organized rent strikes. When one landlord turned off the utilities, the inhabitants were relocated to a local Catholic Church.

In confronting the city over the urban renewal plan for Woodlawn, TWO knew how to "pull out all the stops": TWO organizers rejected Mayor Richard Daley's offer to arrange a meeting to discuss the University of Chicago's South Campus plan—instead, they dispatched ten busloads of people from Woodlawn to City Hall. Some protesters picketed outside while others held a sit in.[1]

James Ralph describes other confrontational tactics of TWO:

> In November 1961, it began a "death watch" of the Chicago Board of Education. At each school board meeting, two or three TWO members, dressed in black, sat silently through the proceedings. Then in February 1962, after Supt. Willis refused to release an inventory of Chicago classrooms, Woodlawn parents formed a "Truth Squad" in order to compile their own. While searching for unused classrooms in nearby all-white schools, the parent investigators, to TWO's outrage, were arrested. Three months later, Woodlawn residents flocked to TWO protests, including school boycotts, against the use of mobile classrooms, at a local elementary school.[2]

During 1962 and 1963, TWO hosted a series of meetings, assembling representatives from various religious and community organizations from across the city to hear reports about discrimination and to discuss the next steps to redress these inequities. It was at one of these meetings that Tim Black presented his report as chair of the Chicago chapter of the NALC.

It soon became clear during these meetings that a more formal organization was needed, one that could pull together all the community and religious groups that had been sending representatives. While there were meetings of local representatives from Chicago chapters of such national organizations as CORE, SNCC, and NALC, until the creation of the Coordinating Council of Community Organizations (CCCO), the civil rights movement in Chicago remained splintered and without a coherent strategy.

CCCO was formed in April 1962, bringing together a score of community, religious, and activist organizations. Rev. Arthur Brazier was selected to head the new organization. He had been the driving force behind the development of TWO and enjoyed wide support. Given that overcrowding of schools had been at the top of the TWO agenda, mobilizing CCCO to challenge the neighborhood school policy that Superintendent Benjamin Willis had implemented was seen as a logical first step.

Before describing the campaign organized by CCCO to force the ouster of Benjamin Willis, the architect of the neighborhood school policy, it is important to understand why the civil rights movement placed such a high priority on this goal. Some might ask: What was so bad about a school policy that dictated that children would attend schools nearby? The youngsters could walk to school, and they would be in classes with their friends from their own block. It might even be easier to involve parents in various aspects of school life if their children were attending schools near their homes.

Moreover, Chicago did not discriminate or segregate children by race as was true for many communities in the South. If a black child showed up to be enrolled at a predominantly white school, the youngster would be admitted if (and this is the big if) he/she lived in the catchment area for that school. Such an event would not trigger the turmoil of the 1950s when black students attempted to enroll at Little Rock (Arkansas) High School, requiring President Dwight Eisenhower to dispatch the National Guard.

At the same time, opponents of the neighborhood school policy pointed to extensive housing segregation that existed in Chicago. Most black families lived on the South Side and Near West Side of Chicago, and given the concentration in these areas, the de facto segregation of students by race in the Chicago public school system was almost complete. Citing some 1964 statistics, Julius Jacobson noted that 86 percent of all black students were enrolled in schools that were more than 90 percent black. Correspondingly, 78 percent of all white students attended schools that were more than 90 percent white.[3]

Some defenders of the neighborhood school policy might have argued, "OK, the schools are de facto segregated, but does that mean that the educational experience is not as good as in the predominantly white schools?" The Supreme Court answered this question in its *Brown v. Board of Education* decision in 1954. That decision concluded that separate was not equal. Backing up this decision was considerable research showing that in schools that were essentially all-black, fewer dollars were spent per pupil, the teaching staff tended to be less experienced, and when teacher absences occurred, substitutes were often not available to step into the classrooms. Perhaps the most serious consequence was that this segregation often led to lower self-esteem among black students.

A practical reason for the emphasis on having African American students attending integrated schools was the reality that central school administrators paid more attention to these schools. White parents tended to be more vocal—or stated differently; school administrators often did not hear the voices of black parents.

In choosing the Chicago school system for its first campaign, the leaders of the CCCO were not guided by any sophisticated research that demonstrated the deficiencies of the neighborhood school policy. They knew from first-hand experience that their children and the children of their colleagues were not receiving as good an education as the rest of the system. Of particular concern were the crowded schools on the South Side and the West Side. Given a much higher birth rate among black families, neighborhood schools grew dramatically more crowded during the post-World War II period. According to James Ralph, "Between 1953 and 1963, the number of Chicago public school pupils skyrocketed from 375,000 to more than 520,000."[4] This prompted Willis and the school board—in order to preserve the neighborhood school policy—to set up trailers in the adjacent grounds of crowded schools to handle the overflow; structures that quickly came to be called "Willis wagons." Rather than transferring students out of crowded ghetto schools into available classrooms in white neighborhoods, Willis followed his "neighborhood" policy and expanded classroom capacity in the areas where schools were already overtaxed. As such, the Willis wagons were viewed as another technique for perpetuating segregation.

It should be noted that the civil rights movement of the 1960s was not the first attempt to focus attention on the Chicago school system. In the aftermath of the *Brown* decision in 1954, the Chicago office of the NAACP had filed a class-action suit, and local residents in communities like Chatham had engaged in sit-ins to protest overcrowding in neighborhood schools located in the predominantly black residential areas of the city.[5]

So, in quick order, the thinking of CCCO leaders moved from general concerns about discrimination to a specific focus: the *subject* was Chicago schools, the *policy* under attack was the trailers, and the *person* who needed to "go" was Benjamin Willis. The strategy did not call for immediately abandoning the neighborhood school policy, but rather removing the superintendent who seemed insensitive to the educational needs of black children in Chicago.

In passing, the question should be asked: When selecting its first direct-action program, why did CCCO not address housing as its first priority? After all, this was the underlying cause for segregated schools in Chicago. (As it turned out, housing did become a focus, but only several years later when the SCLC and Martin Luther King came to Chicago in 1965–66.) For its first target, the leaders of CCCO reasoned that they had higher chances of success in achieving the ouster of the superintendent than the much more difficult task of creating open occupancy and ending the discrimination practices among real estate agents, which had contributed to patterns of housing segregation in Chicago.

On his side of the encounter, Willis provided a natural target for the civil rights movement in its first campaign in Chicago. If he had tried, Willis could not have served as a better catalyst for focusing the energies of CCCO in Chicago. Despite many plaudits, he stumbled during 1963 and exposed himself to attack. What happened? How did the superintendent who James Bryant Conant had praised[6] become the brunt of criticism? How did a person who appeared to be firmly in control of the Chicago school system find himself forced to fight for his job?

Willis made a serious mistake when he undertook a part-time assignment for the Commonwealth of Massachusetts: studying its educational system and developing a master plan. In 1963, Chicagoans found it hard to believe that someone earning $50,000 needed a second job. While Willis would have come under attack in any event, his decision to spend spare time and vacation hours on an outside assignment hastened the attack on his administration.

To be fair, Willis enjoyed substantial support in the years immediately following his hiring in 1955, as Ralph's observation attests: "Willis was a tireless supervisor whose professionalism had won the admiration of Chicago's business community and whose commitment to expanding the school system made him a generous source of jobs and of service and building contracts."[7]

By the early 1960s, Willis was no longer seen as the untarnished leader of the Chicago school system. The praise that had been heaped upon him by such people as Conant was fading. Adding to the growing doubts about the wisdom of his neighborhood school policy was the perception of his arrogance and insensitivity to community feelings. For example, during the years of the Willis regime, parents were not allowed to contact their local schools but instead had to place calls to the central office.

Dan Lortie, a professor in the University of Chicago's Department of Education provided some perspectives on Willis. He had been impressed with how Willis had made himself such a central figure in school government in Chicago and had surrounded himself with persons holding similar views. Lortie recalled an episode involving one of his students who served an internship in the central offices of the school system. Given the assignment to propose adjustments to school catchment boundaries, the intern did a little "squiggling" to achieve a bit more integration. Soon thereafter he was called on the carpet by one of the assistant superintendents, who explained, "We do not make social policy here."[8]

In quick order, Willis was challenged on several fronts. During the summer of 1963, vigorous demonstrations orchestrated by the CCCO took place at several sites where temporary classrooms were being installed to handle the surge of enrollments expected in the fall. About the same time, several parents went to court and successfully challenged the Willis policy, demanding that their children be allowed to attend schools other than those designated by the superintendent. As a result of this court victory and the decision of the school board to permit some transferring between districts, Willis resigned in October 1963. However, his departure was short-lived when civic leaders and other groups urged him to reconsider and persuaded him to return to the superintendency.

The serious confrontation stage was reached with a decision by the CCCO to organize a school boycott to be held on October 22, 1963. The leadership of CCCO had decided that normal methods of appeal and redress were fruitless, especially in light of the fact that they had met with Mayor Daley in February to discuss new appointments to the school board without any positive results.

Most members of CCCO felt that some form of direct action was required, and a school boycott became a fait accompli. All over the city, posters and stickers went up announcing it. Newspapers gave it full coverage. Meanwhile, in the white community, minds were divided, including mine.

The impending school boycott caught the new minister of the First Unitarian Church, Jack Kent, by surprise. He had been in the community for only a few weeks when he was confronted with the fact that the CCCO (which included in its membership several church groups but not Unitarians) was planning a school boycott.

In an effort to evaluate the situation as intelligently as possible, Kent decided to attend an emergency meeting of the Hyde Park–Kenwood Council

WANTED—Thousands of Freedom Marchers

MEET at City Hall
(La Salle Street Side)

MARCH
to the Board of Education

SHOW CHICAGO YOU'RE SICK OF
BEN WILLIS-ISM AND 2ND RATE
EDUCATION—RIGHT NOW!

Freedom Day, OCTOBER 22, is the big day to let Mayor Daley know that it's his job to give Chicago a School Board which will truly serve ALL the people equally. So help to shout it loud and clear by coming to City Hall and marching with the thousands who demand ACTION NOW — for a better future for our children.

This is it! Will YOU be there?

Join the Freedom March on City Hall

TUES. OCT. 22 4 P.M.

You Can Help to do the job

Call your friends! Help spread the word about Freedom Day. Get the facts and leaflets for all — at Headquarters:

Appomatox Club
3632 S. Parkway
Phone: 285–1282

Poster urging participation in the school boycott, October 22, 1963. Courtesy Chicago Urban League records, series III, box 89, University of Illinois at Chicago Library, Special Collections.

of Churches. He asked me to join him. At this meeting, the president of the council and several members of its Community Relations Committee presented a report based on their conversations with leaders of the CCCO. The report took no position on the impending boycott. Immediately, an intense discussion ensued over the merits of supporting the CCCO program. Those opposed framed their comments: "This is not a program we should support. We were not part of the decision, and our best course of action is neutrality." Others felt that, "Regardless of whether we were involved in the decision, this campaign must succeed. If we stay on the sidelines, we have in effect taken sides with Willis and the status quo."

As we left the meeting, Kent remarked, "We have to get involved and be a part of these decisions. This whole thing has come so quickly and found us unprepared." On the following Sunday, an open forum was held at the First Unitarian Church to provide members of the congregation an opportunity to express themselves on the subject and share points of view. I chaired this meeting.

Early in the discussion, several schoolteachers got to their feet and opposed any course of action that would keep children out of school. "We spend all our time trying to convince these kids about the importance of school and trying to develop habits of good attendance. Then the civil rights movement tells them to stay home from school." Others echoed these sentiments by saying, "Kids should not be used in a power struggle. Let parents express themselves, but don't use children as pawns." Several members of the congregation who were active in PTA affairs felt that this rush to engage in civil disobedience was ignoring all of their good efforts. And they pointed to the efforts of the Urban League ("Isn't that an organization for and by blacks?" they asked) and its commitment to keep students in school and to avoid the pressures to drop out.

Some speakers focused on the possibility of violence and felt that urging students to participate in the boycott would be tantamount to breaking the law and could end up landing many supporters in jail. A better alternative, they argued, would be for the congregation to use the day (scheduled for the boycott) for prayer and fasting.

Those taking the other side presented their arguments with equal fervor. "You must remember that for most people in the ghetto, their only form of power is their children. Why kid ourselves; if the schools are no good, keeping the children away one day is not going to hurt their learning." Another point made with emphasis: "Remember, Mayor Daley responds to pressure."

The discussion continued back and forth with the opponents of the boycott playing the dominant role. Toward the close of the session, a soft-spoken lady got to her feet. Leigh Reid and her scientist husband George, both African Americans, had just returned from Switzerland where he had spent a year on sabbatical leave. She related how Europeans often had asked them about racial discrimination in the United States. She felt proud of what was happening in her country, now only to find white liberals in her own church rationalizing and equivocating about a course of action that was aimed at achieving racial equality. With tears in her eyes, she asked the people in the room to support the boycott.

People had been leaving the meeting for some time, and only those with strong views remained. I decided the time had already passed when the session should have been adjourned. In my haste to conclude the forum, I merely summarized the arguments for and against the boycott. Nothing was said about the demonstrations scheduled during the day of the boycott and the role adults might play.

As I gathered up my papers, wondering how the meeting had been received and quietly concluding it had been a good "give and take," several people interrupted: "This meeting lacked closure; why weren't people told how they could participate? All this business about whether it is right or wrong to keep kids home does not settle the issue about our role as parents. Unitarians think they can solve all problems with discussions. We need more personal commitment."

When the day of the boycott came, I remained torn. It was hard to tell from the streets of Hyde Park just how many kids were participating in the boycott. On my way to work at the university, I took a different route in order to pass the local elementary school, serving our neighborhood. Several parents stood in the doors handing out leaflets.

After some soul searching, I decided to participate in the demonstration, scheduled for that afternoon. Unlike most of the other participants who reached the Loop in buses as members of community groups, I traveled to City Hall by myself. From several blocks away I could hear the chanting:

"What do you want?"
"Freedom!"
"When do you want it?"
"Now!"

Feelings of both excitement and unease gripped me as I reached City Hall and saw the line of people two by two, circling the building. At this point, I was still a spectator, and indeed many spectators were just watching in silence. For a few moments, I hesitated as I walked along the side of the street, still in the spectator ranks. I hadn't really made up my mind about whether or how to leave the army of spectators and become a marcher. But then the decision was made for me. Jack Kent came strolling down the sidewalk—he was a marcher. I fell in step by his side and we warmly shook hands. Now that I was on the inside, I relaxed and even began to enjoy myself. The sensation was one of exhilaration—a feeling of accomplishment.

On the far side of City Hall, we spotted another person from the church, Dick Fireman, a freelance writer. He was jotting down notes: "Police are everywhere," he wrote in an essay (portions produced here) that appeared later in the weekly Unitarian Church bulletin:

There seems to be a photographer crouched next to every lamppost. The air is a forest of angry signs:—

DR. WILLIS HIRES ILLITERATES!

WILLIS HAS INCREASED SEGREGATION!

SEGREGATED EDUCATION IS UNEQUAL EDUCATION!

90 OF CHICAGO'S SCHOOLS ARE SEGREGATED!

Police whistles orchestrate the background, trying to keep traffic moving around the edges of the conflagration

And the endlessly moving line of march . . . men and women . . . black and white . . . young and old. The turned collar of the ministry appears again and again.

After circling City Hall for a half hour, the march proceeded to the board of education. A speakers' stand had been erected in a parking lot adjacent to the offices. Fiery speech followed fiery speech. The rally dragged on. Introduction after introduction of people who, until this moment, had not been near the civil rights movement. Long harangues about the Chicago situation went on at length. The only bright spot was comedian Dick Gregory, who told a few delightful "instant Negro" stories.

The first school boycott was judged a success. About 200,000 to 300,000 children, out of a total population of 520,000, stayed away from school. Another 3,000 to 4,000 adults participated in the demonstration. Historians Alan Anderson and George Pickering concluded, "The events of 1963 had expanded Chicago's civil rights coalition, the CCCO had established nonviolent, direct action as the norm of the movement and the standard of commitment. Church groups, labor groups, business and professional groups, new-style and old-style civil rights groups, had all made the transition."[9]

Following the school boycott and for the remainder of the fall of 1963, the activities of the CCCO were not as visible, and race relations stories moved off the front pages. Behind the scenes, representatives of the civil rights movement and various officials and board members of the Chicago schools were meeting. The contentious nature of these meetings is captured in excerpts from several statements issued by the CCCO:

> We are here to serve notice on Mr. Roddewig [chair of the Chicago Board of Education] that his blatant disavowal of any concern with the issue of school integration has rendered him unfit in our judgment either to preside over the Chicago public school system or to deal with us.
>
> There can be no neutral ground between integration and segregation. Roddewig and Willis and their supporters on the Board, by refusing to address themselves to a positive policy of integration, stand guilty of accepting and furthering the actuality of segregation. In so doing, they have betrayed all the children of our city, white as well as Negro, in that both must suffer the handicap of ignorance, or fear, or bigotry, in the absence of an educational program which helps them to understand each other and the world they must share together as adults.

The assassination of President John F. Kennedy on November 22, 1963, heightened already existing tensions. When the CCCO announced in late November that it would resume further direct action, if necessary, to achieve school integration in the city, the chair of the board, Clair M. Roddewig, countered: "There has been too much direct action in this country." Lawrence Landry, a leader of the Student Nonviolent Coordinating Committee (SNCC), in his capacity as chair of the Negotiating Committee for the CCCO, responded at a meeting with the board of education:

> The shadow of President Kennedy's death hangs over our meeting today. For us in Chicago, the shadow is deepened by Mr. Roddewig's reported response last week to our announcement that we shall resume direct action if necessary to achieve school integration in our city. Mr. Roddewig said, "There has been too much direct action already in this country last weekend." The press said that Mr. Roddewig was referring, of course, to the murder of our President.
>
> Only ignorance of the profound meaning of the Negro's movement all over our country today for the benefits of American law denied him for so long—or else hostility to that movement—could engender so irresponsible a comment.[10]

When the board of education finally took a position regarding integration of the schools in a press release on February 13, 1964, its statement stopped short of promising any immediate action. "The members of the Chicago Board of Education believe that this city . . . would be healthier . . . education-ally . . . if [it] reflected the kind of racial and ethnic diversity characteristic of the nation as a whole. . . . However, we see no single overall step or action by which such diversity can be brought immediately to all our schools by the Board of Education alone."

Leaders of the civil rights movement expressed deep disappointment and announced that a second school boycott, which had been under consideration, would now go forward on February 25, 1964. This decision had been taken only after heated discussions during several CCCO meetings in January and February. Bill Berry of the Urban League opposed another school boycott, arguing for more behind-the-scenes sessions with the mayor, while Lawrence Landry spoke strongly for the need to organize another boycott. Landry's position carried the majority. Seventeen organizations supported the motion, three were opposed, and one abstained.[11]

For members of the Social Action Committee back at the Unitarian Church, the latest decision by the CCCO produced considerable consternation as well as surprise. Most had hoped that the first school boycott had been sufficiently persuasive to produce some movement by the board of education, thereby ending the need for more direct action. Their frustration stemmed from a realization that Unitarians were still on the sidelines. In the first school boycott, religious liberals had been caught short because they had failed to appreciate the speed and intensity of the developing civil rights movement. But they had dealt with their surprise by saying, "This thing is moving faster than we anticipated—we had better get on board." With the announcement of the second boycott, the questioning centered on whether such action was wise. "They made their point the first time" some said. "So why is it necessary to have a second boycott?"

Reverend Kent received the news of another boycott with renewed dismay. "Here is another decision we have to react to. We must become a part of CCCO and participate in these decisions." While he did not disagree with the action, as a religious leader he reacted negatively to being in a "follower-ship" position. In fact, during January of 1964, Kent had preached a series of sermons on the "Negro Revolt." I was impressed with his analysis and sensitivity to the complex issues of civil disobedience and his understanding of the different approaches that various groups within the black community were advocating (e.g., the rapidly growing Black Muslim movement).

As I thought about the issues that Kent had raised in his sermon, I focused on two questions. The first: What were the standards for judging the appropriateness of civil disobedience that would justify another program of direct action? This issue had been on the agenda of the adult discussion group for several weeks, and it was very much connected to the themes that Martin Luther King had outlined in his "Letter from Birmingham Jail."

The second question on my mind was: How could the African American community develop its cohesion and self-respect without pulling back and operating independently from the larger (white) community? Re-

Rev. Jack Kent, minister of First Unitarian Church during the 1960s. Courtesy Archives, First Unitarian Church.

lated to this point was an example that had been presented by one of the participants in the adult discussion group about a group of black doctors on the South Side who demanded that they be given the right of "first refusal" for a piece of ground that a businessman (white) from the North Side wanted to develop for a medical center. This developer was forced to withdraw his bid in the face of pressure and insistence from the black doctors and local community leaders that only African Americans be allowed to develop this property.

In the meetings of the Social Action Committee of the church during late January and early February, intense discussions took place over whether we should endorse the impending boycott. As with the deliberations regarding the first boycott, differing points of view were expressed. Many wanted to do something "constructive" in lieu of supporting the boycott. The suggestion was made to develop a brochure that would list the many service programs underway in Chicago that were aimed at improving the well-being of the African American community. Someone suggested that information be included on how to volunteer to work with the various activist organizations. "I may not feel that I can participate in a demonstration, but I want to work in the office of CORE," observed one individual.

A proposal to give additional attention to black history generated considerable discussion. Many thought that it would be desirable to devote several weeks each year in the curriculum of the church school to the study of black history. Reflecting the middle ground, one participant commented: "Let's give it proper attention, but let's not overemphasize it."

Ultimately, the Social Action Committee decided not to take a position but expressed its "deep concern for quality, integrated education"; and noting the lack of agreement among its members on the boycott issue, the committee issued a report presenting statements by Margaret Matchett and myself to bracket perspectives on the subject.

Margaret represented the best of the socially concerned activists frequently found in Hyde Park. She embodied the skills and savvy of a woman versed in how to work for change within organizations. As a schoolteacher, a former president of a local PTA group, and a committee member at the high school, she possessed considerable experience and knowledge about the school situation in Chicago. We frequently walked home together from Social Action Committee meetings. On one occasion, she stated her concerns about the civil rights movement quite openly. She observed that from her point of view, TWO was taking only negative stands. She felt that TWO and CCCO had a responsibility to develop a master plan for the city and especially for Hyde Park. She wanted the civil rights movement to follow a constructive course of action as a way to gain recognition and influence.

I countered that groups like the PTA might have to step into the background and allow the direct-action groups to employ their strategies for changing the status quo. I felt that persuasion and a gradual approach to change had been tried for many years but was painfully slow. I am not sure I convinced her that the use of power and the exercise of coercion were necessary. To make my argument a little more palatable, I predicted that once negotiations started, those who were in the background would be called back "on stage."

The debate over the wisdom of the impending boycott also occurred at my place of employment, the Graduate School of Business of the University of Chicago. A colleague, knowing of my involvement, took me on: "The focus on Willis is not wise. He will be retiring soon. And does the Negro community really dislike him that much? And when he leaves, then what? Integration is not the issue—quality education is the issue." I countered (probably not convincingly) with several points: "Willis has become a symbol. The civil rights movement has adopted a program, and it is important for us to support it, warts and all."

The second boycott also became a political issue, much more so than for the first boycott. This became clear when a leading black alderman, Kenneth Campbell, announced that he opposed the second school boycott and that he was mobilizing his precinct captains to canvass their neighborhoods urging parents to keep their children in school.

Thus, what started out as a confrontation between the CCCO and the Chicago School Board evolved into a larger struggle between the civil rights movement and the black aldermen who represented their communities in the City Council. This development only served to increase my support for the second school boycott. I remembered how Tim Black had attempted to wrest political leadership of a nearby ward away from an entrenched black politician. While Tim had garnered only 3,000 to 4,000 votes, compared to the incumbent's 12,000 or 13,000, his performance was encouraging since he had only entered the campaign a few weeks before the election. However, in another respect, the results were discouraging. Tim had secured most of his votes from the middle-class community of Kenwood, while in the lower-income neighborhoods the incumbent had been overwhelmingly supported.

The Daley machine, with a strong base in the black neighborhoods, demonstrated awesome efficiency. All eight black aldermen were aligned with Mayor Daley. Had these politicians gained the support of their constituents out of ignorance or fear—ignorance, because the people in the "ghetto" did not appreciate the leverage that an independent (like Alderman Len Despres) or another antimachine politician could exercise; or fear, because they believed politicians could strip them of their welfare benefits and other sources of support?

When the day of the boycott arrived (February 25, 1964), I decided that my involvement would not be marching but teaching—and not the classroom at the university but in a small back room of a local church. The First Baptist and First Unitarian Churches of Chicago had agreed to sponsor freedom schools during the second school boycott. The boards of trustees of these two churches had remained neutral about the boycott itself but had agreed to sponsor a type of "Red Cross" service by providing schooling for those students who had decided to observe the boycott.

For the most part, the trustees of the Unitarian Church were more conservative than the congregation and hesitated to endorse the militant activities of the civil rights movement. (Ultimately they did contribute financial resources to CCCO.) Another factor was probably decisive, however—the church was on the verge of a major fund drive. A professional fund-raiser had been recruited, and in his first meeting with the board had urged the church to avoid controversial issues during the campaign.

This same tension between institutional survival and social action had occurred elsewhere: a group of African American ministers had organized a boycott against a large milk company on the South Side. Flyers had been sent to clergymen around Chicago urging them to announce from their pulpits a boycott of the company's product. The ministers, normally 100 percent behind civil rights, refrained from making the announcement "on advice of their fundraisers."

The task of finding teachers for the freedom school was given to the director of religious education at the Unitarian Church. She was not happy with the assignment. Indeed, she had never shown much enthusiasm for the civil rights movement and especially for the idea of a school boycott. But since the board of trustees had voted to support a freedom school, as an employee of the church she set about the task of recruiting staff. I agreed to teach at the school after I learned that my wife, Nancy, had been asked to handle a classroom for several hours. Being inexperienced in teaching and having three young children to look after, she felt unable to accept but suggested that they contact me.

I reached the freedom school about 1:00 P.M. An experienced K-12 teacher had handled the group in the morning, and I was asked to take over for the afternoon. The group numbered approximately twenty, about two-thirds African American and one-third white students. For the first thirty minutes, things proceeded smoothly. Several of the students read stories from a book about black history, and then some freedom songs were played. However, by 2:00, the students had become quite restless.

I am not quite sure what I had expected to find. Perhaps students who would be completely attentive to the purpose and spirit of the day? Or model children singing freedom songs and making inspirational remarks about the civil rights movement? Some of this was present, particularly in the deportment of two white girls who were extremely well behaved and attentive. However, for some students it was a lark, a day away from the routine of their normal schoolrooms. Here they could draw pictures, excuse themselves to go to the bathroom (it seemed as if each student needed to go to the bathroom every half hour), all without the structure and control from their accustomed teachers.

The last hour hung heavy, and I kept looking at my watch hoping the time would pass quickly. About this point, the director of religious education peered through the door and asked how things were going. Things were not going well, as the children were cavorting around the room, and I felt embarrassed at my lack of control over the youngsters. Back at the university, teaching MBA students raised no discipline problems—intellectual issues, yes, but not the challenge of maintaining some degree of order.

Fortunately, the director left the scene before it became too obvious that I was not up to the task, and I continued to struggle for the children's attention.

A few other people looked through the open door, two of them friends of mine from work. They smiled!

At the close of the session, each student was given a certificate. It was an impressive document containing inspirational words about the purpose of the freedom school and the "witness" that these youngsters had demonstrated. I thought about distributing the certificates in a formal ceremony. Instead, the kids crowded around and took them as if I were giving out candy.

The kids were kids: responsive in some ways, easily distracted in other ways. The two girls who had been particularly attentive turned out to be the children of a respected member of the board of education, James Clement. He had heard about the freedom school and had been convinced to send his children after reading the bulletin from the Social Action Committee. One never knows who is influenced by "Conversations with the Congregation!"

Years later, as I was doing research for this chronicle, I interviewed Kim Clement, who was ten years old at the time of the freedom school. Clement recalled that when she came home after her day at the freedom school, her father wanted to know all about it, and to make sure that she and her sister had benefited from the experience. Her parents always talked about social issues, and she remembered sitting around the dinner table and the big impact these conversations had on her. She mentioned that when she was in college, she became a Vietnam War protester and participated in several marches in Washington.[12]

From the perspective of the civil rights movement, the day was successful and meaningful. Over 100,000 students remained home from school, considerably more than independent observers had predicted but many less than the first boycott. Some skeptics pointed to the fact that it was not hard to keep children home from school, particularly those who did not have much zest for education. But if the other freedom schools had anywhere near the same energy and life as my group, then I felt certain that something more than just idle play had occurred around the city.

So how should the two boycotts be evaluated? What function did they serve? Were they useful tactics, given the strategic objective of forcing change in the superintendency and its policy of neighborhood schools?

For his part, Superintendent Willis did not hesitate to express his views about the two school boycotts. In a statement submitted to the board of education on March 11, 1964, he went on record with the statement: "The spectacle of having large numbers of youngsters involved in illegal acts has extremely dangerous implications for every American, regardless of differences in race, creed, religion, or points of view on the complex social issues which confront and divide our society." Willis went on to say, "Violation of attendance laws in this state and elsewhere do a great disservice to those allegedly being helped, the school children. We are a society organized on the basis of law, and no responsible citizen and democracy can condone flagrant violations of duly constituted law. Such practices, if unchecked, can result only in conditions of chaos and anarchy."[13]

At the meeting at which this report was presented, board member Raymond Pasnick criticized Willis for blaming unrest in the schools on the boycotts. In turn, Willis said Pasnick should apologize.

Warren Bacon, another board member, asked for more accurate information on school violence. It was his understanding that violence actually had declined, and he called the statement by Willis "hysterical." For his part, Willis did not provide any data to support his assertions—a pattern often repeated.

On several occasions, the leaders of the CCCO had requested from the board a census by race for all the schools in the system—they wanted to analyze the extent of de facto segregation in Chicago schools. No information was released. Larry Cuban, a keen analyst of school superintendents, especially of the urban variety, commented: "For Harold Spears [superintendent of schools in San Francisco] and Benjamin Willis to reject a demand from civil rights activists for a racial census further enflamed passions rather than defusing them."[14]

Back at the church and in other quarters, the question about the "yield," if any, that the two boycotts had produced, dominated discussions. Some noted reports of high-level meetings involving members of the board of education and various civic leaders, with assurances that changes would take place. Certainly the civil rights leadership, privy to these assurances, could credit the two boycotts with important (implied) concessions coming from the city administration and the board of education, but among the rank and file a deep sense of frustration developed. "We have marched, we have mounted two successful boycotts, and Willis is still in office." Tim Black and the NALC had succeeded in bringing Motorola into face-to-face discussions. But the CCCO had not been able to do the same with the board of education. Anderson and Pickering stated it more succinctly in commenting on the first boycott: "The success of the school boycott was more of a problem for CCCO than it was for the Board of Education."[15]

Of course, the marchers, the teachers in the freedom schools, and the parents who coped with two no-school days could not calibrate the impact of the boycotts on the larger community. These well-publicized, direct-action programs in Chicago presaged and paralleled similar programs in many other cities during 1963 and 1964 and could be seen as part of a larger strategy of sustained and symbolic pressure to sensitize the white community to the need for change in the many arenas of civil rights and race relations.

While the two school boycotts in October 1963 and February 1964 had not succeeded in their stated objective, that is, the forced resignation of Superintendent Willis, they had provided an important rationale for bringing a large number of direct-action organizations, church, and community groups together in one omnibus organization: CCCO. The mobilization of the black community as well as sympathetic elements of the white community had been galvanized by the rallies and meetings that accompanied the two boycotts. The more serious forms of engagement that had been occurring elsewhere in the country, especially in the South—particularly marches that triggered violent backlashes—these were still to come in Chicago during the summers of 1965 and 1966.

5. The Movement Marks Time while the University Plays Catch-Up

Let knowledge grow from more to more,
and so be human life enriched.

—motto, University of Chicago

After the second school boycott in February 1964, the civil rights scene in Chicago quieted down again. Meetings of the CCCO were held infrequently. The first leader of the CCCO, Arthur Brazier, stepped aside and the second line assumed charge. Al Raby moved into the convener's role.

Brazier and Raby could not have been more different. Brazier spoke with authority, with the style of a seasoned preacher. Raby presented the profile of a quiet, behind-the-scenes staffer. A local newspaper described him as "a nervous, thin type man standing 6 feet 1 inch." Ralph offers a succinct summary of Raby's qualities: "Raby was neither a dynamic speaker nor a particularly charismatic leader. But Raby was patient, a good listener, and a skilled reconciler—three essential qualities for a CCCO convener."[1]

At meetings scheduled sporadically during the spring of 1964, Raby's leadership style gradually became evident. He chose the role of a discussion leader. At times, I felt he almost bent over backwards to give everyone a chance to speak—he would not call for a decision until there had been ample discussion and opportunity for consensus to emerge—not surprising, I thought, given his experience in the labor movement and his experience as a seventh-grade English teacher in the Chicago public schools. In this respect, Raby and Tim Black shared much in common: they were educators, and they were both committed to using their organizational talents for the benefit of the civil rights movement and the larger causes it pursued.

The slow pace after February stemmed not just from new leadership but also from a sense of bewilderment—two massive school boycotts had been held and nothing concrete had happened. The city seemed pretty much the same. Superintendent Willis was still in office.

Actually, Superintendent Willis had taken several actions. In May 1964, he announced a plan to change district boundaries, affecting forty schools. And in June 1964, the administration authorized thirty-four more "Willis wagons," the mobile classrooms. To many observers, these moves only served to illustrate that the superintendent was just as intransigent as ever or, at best, only instituting changes at the margin.

This mood of letdown also characterized an educational conference sponsored by the NALC in April of 1964. At the conference, several militant leaders spoke of alternatives to holding more demonstrations. One speaker called upon the audience to join with him in recruiting an army of the unemployed. "By mobilizing the jobless of Chicago, by helping them enroll in government programs, by presenting ourselves in a qualified manner, we can take the fight to another level."

Representatives from CORE told of their plans to operate freedom houses during the upcoming summer months. A few delegates spoke of the need for more direct action, but even they recognized that just as much emphasis should be given to organizing the black community and recruiting individuals to take advantage of new opportunities as to breaking down existing barriers. As I listened to these statements, I wondered why the loss of momentum had occurred so quickly. Only a year before, the focus had been on direct action and demanding equal opportunities for African Americans. Now, just a year later, the emphasis seemed to be shifting—to self-help programs and the mobilization of the residents of the ghetto.

Understandably, the lead was passing from the civil rights movement to community groups and government agencies. Many government programs were coming on the scene: training facilities, neighborhood centers for the unemployed, and other initiatives sponsored by the network of state employment offices. Community groups like the YMCA had undertaken special programs, and well-established organizations like the Urban League were working overtime to meet the many requests for assistance.

Organizing the unemployed was a good idea. The black community needed to assert leadership for the disadvantaged. But where would such a movement go? What could it do? What would be its focus? Help for the disadvantaged was beginning to come from the government, and an army of unemployed could not pressure government—at least in Chicago. And then how many of the unemployed could be induced to march in the streets? Could the residents of public housing, such as the Robert Taylor Homes, be recruited? Many of them were the very people who, for one reason or another, never made it to the nearest employment office. Maybe they could be *hired* to demonstrate, but where would the money come from, and why should they be paid to demonstrate in their own behalf? I thought back to a previous meeting of the NALC, when a trade union leader from the United Electrical Workers Union, in response to a criticism that not many of the marchers were unemployed, remarked, "We can't get out the unemployed even if we bus them." So mobilizing the unemployed might not be a feasible strategy.

And what was the continuing role for militant groups like CORE and SNCC? Perhaps their new role would emphasize black improvement rather than continued direct action; and indeed, groups like CORE were turning to community uplift programs. And while CORE and other organizations had the talent and leadership to make a difference in the ghetto, they did not have the means to cope with the magnitude of the problems of poverty, unemployment, and discrimination. Only the federal government, it seemed, could mobilize the resources necessary to do the job. But the government was not the community, and the community desperately needed to assert leadership and not be forced into a posture of receiving handouts.

Dr. Quentin Young, a well-respected family physician, convened two forums in which he brought together representatives from different community groups and fostered a dialogue with leading members of the civil rights movements. While these meetings had been very well received, to my thinking they were only a beginning.

There did not seem to be any clear or easy answers to these questions. Only time would tell. So I drew together some thoughts that I wanted to share with Reverend Kent. First, I noted that the tactics and thinking of people on the direct-action side of the movement were becoming more extreme while at the same time most members of the white community were becoming less and less tolerant of these tactics. So I saw a growing cleavage between the militants in the civil rights movement and many white liberals with whom I associated. Some type of third force was needed. The CCCO might not be able to provide the bridge, and for myself I felt I was too involved on the activist side to be seen as someone who would have the objectivity to help with this reconciliation

Throughout the summer of 1964, the black community in Chicago remained quiet. The newspapers spoke ominously of simmering discontent. Riots had occurred in Harlem, Buffalo, Paterson, New Jersey (my birthplace), and other Eastern cities. "When will the trouble strike Chicago?" people asked.

In an effort to channel energies and to release the discontent that existed, the CCCO and the Church Federation of Chicago decided to organize a massive rally. The third Sunday in June, the twenty-first, was chosen. The setting was Soldier Field. The assemblage numbered 40–50,000 people sympathetic to the civil rights movement. The featured speaker was Rev. Martin Luther King Jr.

I, along with others who attended the event, judged the rally a huge success. The crowd was impressive in size, and thousands filled out cards volunteering their services. A sense of unity was achieved as all the civil rights leaders from Chicago appeared on one platform and shared their hopes and concerns with the audience. Certainly, in a ceremonial sense, and perhaps in a religious sense, the rally left its mark. As Reverend King moved around the field in an open automobile, the crowd surged toward him. People tried to reach him as he passed nearby. The "Messiah" was in Chicago.

But I also wondered if the day could not have been put to better use. Could the energies of this large crowd have been directed into more constructive channels, organizing community block groups, teaching youngsters, or more dramatically, focusing on discrimination via a mass demonstration in the Loop or even outside the Mayor's home? In Soldier Field, the energies had been dissipated. True, the newspapers covered the occasion but the impact was to a large extent encapsulated in the stadium. The money that was collected (almost $60,000) barely covered the costs of staging the affair. The thousands and thousands of cards (asking for volunteers) that people completed were never processed. The occasion created an emotional high, but would anything fundamentally change?

The emotional release accompanying the Soldier Field rally served as a brief contrast to the lethargy that continued for several more months. It was not until November, as the weather turned colder and the long hot summer ended, that meetings of the CCCO were held once again. No riots had occurred in Chicago, although nearby Dixmoor had experienced some disturbances, but at the same time the civil rights movement could not claim any programmatic success.

The notice announcing the November (1964) meeting represented the first "official" invitation I had received to attend a meeting of the CCCO. Previously, I had attended sessions as a guest of Tim Black or just by showing up. The invitation attested to the fact that the Unitarians and Universalists of Chicago had finally been accepted into the CCCO. Fulfilling Jack Kent's wish, "We have to get involved in CCCO," an application for membership had been submitted. Individual churches could *not* join the CCCO. Rather, membership was only available to denominations and established community organizations. So, for the activists of First Unitarian Church, it had meant persuading the Social Responsibility Commission of the Chicago Council of Liberal Churches to make application for membership. Richard Nash, chair of the commission, and I were nominated to serve as the two delegates to the CCCO.

However, the secretary of the CCCO had lost the council's first check, and it had taken another two months before Nash and I became official members of the CCCO. I wondered how tolerant the civil rights movement would be of employers who took such a long time to process applications for employment.

Only a handful of people attended this meeting. In contrast to the 50 or 60 delegates who had attended sessions when school boycotts were on the agenda, only a few stalwarts were on hand—and they were not the key leaders of the member organizations. They were the operatives of the civil rights movement. The main purpose of the meeting was to decide future strategy regarding the Chicago schools. Al Raby, the convener, wanted to appoint a subcommittee and asked the group to make suggestions regarding possible courses of action. Tim Black suggested that a large conference be held to examine the Chicago school system. This conference would consider several reports being prepared on the Chicago schools. Another delegate countered, "We don't need another conference. Everyone knows how bad the Chicago schools are. What we need is action, some way of getting Willis out of office."

Philip M. Hauser, professor of sociology, founder and director, Population Research Center, University of Chicago. Courtesy Special Collections Research Center, University of Chicago.

Tim Black's mention of reports being prepared on Chicago schools referred to work by two University of Chicago professors, Philip Hauser and Robert Havighurst. These studies had been commissioned by the board of education, and Hauser reported first in March 1964.[2] The Hauser report did not advocate busing, but rather it outlined modest steps toward eliminating segregation.

In August 1964, in a speech to the American Federation of Teachers, Hauser noted that five months had passed since his report, and he expressed frustration over the lack of action on the part of the superintendent and the board of education. "The Chicago Board of Education has proved to be weak and vacillating." He went on to say: "The two forces that have beaten the Board into an inactive and inert body have been: (1) a reluctant general superintendent, and (2) a vociferous minority group which is blatantly anti-Negro and constitutes the local version of the 'white backlash.'"

Shortly before the CCCO meeting in November 1964, Havighurst released his five-hundred-page report entitled "Report of the Advisory Panel on Integration in Public Schools."[3] It opened with the statement: "The time has come for this city . . . fully to recognize the unprecedented crisis that confronts the public school, and to weigh the cost of improving education against the cost of not doing so." The report by Havighurst concluded that residential segregation was the basic problem confronting the schools. He advocated the board of education's promoting integration by breaking the school system into regions and creating a new position of assistant superintendent for integration and community development.

Several months after issuing his report, in February 1965, Havighurst expressed the same frustration that Hauser had earlier voiced. In his speech, Havighurst noted that a subcommittee of the board had spent considerable time meeting with representatives from various local communities to consider proposals for both stabilizing the integrated schools and encouraging more African American pupils to transfer to predominantly white schools. He concluded by saying, "The superintendent has not yet declared himself on the matter of integration, although the Board of Education adopted in April 1964 [almost a year earlier] a set of recommendations regarding the integration of the school system."[4]

For his part, Willis outlined his views in an interview in the magazine *Phi Delta Kappan*. He argued that his job was to focus on educating all the children, regardless of color or race. He went on to describe what he saw as the problem. The districts with disadvantaged pupils were also those that were growing rapidly. He felt that race was educationally irrelevant and that the focus should be on dealing with overcrowding. He

Robert J. Havighurst, University of Chicago professor of education and member of the Committee on Human Development. Courtesy Special Collections Research Center, University of Chicago.

summarized his position: "We do not have a problem of segregation, only a complicated problem of education. This is not evasion; it is keeping our eye on the educational ball and refusing to be distracted by highly charged emotional issues. Concentrating on racial aspects of a problem only creates more problems."[5]

At the CCCO meeting, a Catholic priest in attendance expressed concern about staging any more school boycotts, fearing that another school boycott would split the community wide open. He thought the movement had already experienced considerable backlash and that, for example, people on the Southwest Side might mount their own demonstrations if the CCCO sponsored another boycott. The question of backlash was real. Alabama Governor George Wallace had been campaigning in the North and speaking about the race question. Everyone was "holding their breath" about the growing negative reaction within the white community to the tactics of the civil rights movement.

Toward the end of the meeting, Norman Hill, a leader from the West Side SNCC organization, stood up and delivered an impassioned speech about the quibbling and the hesitant help of white liberals: "We have been hurt in the past and we will be hurt again. We have gone along with our friends in the past who have told us to take it easy and let the forces of change play their role. I say that the time has come for us to act now and do it whether our friends are with us or not." It was clear to me that by "friends" he meant the white people sitting in the room.

I had observed Hill on several previous occasions. He spoke eloquently and calmly, but behind his cool manner burned a fire. I hoped it was a fire that could drive the engines of the civil rights movement and not a fire that would destroy it. Earlier I had interacted with Hill at a planning session of the NALC. Tim Black, president of the organization, had been careful not to invite me to such meetings. After all, the NALC was an organization for blacks, not whites. However, on this one occasion, Tim needed help planning a major conference and he had asked several people from the University of Chicago to chair workshop sessions. Hill was at this meeting, and he gave me an icy stare (or that is the way I perceived his demeanor). In fact, he carefully avoided shaking hands or offering any recognition. When the agenda of the meeting turned away from the conference and to a discussion of strategic questions facing the NALC, I felt uncomfortable and found an excuse to leave the room and head home. In fact, Tim diplomatically conveyed the message when he said, "Bob, don't feel you have to stay; we don't want to take too much of your time."

Hill represented an important element in the CCCO. Militants such as Hill possessed a consuming passion for the direct-action agenda of the civil rights movement. Some of them sat in sessions biting their lips until they got an opportunity to speak. Others drummed their fingers on the table as they stared out the window.

It was awesome to see the devotion of these people. It was also fearsome to observe their determination and militancy. They liked controversy, and indeed, they seemed to thrive on situations in which they were in the minority. At times I wondered if the militants were not glad the superintendent of schools, Willis, was so obstinate and aloof. He provided a perfect target for their militancy. If the superintendent were more charitable and constructive, it might have frustrated these activists. They needed an anvil on which to hammer out their anger.

The CCCO provided an important venue for talented individuals. Similar to the labor movement, the civil rights movement was a proving ground for "diamonds in the rough." Where else in our society could people with this leadership potential find expression for their energies? Many activists without substantial formal education were writing brilliant letters of protest—letters filled with anger but also containing valid points and persuasive arguments.

Eventually, Al Raby took control of the discussion and said that in his opinion the best strategy would be to work for the quiet removal of Willis. Apparently a committee of influential citizens had been meeting with the mayor, and there was every hope that Willis would not be reappointed when his contract expired in mid-1965. The choice, as Al saw it, was whether to keep up the pressure via more demonstrations, which would dramatize continued opposition to Willis, or to lay low and give people behind the scenes an opportunity to develop a graceful exit for the superintendent. Al believed it might be difficult for Mayor Daley to bring about Willis's removal if he appeared to be giving into pressure. For this reason, Al favored a go-slow policy.

It was unfortunate, I felt, that so much time was being spent debating the Willis matter while critical issues at the community level remained unresolved. In Hyde Park for example, a battle was raging about how and where to provide additional high school capacity. Should it be an extension of the existing facility located in Woodlawn or should it be a new building within Hyde Park proper? The Hyde Park community was very ambivalent and could benefit from the input of an organization like the CCCO. Some liberals supported the comprehensive plan—it was a way of staying related to Woodlawn and not dodging the problem of educating large numbers of black children. Others in the community with equally good intentions wanted a school that could achieve a viable racial balance and not end up being overwhelmingly black. They expressed concern about the social atmosphere of the existing high school and questioned whether any school, however comprehensive and imaginative, could ever be viable when located at the edge of the large black ghetto. The CCCO seemed remote from these gritty problems of designing a new high school and the need to achieve some workable consensus given such divergent community attitudes.

Shortly before the meeting adjourned, the attendees heard from a visitor who had been waiting patiently to make a report about efforts going on around the city to secure an open occupancy bill. (The concept of *open occupancy* envisioned a real estate market in which a prospective renter or buyer of housing could not be barred on the basis of race or national origin.) The visitor addressed the delegates assuming they exercised considerable influence within the black community. But could these representatives rally the community behind open occupancy? The delegates nodded their heads, but were they as powerful as the visitor believed?

I also wondered why CCCO was spending so much time on so many different subjects. It had barely come to grips with the school question, and now it was mulling over the housing problem. In addition, several other subjects had been put forward for discussion during the long meeting, which ran from 10:00 AM (when participants went to the cafeteria to get breakfast) until after 2:00 (when people went to the same cafeteria to get lunch). The meeting ended abruptly when Al Raby suddenly headed for the door saying, "The TV and newspaper men are outside waiting for a statement. Will someone else chair the meeting?" The rest of us decided to adjourn. Without Al's leadership, we might as well go home.

While the civil rights movement was quiet during the summer of 1964, Dean George Shultz took the initiative at the University of Chicago to design a program that responded to the crisis. The program taking shape at the Graduate School of Business initially carried the official title, "Careers for Negroes in Management"; later it came to be known as the Black MBA Program. The program brochure observed, "There is substantial evidence of the growing desire of business organizations to employ capable Negroes in management positions. Because able Negroes intent on professional careers have sought them in fields other than business, the present demand for Negroes trained for business careers is far greater than the available and immediately foreseeable supply."

Later, in correspondence reflecting on the impetus for the program, Shultz recalled, "Prior to the program, we had received no applications from [African Americans] because: (1) they could not afford the cost; (2) they could

Dean George P. Shultz, architect of the "Careers for Negroes in Management" program, standing in the library
of the Graduate School of Business, University of Chicago. Courtesy George Shultz.

not imagine being accepted for a job in management; (3) they had no human
contact with anyone—either a father, brother, uncle, or friend— in management; and (4) so management education seemed to be expensive and an
alien unknown."[6]

The financial support for such a program would come from business itself.
Large companies would be approached and asked for fellowship money and
slots for summer employment. No guarantee would be asked for employment
of enrollees after graduation. The resources received from the companies
would cover each student's tuition and provide a modest stipend for living
expenses. Summer internships between the first and second years at the

Careers for Negroes in Management

Graduate School of Business
University of Chicago

Brochure for recruiting sponsor companies and applicants for "Careers for Negroes in Management." Author's collection.

sponsoring companies would offer a valuable "look-see" for both sides as well as supplemental income.

Early in the launch of this new initiative, Shultz organized a luncheon and invited Bill Berry, executive director of the Urban League, to attend. Shultz asked me if I would round out the table with another guest, and I immediately thought of Alex Poinsett, from *Ebony Magazine*, someone I knew well as a fellow Unitarian. The luncheon went well. Shultz outlined background information on the program, summarized the impetus behind it, and presented steps to be taken to acquaint prospective students with opportunities in the field of business. After about twenty minutes, Bill Berry interrupted Shultz to ask: "It seems to me you're a bit timid about promoting this program. Are you embarrassed by your effort to help Negroes?"

Well! Berry had hit the dean with a tough question. Berry knew how to challenge white people, and he relished the task of exposing what he suspected might be the ambivalence of liberal whites toward improvement programs for blacks. He was a favorite speaker at church groups and community associations, where he skillfully created feelings of "guilt." The strategy, of course, was to place people in a position where they could only live with themselves by "getting involved." This might mean personal participation; or it might mean financial support. Whatever the response, the result was the same, namely, to enable white people to work off what psychologists call "dissonance."

In many respects, Berry resembled a clergyman. He was both a prophet (creating the sense of shame) and a father confessor (providing avenues by which people could relieve their feelings of guilt). But just as churchgoers may tire of being put through emotional highs and lows, some members of the white community grew tired of hearing the same rhetoric over and over again. At a first encounter with him, one was quite impressed; as the number of encounters increased, one found his message less compelling.

For Shultz, this was his first meeting with Bill Berry. The question, "Are you embarrassed?" derailed the dean's organized presentation—not because the dean was not used to interruptions (after all, he governed a spirited group of faculty members), but because the school's sponsorship of a special program for black students had indeed raised some issues with corporate supporters and faculty of the school.

The original idea for such a program had originated with Inland Steel. Characteristic of its liberal and somewhat independent outlook, the company had decided that business should take the lead in increasing the flow of blacks into American management. The genesis of the program had developed in an interesting way. When Neale Stearns (associate dean for development at the school and a former Inland vice president) died, George Shultz approached Inland regarding a contribution in Stearns' memory. Inland replied that they did not want to make a contribution for this purpose, but would be interested in supporting a program to attract blacks to study business administration. As a result, Shultz met with Frank Cassell and several other Inland executives, and their discussions led to the concept of the Black MBA program.

Joe Block, chairman of Inland, hosted a luncheon in the company's dining room, presenting the program to representatives of about a dozen companies. I attended this luncheon. Both Shultz and Block made very persuasive presentations. Most of the companies in attendance joined the program, including Brunswick Corporation, Carson Pirie Scott, Commonwealth Edison, First National Bank of Chicago, Hart Schaffner & Marx, Inland Steel, Spiegel, Standard Oil of New Jersey, and United Airlines.

To publicize the new program, George Shultz and William Lowe, vice president of finance at Inland, visited several predominantly black colleges. Following up on those visits, a black assistant from the school's placement office, second-year MBA students, and Yoxall visited black colleges to meet with faculty and students to tell them about the program. I visited Fisk University, one of the schools that supplied a substantial number of enrollees in the program.

Difficulties soon developed, however. Several other firms declined to participate when approached about supporting such a program, some offering negative reactions: "Since when have we set up a special program for Caucasians? The business school must be misguided to support such preferential treatment for blacks."

From within the faculty ranks at GSB, questions (some bordering on opposition) also emerged. One response occurred when I asked Professor Yale Brozen whether small Negro colleges were included on the solicitation list for a special summer program for faculty in economics. I was prompted to ask this question when the liaison person from the GE Foundation (which was financing the program) inquired about how widely nets were being cast for applicants. In a note to Brozen, I said: "I am just checking with you to see if the small Negro colleges (I believe there are some 30 or 40 of them) are on our mailing list for our summer GE Institute for faculty teaching economics." Brozen responded that all four-year liberal arts colleges were on the mailing list. He indicated that usually one or two professors each summer came from what he called "Negro derivation." His final paragraph spoke to his irritation with my request: "I remember only one case of rejection, which I am sure was an applicant from a Negro school. The applicant was a white man of Czech origin. I am sure we must have rejected many more than this from Negro schools. We make no effort to practice discrimination against white schools."

All of these events and ramifications must have flashed across Dean Shultz's mind as he formulated an answer to Bill Berry's query. Despite Shultz's agile mind, the time interval seemed awkwardly long. Finally he answered, "Perhaps we have been a bit timid, but it has not been out of embarrassment but out of modesty. We haven't wanted to talk too much about the program for fear we would seem to be boasting. I feel there is too much attention given to programs that are mere ideas. We wanted to accomplish something before we talked about it publicly. I can see, however, where we need to talk about it so people will learn about it and apply. No doubt we should do more and perhaps the Urban League can help us." I thought to myself, "Nice job, Dean. You sure handled that one skillfully."

Dean Shultz had that way about him. He exuded sincerity and modesty. One summer, I collaborated with him on a research project for a large oil company. Quite often during that long hot summer, we called on district managers and other executives, only to have them appear unimpressed—at first, that is. Then Shultz would start talking in his soft and measured manner. Their glances out the window continued until they quickly realized that behind this seeming "uninspired" manner was an incisive mind and considerable perseverance. These same qualities prepared him for distinguished service in Washington, which culminated in his role as secretary of state under President Ronald Reagan.

The dean's response appeared to satisfy Berry. He matched Shultz's response by offering assistance from the Urban League to promote the new program "around the circuit." Associate Dean Walter (Bud) Fackler continued to frown, however. Charged with responsibility for external relations, especially contacts with the business community, he was most sensitive to the backlash sentiment in companies. As it turned out, to secure ten sponsors, he found it necessary to contact over sixty firms.

The person who seemed most pleased with the course of events was Alex Poinsett, the *Ebony* editor I had invited to the luncheon in the hope that agreement would be reached about publicity for the program. *Ebony* wanted to do a story on the program, but the dean hesitated, not refusing but not saying yes either.

In fact, no story was released to the media about the program. At a conference for industrial relations practitioners in October 1964, as part of a talk that I gave on efforts by business to find jobs for African Americans and to upgrade their talents, I reported that "several corporations are supporting a University of Chicago program to train Negro college graduates for business careers through scholarship help and summer job opportunities."

The unresolved issue of whether and how to handle publicity for our efforts at the business school to respond constructively to the challenges posed by the civil rights revolution continued to bother me. At some point in 1966, I drafted a note to Dean Shultz expressing my concern about our reticence to talk about what we were doing to improve conditions facing African Americans.

Looking back at the summer of 1964, and the months immediately preceding and following, I found it noteworthy that the inner-city neighborhoods of Chicago remained quiet, unlike a number of cities across the United States that had erupted in serious violence. A good deal of the credit for the summer calm needed to go to the leadership of the CCCO, and the two boycotts that had relieved some of the pressure and resentment that had been building over the years in the black community. While considerable frustration over the lack of progress had been voiced publicly by two analysts of the Chicago educational system, Professors Hauser and Havighurst, the average resident in the black community remained hopeful that change was on the way.

Within the councils of the CCCO, most delegates opted for a wait-and-see strategy: Would Willis be eased out? A few of the more militant delegates argued for keeping the pressure on with new demonstrations and boycotts, but they were in the minority.

Meanwhile, within the establishment, change was taking place. For example, the Black MBA Program being inaugurated by the University of Chicago. One of the early enrollees in the program, with whom I have maintained contact, is Hassell McClelland, now (2012) on the faculty of the School of Business at Boston College. He observed that by getting started when it did, the GSB got the jump on other business schools. In fact, it was able to attract most of the fourteen students in the first class from historically black colleges. With only one exception, all graduated on schedule and entered business.

McClelland explained that he chose the University of Chicago over a PhD program in economics at Cornell University in large part because of the financial package and summer internship, which gave him an opportunity to learn more about business. Before entering the University of Chicago, he could not identify anyone of color whom he knew as an investment banker. Thus, for him and the other black students, the program was like "learning to play baseball while you were playing in the World Series."[7]

6. Spring and Summer 1965: Marches, More Marches, and Al Pitcher

The voice of dissent must be heard.

—Henry Ford

Two dates serve as markers for the spring of 1965: March 21, when my wife, Nancy, marched in Selma, and April 19, when the CCCO mounted the Good Friday demonstration in Chicago.

Selma is important to the Chicago story in the same sense as the impact of the march on Washington two years earlier. By recruiting participants from Chicago and by drawing attention to the national scope of the civil rights struggle, these two seminal events served to energize the movement back home. While many others have presented their Selma stories. Nancy's decision to go to Selma and her reflections on that experience are important to record. She represented our family.

To recap briefly: on March 7 and 9, 1965, two civil rights marches in Selma led to major confrontations at the bridge where the marchers, who had set out for Montgomery, were turned back. There was considerable violence, and Rev. James Reeb, a Unitarian minister, among those who were attacked, died a few days later. A new march was quickly organized on March 21, and people from all over the country traveled to Selma to demonstrate that the movement was not going to be deterred from marching from Selma to Montgomery. Six individuals from the Unitarian Church, including my wife Nancy, made the trip; I couldn't go because of my teaching obligations.

The entire operation was well organized. Nancy recalls that in spite of the fact that thousands and thousands of people were pouring into that small area, several young black men met her group at the train station in Selma and brought them to the location where others were gathering to begin the march. Before the march started, they visited several homes where black people greeted them warmly and provided food and bathrooms. She was impressed by how many incredibly talented, young black people were involved. "Here was this raw talent that had always been there in the black community but had never been heard, really, never understood, never appreciated, never before allowed to come out."

For most of the hours that they were in Selma, the atmosphere felt like a festival, like "old home week." Nancy recalled seeing Harvey Cox (a roommate of mine from the University of Pennsylvania) sitting on the grass with a bunch of people, looking like everyone was enjoying a midday picnic. The amount of time spent marching was relatively short, probably not more than an hour or two. So there was a lot of down time—not a day of great momentum, but a day full of great emotion. There was considerable praying and many speeches, from Martin Luther King, Walter Reuther, and other dignitaries.

Nancy especially remembered going to hear Walter Reuther speak. "All of us in the Chicago group decided to go to the meeting. By the time we got to the church, it was jammed. There were only a few seats left, up in the balcony, where we decided to sit and hear the speech. Some might say we were probably tempting fate because there were about three times more people in that balcony than should have been there. It was an old wood-frame church, and how everyone managed to squeeze in and not break that balcony was, in retrospect, something to marvel at. It was fortunate for us that we escaped without injury. But no one considered leaving. Everyone was going to stay there! Thoughts of danger never entered our minds—although I should have been concerned since I had left three small children behind in Chicago."

During the march the police, who were keeping people in order, knew the eyes of the nation were on them, so they didn't do anything untoward, and the marchers were very disciplined. They marched up to the bridge, which served as a "mission accomplished."

Another anxious moment occurred on the way out of town. At the end of the day, the group got back into their van to drive to the airport and fly back to Chicago. It was later than had been planned, so people were anxious to get to the airport. As they sped along the dark roads deep in the South, the van passed a car, filled with black teenagers, which had broken down. But the van just kept moving; the driver refused to stop and help anyone.

Even today, Nancy thinks about the group's responsibility, and she believes the group should have stopped and done something for those young people. What would have happened if the police had come along and found them?

Left to right: Walter Reuther, president, UAW; his wife, Mary Reuther; and Harry Van Arsdale, president of the New York City Central Labor Council, marching in Selma, Alabama, March 1965. Courtesy UAW Collection: Public Relations Dept. Contact Sheets, 1965; Reuther's visit to Selma, Alabama (negative no. 23a–24); Walter P. Reuther Library, Wayne State University, Detroit.

Would they have been thrown in jail? Would they have been beaten up? It was just the kind of scene that often has been talked about—the dark roads, the fear, and the unconscionable actions of man against man in areas like that. The irony was that a driver who was very concerned about the group's welfare—one of the talented young black leaders—was taking this group of mostly white people in the van back to the airport. And it was his decision to pass by the black young people on the side of the road who needed help.

The Selma story would not be complete without mentioning Mrs. Simmons —a wonderful black woman—and there were many of them—who worked for families in Hyde Park. She helped our family at a time of great need, when Nancy had her hands full caring for three young children. Mrs. Simmons came to the house and cared for the children, ironed, and cleaned the house. She didn't come every week, but she came fairly frequently. In Nancy's words: "She knew the children, and knew the house, and knew us, and she was always very helpful, and an extraordinarily dignified woman."

So when it came time to find someone to stay with our children while Nancy was in Selma and I was in the classroom, Mrs. Simmons was the person who got the job. Nancy recalls that when the civil rights movement in Chicago began, we had conversations with Mrs. Simmons and learned that she was uneasy about the marches and demonstrations. When Nancy decided to go to Selma, Mrs. Simmons said something to the effect, "Well, I'm not sure that's the right way for things to move forward." Nevertheless, Nancy decided to go, and in the end there was no hesitation on Mrs. Simmons's part about watching our kids; and in fact, she would not take any pay for that long day. Nancy and I think that deep down, Mrs. Simmons was really pleased, maybe she even felt good about it. Nancy recalled her saying something like, "Well, you know, you're doing something for my people."

In reviewing this story one reader asked that the first name of Mrs. Simmons be added. If the truth be known, we never knew her first name. Not wanting to perpetuate the practice (from plantation days) of only addressing blacks by their first names, we only used her last name and the rather formal prefix of "Mrs."

Nancy's return to Southside Chicago after the trip to Selma brought things into sharp relief. While in Selma, she felt safe in the care of the black leadership, in the hands of the black community. Living in Hyde Park, however, we didn't necessarily always feel safe going into Woodlawn, the black community to the south of Hyde Park.

Nancy spoke to this contrast: "Selma was theater as opposed to real life. Woodlawn is real life. Woodlawn illustrated what happened to blacks, with people not paying attention to them. In Selma, the eyes of the world were watching; it was like a stage, a temporary thing. I don't know—if we went into the black community at another time in the South, would we have felt as welcome?"

The subject of a real or imagined sense of safety for a white person venturing into a black residential neighborhood requires some additional comment. As members of groups involved in demonstrations, we always felt perfectly safe in the black community because the presence of fellow black marchers signaled to residents that something "good" was taking place. Such a message would not be present if we, by ourselves or with a small group of white friends, ventured into Woodlawn, especially after dark.

Meanwhile, back in Chicago, another season for direct action was approaching, and the leaders of the CCCO decided the time had come to escalate the pressure. Along with other delegates to the CCCO, in March I received a letter from Al Raby announcing a meeting to organize a demonstration the council was planning for Good Friday. The demonstrators would march from Grant Park to City Hall where they would meet with Clergy for Quality and Equality in Education. Raby's letter advised:

> WE WILL NEED YOUR SUPPORT, since we are hoping that this will be the largest demonstration of its kind in support of "quality and equality" in public education for this city.
> WE WILL NEED MONEY ... or the operation will "die aborning..."
> If you believe education is a public trust that has been publicly distorted and crippled by the present administration ... let us see you on Saturday ... ready to work.
> THE CROSS OF POOR EDUCATION MUST NO LONGER BE BORN BY THE POOR ... AND THE BLACK. LET US REMOVE IT ... on Good Friday, 1965.

As was becoming my habit, I decided not to attend this CCCO meeting, or if I should get there, to arrive sufficiently late to miss crucial votes. As it turned out, for this meeting I did not even make an effort. Increasingly, I viewed these Saturday morning meetings as an imposition. After a week of work at the office, I looked forward to the undemanding routine of cutting grass and doing odd jobs around the house. More was involved, however, than jealously guarding my free time. I frankly wondered about the usefulness of yet another demonstration. I wondered: Hasn't the civil rights movement made its point painfully clear? Haven't all possible forms of direct action been tried? What would a pilgrimage on Good Friday really accomplish? These were questions that I could not raise in a floor discussion at the CCCO, but these were issues that bothered me.

Rather than attend the meeting and make my reservations known, I took the easy alternative—I avoided any encounter. I was under no delusion that I possessed any influence in the civil rights movement. While I did enjoy the friendship of several key leaders of the CCCO, I chose not to alienate myself further from the movement since matters had reached the point where it was clear: "If you are not with us, then you are against us." One could not raise serious questions and at the same time retain any influence. One could make suggestions about reshaping the action, but one could not challenge the need or appropriateness of the action program itself.

However, I did feel free to express my concerns at the next monthly meeting of the Social Responsibility Commission (SRC) of the Chicago Council of Liberal Churches. The Good Friday Pilgrimage was going forward, and the liberal churches once again found themselves in the position of debating a program that would take place regardless of their support. For this reason, some of the commission members urged that no vote be taken. Others objected: "We are too deeply involved in the civil rights movement at this point to remain neutral; if we do not actively support the pilgrimage, we will be criticized."

Tim Black, who also was attending the SRC meeting, agreed with some of the points, particularly those questioning the usefulness of another demonstration. He also agreed with the argument made by several members of the commission that the confrontation with the school board had degenerated into a test of personalities. The whole issue of quality and equality in education had been over shadowed by the "get Willis" psychology. The movement had developed a fixation on the superintendent. It was pushing itself into a world of unreality with the view "If Willis goes, then everything will be different in the school system." Some felt the city could easily be worse off with a weak superintendent. At least Willis told you where he stood and provided strong leadership in carrying out the policies of the school board.

The discussion concluded by passing two motions, and I was asked to communicate these to the CCCO, hopefully by making a report at one of the next Saturday morning meetings. I wondered about this instruction and, given my hesitancy to take a stand against the thrust of the CCCO, I drafted a letter to Al Raby. In it I reported that the Commission of the Chicago Area Council of Liberal Churches had voted to support the Good Friday pilgrimage and to urge our local churches to participate. But the commission also wanted to emphasize that the focus of the pilgrimage should be on achieving high-quality integrated education, and not on the removal of Superintendent Willis.

I knew this letter would be lost in the pile of correspondence and papers at CCCO headquarters. One did not communicate with the leadership by letter, one did it person-to-person, either on a face-to-face basis or over the telephone. Consequently, I was not surprised when, at the next CCCO meeting, no mention was made of the motion adopted by the Commission of the Chicago Council of Liberal Churches.

As a way of implementing the resolution and working through my ambivalent feelings, I pitched in to organize a delegation from the local church to participate in the Good Friday demonstration. I prepared an announcement for the church's weekly calendar and made several phone calls to people asking them to help recruit others. On previous occasions, I had enlisted the help of the Social Action Committee and the board of trustees, but on this occasion, I decided to recruit participants myself.

The task of garnering additional support within the congregation was not easy. Those who supported direct action could be counted on, while those who were opposed or apathetic would remain so, and comments on my part would not make much difference. The church liked discussions—they were stimulating—and this give-and-take made people feel they were in touch with important developments. However, such discussions seemed to have little effect on personal involvement. The debate did air the issues and perhaps telegraphed to others in the community the thinking of the church, but in terms of measurable additions to the movement, nothing! With these thoughts in mind, I wrote a parody entitled "Birds of a Feather":

This Sunday morning at 6:00 AM, all Unitarian Crows ("U.C.-ers" for short) will meet on the church roof. This flocking has been made necessary by the recognized disparities in the established pecking order. To put it crudely, most of our brethren do not occupy the top branches and we all know what happens when we find ourselves sitting beneath other birds. . . .

Aside from the demeaning position that our brethren occupy, they are being changed against their wills: their black bodies are being whitened by "fallout." And what is a crow without his black coat?

Thus, the purpose of our gathering is to proclaim the plight (rhymes with flight) of our fellow crows rather than any difficulties that we Unitarian Crows have experienced, especially at First Church. Rather than being shot at (as happens in rural America) or being forced to survive on the crumbs of affluence, our lot has been relatively pleasant—indeed, some of us have gotten fat and forgotten our lean brethren.

Spokesmen for other species have asked whether they might fly in for the meeting. Reluctantly we have concluded that only black-bodied creatures can attend.

But I relegated it, like other pieces created to release frustration, to the oblivion of my files.

Good Friday, April 19, 1965, turned out to be a pleasant day, not at all like the dark and ominous day of biblical times centuries ago. At the church, a delegation of about ten people gathered. Two cars were parked outside, my own and one belonging to Leon, the husband of the chairperson of the Social Action Committee. I was surprised to see him on hand for the demonstration. In the Adult Discussion Group, he had criticized, clearly and powerfully, the penchant of religious liberals to demonstrate on the street but then fail to devote any energy to providing practical value to those in need, for example, at a nearby tutoring and study clinic where he spent many hours as a volunteer. I wondered if his wife had asked him to participate; was he there as a participant or just as a chauffeur?

Most of the soon-to-be-marchers were housewives. This created some discomfort for me. In a way, I envied the people with formal jobs in banks and other organizations—they knew they couldn't get the time off and didn't have to wrestle with a decision whether to participate.

As I was making car assignments, one of the ladies came up and said, "Don't put me in Leon's car. I can't stand him."

"Very troubling," I thought, "none of us is completely devoid of biases and hang-ups." We might have conquered racial discrimination, but there remained a subtler closing of our minds to certain personality types. At a congregational meeting the previous year, there had been another unpleasant illustration of this reality. The chairman of the House and Grounds Committee had been nominated, along with four others, for the church board. Never had the church seen a more dedicated and effective worker. Without a doubt, he was the number one layman in the congregation. But for all of his strengths, he had an abrasive personality. He told people what he thought; he dominated discussions with his ideas. Clearly, he did not fit the image that people had of a "good" board member. As a result, a telephone campaign took place within the church; and it was effective, with the result that this hardworking volunteer was defeated and several others—possessing far fewer qualifications and far less service to the church—were elected to office.

On our way to the Loop, one passenger asked if her boyfriend could be dropped off near his home. I mused about the nature of the relationship between this attractive white teenager and the young man, a handsome African American youth. Clearly, this girl was making her own statement about racial integration. Her mother, who was also in the car, apparently approved of the relationship. Curiously, though, this mother was the same person who had asked to ride separately from Leon.

At Buckingham Fountain in Grant Park, as the demonstrators began to assemble, a festive air prevailed. Other religious liberals had arrived, some from the Unitarian Church and others from the SRC. Our minister, Jack Kent, who had been in the Loop for a luncheon with the chairman of the church board, arrived in his characteristically brisk fashion. Then the chairman of the SRC, Dick Nash, arrived carrying a very large banner rolled between two poles. With pride he unfurled the banner, which read: CHICAGO COUNCIL OF LIBERAL CHURCHES SUPPORTS THE DEMONSTRATION, FIRST UNIVERSALST CHURCH.

Then someone started to laugh. "Dick, you've misspelled Universalist." Sure enough, an "i" had been omitted. Someone commented, "What else can you expect from the Willis school system?" Some pictures were taken of the misspelled banner alongside a placard that had been made at the church, which said, "I learned to spell in the Chicago Schools."

Several teenagers from the church had prepared a dozen signs, demonstrating their artistic talents. Many of the signs focused attention on Willis and contained sarcastic epithets. I grabbed a sign that said something about achieving quality and equality in education. The march was underway.

Since I had participated in several marches before, marching along the streets of Chicago was losing some of its exhilaration. Just the same, there was something impressive about such a large assemblage—the feeling of camaraderie in juxtaposition to the apathetic and hostile faces of the passersby. The police on detail cooperated fully, and the marchers were quickly marshaled along to City Hall.

About midway into the march, Jack Kent looked up, pointed to a tall office building, and said, "I bet Doug Anderson is up there watching us. I had lunch with him today, and he said the closest he could come to the march would be to wave to us from his office in the building." Doug, chairman of the church board and active in political affairs (he ran the Chicago office for Senator Paul Douglas) was one of the first from the church to sign up for the second Selma march in March 1965. He and his son had taken the train down (Nancy was also on board, along with George Sikes). How ironic it was that Doug

WE MARCH TO SECURE QUALITY EDUCATION AND A BETTER LIFE FOR ALL THE CHILDREN OF CHICAGO.

"Why We March," CCCO flyer, 1965. Courtesy Chicago Urban League Records, series III, box 102, folder 1123, University of Illinois at Chicago Library, Special Collections.

could take a strong stand about civil rights in the South but remain quite aloof here in Chicago. Working for a politician, he was sensitive to the power realities of the city and he was well aware that Mayor Daley would deal severely with any member of his Democratic machine who took part in local demonstrations. The dilemma was not unique. Indeed, many who had participated in Selma and experienced exhilaration and a sense of purpose were stymied when it came to playing a meaningful role in the North. A psychologist friend of mine in Washington had studied the question and concluded that the biggest problem for the participants after Selma was dealing with the sense of letdown and the frustration of trying to figure out how they could make an equally dramatic statement in their own communities.

At City Hall, several thousand people had assembled for the rally. All the dignitaries were introduced, each one feeling compelled to make a speech, although it was hard to hear what was being said because of a poor public address system. I remember thinking it was a marvel how the civil rights movement handled the logistics of a demonstration: organizing buses, distributing leaflets, making arrangements with the police, and attending to many other details. Yet, other organizational arrangements were quite inadequate: not enough marshals and a totally inadequate public address system.

For me, the big problem with the speeches was not that they were barely audible but that they lacked originality. Everyone said the same thing, and all of it had been said hundreds of times before. Of course, the real point of the rally was not to say something new, but to assemble several thousand people on the symbolic Good Friday afternoon to make a personal witness to their conviction that something must be done about the deep social and racial problems in the city of Chicago.

The ultimate question really was: Did two or three thousand people make an impact on the consciousness of the city of Chicago? The answer was not clear. Thousands of commuters on their way home from work observed and must have wondered about the demonstration. The newspapers gave it some publicity, but not much; the explanation often voiced was that the newspapers were under the control of the Daley machine.

About fifteen minutes into the speechmaking, I asked my colleagues from the church whether they wanted to leave, and we quietly departed the crowd. Shortly after the demonstration ended, CORE and several ministers began a round-the-clock vigil at City Hall.

At the next meeting of the CCCO, the demonstration was evaluated as only a partial success; some even termed it a failure. Against predictions of 10,000 to 15,000 expected attendees, the turnout of only several thousand was indeed disappointing. At the meeting, several speakers engaged in pointed criticism of organizations that did not give full support. Rather than commenting on the positive aspects of the Good Friday Pilgrimage, a considerable amount of time was spent in rancor and debate about how the march could have been better organized. The first convener of the CCCO, Reverend Brazier, who was in attendance only because he had attended an earlier meeting in the same building, explained away the poor showing by saying, "How can you expect people to demonstrate on a religious day? People are supposed to be reflective and not agitating for social reform on Good Friday."

In many respects, the march and the follow-up meeting represented a turning point for the civil rights movement. The CCCO meeting had been scheduled to follow a luncheon sponsored by the Urban League—the main purpose of the luncheon being to raise funds for its operating budget. Some of the Urban League people, like Bill Berry, stayed on for the meeting of the CCCO. However, most Urban League dignitaries left the building.

Those who attended this CCCO meeting were the militants of the movement. As the discussion unfolded and people continued their pointed criticism of different organizations, Al Raby took control of the discussion and toward the end of the meeting offered some personal observations about the future of the civil rights movement in Chicago: "I think we have come to the point where we have to be ready to go to jail. We have to create the kind of crisis that Selma experienced. It is clear to me that just another demonstration will not do anything. We have to get rid of Willis and to do that we have to bring about a political crisis in this city. This business of orderly demonstrations is not going to do a blessed thing. We have to be ready to get hit over the head and to be jailed for our beliefs."

Al's forceful talk drove home the realization that we were on the threshold of a new stage in the battle for racial justice in Chicago. A Catholic priest, the secretary of the CCCO, spoke passionately about the importance of getting rid of Willis and the need for something dramatic. His position had changed considerably from earlier meetings, when he had spoken against just focusing attention on Willis. He had been afraid that if the CCCO pushed too hard on Willis, it would only stiffen resistance within the white community, and the resulting backlash would intensify.

Bill Berry continued to urge moderation and assured participants in the CCCO meeting that discussions were taking place behind the scenes to work out a compromise. Of considerable significance was the fact that Berry had been meeting with Phillip Hauser, and as a consequence had received a letter from Hauser dated January 15, 1965, in which Hauser said, "I have reached the conclusion that Dr. Benjamin C. Willis should not be reappointed as General Superintendent of Schools. The evidence is clear that Dr. Willis regards the public school system as his own principality, which should be operated as an independent entity without regard to the problems that beset the city as a whole." Berry and the Urban League had released this letter, thereby placing the credibility of Hauser solidly behind the effort to remove Willis from his position as superintendent. Berry was orchestrating a strategy of pressure, but not too much pressure, on the board of education and the mayor.

I wondered about all of this. Going to jail might produce a crisis, but should it be the objective? The civil rights movement had worked itself into a position where it felt compelled to escalate its tactics. Would it not be better to shift direction and tackle concrete projects? Could the movement work at the local school level and focus attention, locality by locality, on the problems of overcrowding and inadequate facilities in the school system? Everything was being interpreted in terms of one person. Instead of the problem of overcrowding, it was Willis wagons. Instead of Willis's policies, it was Willis the person; instead of an emphasis on quality education, it was exclusively the issue of integration.

But more important, I thought, any program of direct action should be chosen only if it had some chance of success. Fixating on the removal of Willis was a long shot by any objective estimate. If the campaign succeeded, the civil rights movement would be greatly strengthened, but if it failed, the movement would find itself more and more marginalized.

On May 22, 1965, the bombshell hit: the board of education voted to reappoint Benjamin Willis, thereby guaranteeing that Chicago would see another summer of protest. On hearing the announcement, the NAACP immediately announced a weeklong boycott of the schools and daily demonstrations in the Loop. Al Raby called a special meeting of the CCCO to decide whether to endorse the program being sponsored by the NAACP.

When the school board announced the reappointment of Willis, no one in the civil rights movement knew about the behind-the-scenes discussions that had taken place within the board. Kay Clement, wife of the late Jim Clement, a board member at the time, recalled: "I think it was the mayor who felt he couldn't give in. Because they had quite a session during that meeting when Willis was rehired. Because he was going to stay just so long before he retired, and they kept saying 'Do you promise to retire?' They just had to pull it out of Willis that yes, he was planning to retire at some point in the future."

Kay Clement also described the steps taken by the mayor's office to protect board members in the aftermath of the reappointment decision. Security personnel were assigned to the homes of board members twenty-four hours a day, and this "protection" continued throughout the summer. At one point, when the Clement children decided to "camp out" in tents in their back yard, the security detail shifted their post outside and kept watch during the night.[1]

As I drove to the Washington Park YMCA for the CCCO meeting following the school board's announcement to reappoint Willis, I remembered the old adage: "God grant me the serenity to accept the things I cannot change, courage to change the things I can, and the wisdom to know the difference." What would another demonstration on the Willis question achieve? Wasn't the city well aware of the feelings and fervor of the civil rights movement on the Willis question? Hadn't the time come for the civil rights movement to turn its energies in other directions, either to advocating concrete changes to improve education in Chicago or to other important issues like housing and employment?

With such questions running through my mind, I decided to sit in the back of the crowded meeting room. The discussion proceeded, with no one questioning the wisdom of direct action. People expressed their sense of dismay, their bitterness, their complete sense of frustration, in extremely eloquent language. Bill Berry from the Urban League reviewed three major defeats: "They defeated us on the Charles Gray issue; they are about to kill the open occupancy bill; and now this slap in the face from the board of education."

For the first time in many months, attendance was back to full strength at the CCCO meeting. The atmosphere resembled the earlier days of the organization when it was planning the first school boycott. People were more seasoned, yet in some ways feeling more desperate. The meetings during the formative period of the CCCO had projected an air of anticipation as well as uncertainty as the delegates searched for ways to develop and assert power. Now people were much more realistic; they recognized they possessed power, but power rose and fell with events and depended on the willingness of a dedicated minority to engage in street actions that might involve civil disobedience.

The chairman of the NAACP took the floor and spoke in favor of his resolution calling for the school boycott and a massive march on City Hall. He acknowledged that, on the advice of other civil rights groups, his organization had decided to limit the boycott to two days and the demonstrations to one or two days.

This reduction in the length of the proposed boycott was not as important as the fact that for the first time the NAACP was getting behind the civil rights struggle in Chicago. The chair of the local chapter had just been transferred from New York City, his predecessor having taken a leave of absence for health reasons. His newness to the Chicago situation was an advantage for the civil rights movement, primarily because he was not beholden to the Democratic machine. He was expressing his outrage at the reappointment of Willis.

Raby rose from his seat and gazed out the window (he usually looked away from his audience, as if he were scanning the horizon) and told of the events leading up to the recent school board decision. He shared some developments that, until this meeting, he had kept confidential: specifically, how the top leadership of the CCCO had been assured by key city officials that if they laid low and let influential leaders within the city work behind the scenes, a way would be found for easing Willis out of the superintendency. Clearly, the expected had not happened, and Raby felt double-crossed.

Tim Black was not at the meeting; he was attending the national convention of the NALC in New York City. However, he had been quoted in the newspapers as expressing doubt about the value of additional direct action. I wondered whether Tim would have difficulty maintaining his influence in the movement given the sentiment and support for direct action being expressed in this meeting.

The resolution to support another school boycott was passed unanimously. The meeting then considered a resolution urging the three members of the board of education (Bacon, Clement, and Pasnick) who had voted against the Willis reappointment (the vote was 4 to 3) to resign as an act of protest. The person who proposed the motion said that the point had been reached in the city where people could no longer work within the system. They had to challenge the ability of the system to bring about change by removing themselves from the system and working from the outside. He therefore urged members of the board who were sympathetic to the objectives of the civil rights movement to resign.

Others felt that the presence of the three sympathetic members on the board was better than nothing and that they should remain as minority spokesmen. It would be presumptuous of the CCCO to call upon these individuals to resign, and it would also place them in an embarrassing position, even though some of them might be contemplating such a move.

Toward the end of the discussion, Al Pitcher spoke up. He had been sitting quietly on the side, scribbling some notes. He acknowledged that it might be necessary for the three board members to resign, but he said it should be part of a long-range plan, that it would achieve nothing at the present time. Better, he thought, in the future when the point was reached where they needed to withdraw and fight a type of guerilla warfare. But he felt that point had not yet been reached and that the group should think through a long-range strategy.

Al's appearance at the CCCO meeting was significant. He was not a delegate, since his religious denomination (Baptist) had not chosen to affiliate with the CCCO. However, as a minister and as a white social activist, he had been involved in the race relations struggle for some time.

I remembered my first meeting with Al Pitcher, about a year earlier, over lunch at the Quadrangle Club of the University of Chicago. A neighbor had suggested that the two of us get together because of our mutual interests.

Clockwise from top: Al Pitcher, Al Raby, and Martin Luther King Jr., key leaders of the Chicago civil rights movement. Courtesy Mrs. Al (Sara) Pitcher.

Al had just returned from a sabbatical leave in Europe, and although back in Hyde Park for only a few weeks, he had entered quickly into the race-relations arena. He joined with several other influential people to form "Protest at the Polls," an organization aimed at giving the black community new political power. He had also met with several black ministers and helped them organize consumer boycotts against several milk companies.

Al was older, and I wondered about his career. His rank of assistant professor in the divinity school, given his age (probably early fifties) puzzled me. We talked about many things during lunch. One of the subjects I remember because it hit a sensitive nerve with me was the subject of "publish or perish." Al spoke quite bitterly about the pressure on him from the divinity school to "write one article after another." He felt that his activities with social action groups, his work in the local Baptist Church (he was chairman of the board of trustees), and his community involvement were not valued. "The school is not interested in ministers; it is only interested in writers."

He outlined his philosophy of not creating new institutions but working within existing organizations to help them become more effective. In this respect, he wanted to model himself after his father-in-law, a practicing minister who addressed many social issues. Al referred to him affectionately as a professional "do-gooder."

Our association continued on a casual basis. Sometimes we saw each other on campus and exchanged a few words. On one occasion, Al invited me to deliver a talk before a group of ministers in which I explored the question of ethics and decision making in the modern corporation. After our initial meeting, the first real chance to talk came at the home of Julie Ashenhurst on New Year's Eve. Al and his family lived across the hall from Julie. Ashenhurst, a recent divorcee, who had invited an eclectic group of people to celebrate New Year's Eve. Some of those present were like herself, going through "passages." Others were longstanding friends. And some others were neighbors like Al and his family. Three of his four children attended. One would be graduating that June from Oberlin; another was on the verge of entering Oberlin; and one was still attending Hyde Park High.

The two of us huddled off to one side and quickly started talking "shop." Al was serving on a committee of the Chicago Church Federation, and they were seeking to formulate a position on the school question. He had urged support for a statement emphasizing the need for equality in education. He felt Willis would have to go, but it would be better not to focus too much attention on him.

The next time I saw Al was one Sunday morning a few weeks later as we both walked home from our respective churches. Al reported on the "tremendous" reception generated by a petition signed by many faculty from the university asking the board of education to let Willis go. Several days earlier, a one-page ad had appeared in a number of Chicago newspapers signed by hundreds of professors from the Chicago area. The point of the letter was: Willis had lost his effectiveness, a new superintendent was needed who could deal with the problems, Willis should be let go, and a search commenced immediately for a successor.

I mentioned that I was disappointed not to have been included in the petition. I had expressed such thoughts in a letter to him the day before, but seeing him face-to-face on the street I decided to raise the issue. As we parted, Al said, "We ought to establish a standing faculty committee at the university, one that can consider social problems and, when appropriate, issue statements."

Thus, Al Pitcher's presence at the CCCO meeting was not surprising given the considerable time and energy he had invested in lining up a large group of faculty to support the petition. The petition itself generated attention and hopes ran high that Willis would go. And then this reappointment. Like the rest, he too had been led to believe that Willis would retire.

As it turned out, the school boycott was never officially held. Unlike earlier boycotts, this time the board of education went to court and sought an injunction, and a judge granted its request. Previously, the board had remained in the background, letting the civil rights movement proceed with the two school boycotts. Clearly, the decision had been made by the authorities to push back. Willis was going to stay, and city officials were not about to let the movement challenge this action.

Despite the injunction, some students stayed away from their classes during the first week in June. And as was the case in the first two boycotts, several freedom schools operated.

Given the injunction preventing leaders of the CCCO from openly mobilizing support for a boycott, attention focused on sponsoring two demonstrations. During the first march, thousands of people participated, marching down State Street arm in arm, and CCCO leaders judged it a huge success. For a different assessment, consider the following: "CCCO and the clergy turned out only 2,500 demonstrators for a poorly organized event that more or less marched from Grant Park to City Hall during rush hour."[2]

But more significant than the size of the turnout was the increased participation by black clergy. White clergymen had played a prominent role in the civil rights movement from the outset in Chicago, but the black clergy had been conspicuously absent. Some leaders had criticized their absence as "Uncle

Tom-ism." Others had attributed it to the influence of the Daley machine. However, their participation evidenced a growing militancy within the black community: a stalemate had been reached in the city, sides had to be taken, and the clergy felt compelled to join forces with the civil rights movement.

When the second demonstration took place on Friday, June 11, a number of marchers were arrested by the police, including Al Pitcher, Al Raby, and several other leaders of the CCCO. When the police sought to restrict marching to sidewalks and one curbside lane, a dispute arose over the use of the curb lane, with the police claiming that the demonstrators had violated the guidelines. The arrests of key leaders signaled that a new phase in the struggle for racial equality had been reached in the city of Chicago.

The arrest of Al Raby in particular represented an ironic turn of events, given that he had received a phone call earlier that day from the office of Mayor Daley, asking if he "still wanted to meet." Raby later remarked at a CCCO meeting, "I started out to see him—with CCCO delegates, of course— but we were ambushed before we got there."

I did not participate in either of these marches. I felt ambivalent about the rationale for the marches and harbored the same reservations I had experienced at the CCCO meeting. Then too, I shuddered at the thought of being arrested. I wanted to stay invisible, not pictured in the local newspapers.

What had begun as just two days of demonstrations soon shifted to a campaign of daily marches. Al Raby announced they would continue to march on a daily basis until Willis was removed. More arrests occurred the following Monday. In fact, on this particular day the marchers willingly engaged in civil disobedience as they dashed from the sidewalk and sat down at the "busiest corner in the world"—State and Monroe Streets.

Within the ranks of marchers, however, not everything was "Solidarity Forever." At one point, a group of blacks from CORE refused to march behind a white leader. The awkward situation was quickly resolved when a CCCO leader reshuffled the lineup and explained that the CORE participants had just been "resting."

And most significant, the decision-making venue for the civil rights movement had shifted from the conference room at the Washington Park Y, where CCCO meetings had been taking place, to the meeting ground behind Buckingham Fountain, where the marchers gathered each day. On an ad hoc basis, decisions were taken about whether the day's march would be conducted peacefully along the sidewalks or whether some participants would engage in civil disobedience. If the leadership felt that the police were acting aggressively or those in jail were not receiving fair treatment, then more marchers would be asked to subject themselves to arrest. The decision-making process involved input from those who had assembled, and all demonstrators had the option to do what they wanted—march, be arrested, or not be involved at all. (The next chapter details a CCCO meeting when the leadership sought authorization for these daily marches.)

During the third weekend in July, Martin Luther King arrived in Chicago, met with professionals, business people, and labor union officials, and led a march of more than 10,000 from Buckingham Fountain to City Hall. No one was arrested on this occasion.

As the marches continued, day after day, I grew more and more concerned. I excused myself from actively participating due to "the press of work at the office." Inwardly, I wondered whether I was just scared or whether remaining on the sidelines was the better part of wisdom. Had the civil rights movement entered upon a course of self-destruction? Had they lost all reason and were now just exhibitionists? Or were they people acting out of deep conviction?

After three weeks of daily demonstrations and after several hundred arrests, the *modus operandi* for the protests was modified significantly. Each day's march would focus on the problems of a different community. And for one of these days, the organizers decided to highlight issues facing Hyde Park. On this particular day, my wife and I had agreed to spend a few hours having lunch and then visiting the Art Institute. Nancy was already in the Loop, having gone there early to do some shopping. As I journeyed to the Loop, I noticed a crowd gathering at Buckingham Fountain and then remembered that this was the day scheduled for the Hyde Park march. How could I be in the vicinity and not participate? When I joined Nancy on the steps of the Institute, I asked, "Shouldn't we be over at Buckingham Fountain and joining in the march?" She answered, "Yes, I've been bothered about this for some time. Ever since I got back from Selma I've been wondering whether I have been doing enough." Putting off lunch, we walked quickly toward Grant Park. As we reached the fountain area, there was no one to be seen and Nancy said, "Now that we've decided to march, I hope we don't miss it. Let's run."

We fell in at the tail end of the march as it crossed Michigan Avenue and moved into the heart of the Loop. At the end of the line was a man on crutches who had walked all the way from Selma to Montgomery. His picture had been in many newspapers and magazines. The spirit of the marchers was much more subdued than earlier Chicago marches. Nancy observed, however, that the spirit, by contrast, was more buoyant than at Selma where "no one talked and everything was deadly serious."

As we came up Wabash Avenue, there were Dick Gregory, Al Raby, and Tim Black in a huddle. The marchers continued several blocks beyond them while they remained in intense discussion. Nancy and I wondered whether they were planning some form of civil disobedience. I ventured a guess that Gregory was anxious to do something dramatic and Al was trying to dissuade him.

As we reached the busiest corner of the world, no confrontation occurred. Traffic was stopped and we all moved quietly by. I helped a little girl across the intersection—not one of my own children, who were home with a baby-sitter. This was the daughter of Rosemary Snow, a church member who was heavily involved in the movement. She had participated in all the earlier demonstrations.

Toward the end of the march, who should stroll by dressed in a smart business suit and wearing a straw hat but Al Pitcher. He shook our hands and said he was glad to see us in the march. I was glad Al had seen us. An important reason for participating in these marches was to make a public statement, that is, to make friends aware of your witness. In fact, to be frank, I found myself a couple of times going out of my way to shake hands with Tim Black so that my presence and commitment would be recognized.

Al Pitcher and I met again at Julie Ashenhurst's home in June 1965—this time at her wedding, at which Al performed the service—and he mentioned that he needed a place to live during the summer. One of his daughters had just been married and was honeymooning in his Hyde Park apartment. Being a sensitive father, he felt it inappropriate to live with the newlyweds. Yet, attempting to commute from his summer home in the Indiana Dunes would have made it difficult to participate actively in the civil rights movement. As he put the challenge, "To be a part of this fast-moving crusade, you really have to live with it. I envision being at meetings half the night and then needing a place to sleep for several hours." My response was to immediately offer our home.

This opportunity was too important to pass up—a chance to have a warm and wonderful person like Al in one's home, a chance to have a window through which to look into the inner leadership circle of the civil rights movement—all this was too good to be missed. And so Al came to live with our family during the summer of 1965. In fact, he came to live with us the day after the wedding. The marches were continuing and the civil rights scene was rapidly intensifying.

The first thing Al did after joining our family was to learn the names of our three children. As he put it, "I want to develop a relationship with your family." And this he did. Like the Master himself, he had a way with children, even if they were young or small. Jody Ashenhurst (Julie's daughter by a previous marriage) also lived in our house that summer. Al knew how to handle her better than anyone else. He used a combination of humor and directness that shattered the nonchalance of a teenager. At one point when she was complaining that her towels never got dry, Al said "Don't leave them in the corner of the room, just hang them up."

Whenever our infrequent interactions with Al took place, they were intense and friendly. He only slept three or four hours a night and was constantly on the go. The most leisurely moments were over breakfast, when he would recount the events of the preceding evening. In one conversation he told about the function of the daily executive committee meetings that had replaced the parliamentary procedures of regular CCCO meetings in favor of a "command headquarters" approach. While some individuals complained about the lack of participation by the duly constituted groups in the CCCO, this concern did not bother Al (nor me) since the movement had entered into a "warfare" phase and who would ask for town meeting democracy when the "enemy" (Mayor Daley) was well known and the troops had to be deployed on nightly marches? And what folly it would have been for the full CCCO membership to deliberate over decisions about civil disobedience.

Indeed, on one occasion the complications of democracy had been vividly illustrated. After lengthy deliberations at a CCCO meeting, a particular course of action had been endorsed only to be vetoed by the marchers who were prepared and anxious to do something different. This new reality meant that henceforth, decisions on strategy would need to be made by the small leadership group at CCCO headquarters and decisions on tactics by the groups that assembled each day for the premarch caucus at Buckingham Fountain. Decisions had to be made about a number of options: when and whether to shift the demonstrations to different sites, for example, when to march on Mayor Daley's home or Superintendent Willis's. (Dan Lortie, retired professor from the University of Chicago, recalled in an interview that at a meeting of the American Sociological Society held in Chicago during 1965, a delegation of professors was assembled, and they traveled to Willis's home, located in one of the northern suburbs, to express their support for the CCCO campaign.)[3]

The substance of these meetings that decided strategies and tactics provided the morning "scoop" that we received from Al in our conversations at the breakfast table. On one occasion, Al talked about a television program he had just taped. As an articulate and charismatic person, he found himself assuming a bigger and bigger role as a spokesperson—not as much inside the movement but more as an interpreter to the public in general.

One Saturday afternoon he dashed back into the house to quickly change into a blue shirt, the garb of a television personality. As he was leaving, he asked, "Would you drive me down to the studio?" With the kindness and yet the authority of Jesus asking Peter to leave his fishing nets, Al asked me to leave my bluebooks (it was the end of the quarter and grading was in full swing) and drive him and several other leaders down to the Loop. I quickly agreed and asked our children if they'd like to go along (my habit of trying to pack as much into every event as possible). While it was quite possible that Al wanted quiet in the car so he could think about the upcoming presentation, nevertheless I put our three young kids into the back of the car.

On the way to the Loop we stopped to pick up Al Raby's wife. Al was already downtown, having attended several meetings earlier that day. She had a suitcase with her. Rather than talking about civil rights, she talked about a weekend vacation that she and her husband were planning. As she talked about the retreat where they were heading after the television program, I thought about their contrasting worlds. How important it was for them to be able to get away from it all. They needed a respite from Hyde Park and the telephone. Yes, they had an unlisted number, but their address had been published in the newspaper several times and they had received threatening visits. And then there was the ever-insistent press. By going to Michigan for a weekend, they could escape this constant pressure.

Here were the Rabys, going off to Michigan for a respite, in a way reminding me of a businessman flying off to a vacation spot to escape the pressures of his organization. In this sense, Al Raby seemed no different than any other executive or administrator. I wanted to think of him as someone quite unlike our MBA alumni. But I concluded that he was a manager; yes, managing protest, and subject to the same unrelenting pressures of an executive in a large firm.

On the way back from the Loop, I decided to take the three youngsters for a tour of the local park district. We drove by the Aquarium and the Observatory. It was a gorgeous spring day, and people were sunning on their yachts, if they had not already headed for the beaches of Lake Michigan. I wanted to shout to them as we went by in the car, "Don't you know there is a revolution going on in this city? How can you sit here in all your affluence and enjoy yourself when there is a confrontation going on between blacks and whites in this city?"

That night Nancy and I stayed up late to watch the television show that had been taped that afternoon. Al Pitcher, who certainly needed the change of pace at his cottage in the Dunes, expressed little interest in seeing himself on television. In fact, for all the times he had appeared on television, he had never seen himself, even once. This did not bother him, but his family was upset. They did not have television in their Hyde Park apartment, and out in the Dunes it was awkward to bother a neighbor.

One evening, Al was relaxing in our house while a television program in which he appeared was being aired, and he never said a word about it. Nancy was upset with herself, for she had forgotten to look at the *TV Guide* and a half hour later realized that we had missed the interview with Al. He said something to the effect: "You didn't miss anything," as he continued to make light of his public appearances. On another occasion, he told us how happy he was when a list of the leaders of the civil rights movement of Chicago appeared in the local newspapers and his name was not mentioned.

However, a television program on one particular evening proved fascinating. Nancy watched it in its entirety until 3:00 A.M. I gave up about 1:00 A.M. and went to bed. I found the discussion repetitious of earlier forums and, to some degree, stressful when I compared my largely observer role to that of Al Pitcher, a friend and now a boarder who was totally immersed in the movement.

This particular television program presented the spectrum of perspectives on the race question. There was a representative from Congress who spoke in glowing terms about the legislation (the Voting Rights Bill) just passed by the Democrats. He expressed disappointment that the civil rights movement did not stand up and say, "Well done" to the passage the previous year of the Civil Rights Act of 1964, the War on Poverty, the training legislation, the new education act, and the other items that were pouring forth from President Lyndon Johnson's administration. Then there was a businessman who said that he had always been friends with African Americans. "Why, some of my best friends are Negroes." He talked about a classmate of his who had gone to Dartmouth College and how through hard work had become a successful and respected man in his community. He likened the African American to the Jewish immigrant who worked hard to integrate himself into society and to succeed through his own efforts.

Al Pitcher dealt with these panelists most skillfully. He lifted the argument to a completely different plane. He talked, almost in the language of a prophet, about the insensitivity of the white community. He pointed to all of the rationalizations, all of the legalisms, all of the theoretical arguments that the white community was making about how black citizens should advance in the United States. Such an approach overlooked the facts of despair, the reality of centuries of discrimination that needed immediate attention. It was not enough to say that considerable progress had been made and that there was a good prospect for more progress in the future. "We have a situation where expectations are outrunning realizations. We are in a dynamic revolution where people have begun to taste freedom and equality and they want all of it now."

To my mind, the disparate perspectives could be collapsed into the difference between the ethic of justice and the ethic of love. With the exception of Al Pitcher and a white racist from the southwest side of Chicago who had been brought in to complete the spectrum of opinion, the other speakers endorsed traditional strategies. People should be rewarded according to their contributions to society. One group should not be given more preference than another. This was the essence of justice. Al was speaking in favor of compassion, of identifying with another person's plight and taking that person's plight as your own personal burden.

Al wound up his presentation by saying in very direct, theological terms that the judgment of God was upon the United States. Much as a prophet of the Old Testament pointed to the judgment of God manifested in threatened harm to the Jewish community, Al interpreted the civil rights movement as a sign that the white community had lost its way, especially with respect to race relations. The other panelists squirmed. Their self-concepts of being people with good motives were being challenged. How did they deal with the inconsistency between their self-concepts and what Al was saying so pointedly? They grabbed at the ethic of responsibility. They blamed the plight of the black community on the black community.

One morning at breakfast, Al Pitcher announced that Martin Luther King had agreed to come to Chicago for an extended weekend. Several weeks earlier, King had announced that the SCLC was moving the focus for his civil rights campaign to the North. With this latest news, it was clear that King was close to choosing Chicago as the first site.

Al groaned out loud as he reviewed the logistical challenges that the King visit posed: "Except for Al Raby, no one is on hand to plan and coordinate this visit. I guess the job will fall to me."

Being the impresario for the King visit seemed like an inevitable step in a series of steps that had placed more and more responsibility on Al Pitcher for managing the civil rights movement of Chicago. From that moment several months earlier when he had spoken up toward the end of a CCCO meeting about the need for a long-run strategy, Pitcher had moved steadily to the center of the small leadership circle. It may have not been his plan, but the progression occurred so inexorably that the result seemed almost predestined.

Martin Luther King Jr. speaking from a car. Courtesy Chicago Urban League records, CULR_04_0120_1392_004, University of Illinois at Chicago Library, Special Collections.

His revelation at breakfast about how limited the leadership capacity was at the center of CCCO came as no surprise. Outsiders may have assumed that the organization was the model of military efficiency and run by a series of able lieutenants. Nothing could be farther from the truth. True enough, many volunteer workers were on hand to make phone calls and type correspondence, but they could not plan and make policy decisions nor handle the job of recruiting persons with "clout." This job fell to people with connections and influence in the city.

The office was well staffed with "hippie" types. These were teenagers and other "soldiers of fortune" who spent their days in the office and their evenings marching and demonstrating. Some of them had leadership potential, but they required seasoning—to spend time in a type of apprentice system—ideally learning under the guidance of a pro like Al Pitcher. Unfortunately, too many of the "novitiates" expressed little patience for organizational matters, wanting instead to go forth and challenge and change the world immediately.

Pitcher spoke about the problems posed by the "teen rebels" in the office. Several who had come to Chicago for the summer from other cities slept in the headquarters. At first Al and the other adults had sanctioned the practice, as it afforded protection for the office. However, as the office became more and more unkempt, and as rumors circulated about improper conduct at night, the decision was taken to close the office each evening, and no one was allowed to stay over.

This decision provoked considerable controversy. Some of the teenagers from Chicago defended their out-of-town colleagues, saying, "These people have come to Chicago to work for us, the least we can do is to give them a place to sleep at night." Pitcher appreciated their point, but they'd have to find another place to sleep at night. Pitcher's concerns were confirmed a few days later when an adult volunteer reported that some whiskey had been stolen from her car while it was being used by several teenagers to take a group to a nighttime rally.

I asked Al whether he enjoyed his role as office disciplinarian and general manager of all details. He responded, "No job is too small for me. I am the person who has the only key to the storeroom. If I didn't keep control of it, we'd never have any supplies on hand. My job is to serve, whether it's a small assignment of disciplining rambunctious youngsters or making important policy recommendations to Al Raby."

Al's daughter Kathy, who worked in the office as a volunteer, offered another perspective on the tensions in the office. While working in the office, she had occasion to call her mother. As she picked up the phone, her father asked her what she was doing. He told her not to make any personal phone calls from the office. She felt humiliated by the incident but understood his reason after he explained that CCCO had received a $300 phone bill the previous month due to the "kids" calling all over the county to talk to their friends.

His willingness to tackle the nitty-gritty was illustrated by the role he played in planning for the upcoming visit of Martin Luther King in late July. He had to organize transportation so people could travel from their communities to the center of Chicago for what was hoped to be a massive march that King would lead. This meant contacting bus companies, assessing the transportation needs of many different communities and merging those of certain localities in order to conserve expenditures, and planning an operation as complex as a military invasion. It didn't require much imagination; it required attention to detail and many hours of work and endless phone calls. And Al was happy to play this role and deal with all the necessary details.

Occasionally during the summer one or two of the teenage volunteers would pack up their gear and head off, accompanied by comments from the adults like, "Well, there go our 'soldiers of fortune'—off to save Mississippi." Those who stayed behind and continued to type letters and serve as "go-fers" often felt envious of the adventures presumed to be ahead for those who were moving on to other action sites.

If Al Pitcher had not come to live with us during the summer of 1965, I doubt that I would have remained active in the civil rights movement. Here was a talented white person serving the civil rights movement, managing the CCCO office, providing counsel to black leaders, and doing all of this in a self-effacing way and without much sleep. His dedication was inspiring. If he could throw himself into the mix, the least I could do was continue to be a delegate to CCCO and to offer my legs when the next march took place.

7. A Peaceful March in Kenwood and a Not-So-Peaceful March Led by Dick Gregory

Strength does not come from physical capacity.
It comes from an indomitable will.

—Mahatma Gandhi

While the marches from Grant Park to City Center continued on a daily basis, other marches took place, in some cases outside of the Loop. It is instructive to describe two examples of what could be termed more bottom-up, instigated marches: an evening march in Kenwood, a community just to the north of Hyde Park and a march led by Dick Gregory to the mayor's home neighborhood, Bridgeport.

The new neighborhood rallies followed roughly the same pattern. They were held in the early evening to allow working adults to participate; they took place in the inner-city communities so there would be maximum involvement by and impact on the residents;, and they usually concluded with a rally at the local alderman's office.

In early July 1965, two teenage girls launched a series of rallies in the Kenwood community. Their first efforts drew only a handful of people. By the third week they decided to call for "guest" marchers from Hyde Park. So on one Friday night, I decided to participate, and the evening took on many attributes of a pilgrimage. The group gathered at a schoolyard for a pre-rally pep session. Several black teenagers were playing drums, and the small group that had gathered joined in the boisterous singing.

As the crowd assembled, clearly two distinct groups were present, white adults and black teenagers (in fact, the whole effort appeared to be in the hands of these energetic and talented leaders). Interestingly, only a few black adults were on hand.

About dusk, the march proceeded into the depths of the Kenwood community. Like a snake, it moved down the dark byways, around corners, seemingly without any preconceived plan. A young boy carried a lantern at the head of the march. The line of participants extended over several blocks, an impressive measure of the number of participants.

As the march moved forward, scores of youngsters came up. The teenage girls invited them to participate, making sure that there was an adult present in the line of the march to look after them. Some of them fell in step with the march for a few blocks and then dropped out.

A carnival atmosphere prevailed. People hung out of windows. Others stopped what they were doing. A man who was putting a suitcase into a well-polished car looked up for a minute and then went back to his packing. Many waved supporting gestures as the march went by. However, no adults ventured forth from the porches to join the march. Was it because they had not been invited? No. The youngsters took it upon themselves to invite everyone within range of their voices to join the march. Was it apathy? Perhaps. Was it ignorance about the purpose of the march? Perhaps. Yes, we held signs about education and integration, and we chanted: "Ben Willis must go." But the leaders needed to keep the march moving, and there was little opportunity to elaborate on the issues and to tell the bystanders why they should join the march.

Some of the onlookers appeared troubled, seeming to wish that they not be confronted with the choice of remaining observers or joining the march. Those who reacted this way tended to be the younger men. One young man was working on a beautiful car and looked up as we passed. I wondered whether for him the best feature of his prized possession was that it allowed him to regularly escape from his neighborhood. Steadily, the number of marchers grew to several hundred and soon stretched over three or four blocks. The singing increased in fervor and everyone felt in high spirits. As the march turned the corner onto Oakenwald Street, Sullivan House, now a community center, loomed in front of us. Named for its famous first resident and architect, Louis Sullivan, it stands as a reminder of a by-gone era, when this section of Chicago housed wealthy families who wanted to live near both the lake and their places of work in the Loop. One could easily discern the quality of the construction of Sullivan House, especially its wrought iron work, a hallmark of the Sullivan era. However, much of the wooden trim had decayed and the building appeared quite dilapidated.

Significantly, the juxtaposition of this civil rights march and the social service function being served by Sullivan House underscored a crucial difference in strategies for dealing with the problems of the inner city. As a result of the efforts of a visionary social worker, Sullivan House had been saved from urban renewal and converted into a neighborhood settlement house with emphasis on club work for teenage boys. I learned that a dedicated soul by the name of Dillon had quit his regular job and taken up residence with the purpose of helping local youngsters make conga drums and coalescing them into a performing group.

While the settlement house strategy only served a small number of local residents, hopefully it created lasting value for the individuals involved. By contrast, the civil rights movement and this march espoused more ambitious goals, but in the end the impact was less certain. Clearly, both approaches needed to be in play. Unlike the preaching of sermons or the arguing that occurred at endless meetings, both marching and building conga drums could be seen as useful and necessary forms of social action and service.

The march moved on. By now it was quite dark. Down a dingy and poorly lit street we continued. A group of teenage boys had gathered on a front porch with a phonograph. It blared forth the latest beat music. Some of the teenage girls in the line of march, who knew the boys, asked them to join us. They laughed and responded with several sarcastic remarks. Not coincidentally, this block had the most broken glass and rundown houses.

As we emerged from the narrow streets onto 47th Street, a main thoroughfare, we were met with a cold stare from the pastor of a large Baptist church. Why was he so negative? Was he afraid of another group exercising influence within his community, would his role be lessened? Or was it more ideological? Perhaps he believed in change through persuasion rather than through demonstration and pressure tactics. He was neither apathetic nor frightened. On the contrary, he appeared agitated and upset.

The march stopped at the park at the western edge of the community. A makeshift platform was quickly erected and the closing festivities began. Al Raby, who had joined the march as it neared the end, came to the platform, and in his usual diffident manner, said: "My name is Al Raby. I am referred to as the so-called 'leader' of the civil rights movement. I came here because these two girls who organized the march asked me to come. I go wherever I am asked to help. I don't see what they can gain by having me here, but I'm happy to come. There is a CCCO meeting going on right now, and I will be late for it. But let me say that these neighborhood rallies are the start of something important. We're going to move and move until we throw off the yoke of these ineffective aldermen."

About that point, a large loudspeaker appeared in a window overlooking the park. It blared forth voluptuous dance music and several silhouettes appeared in the dimly lighted room. Raby remarked, "Looks like Mayor Daley has turned on the music to keep us from having a rally."

Several other leaders took the platform, without the benefit of a mike, since no public address system was in place. A few hymns were sung and the meeting was about to end when someone shouted, "Let's hear from Tim Black." People in the crowd looked around, and Tim made his way forward to the platform. This was Tim's home community where, as mentioned earlier, he had run against the machine alderman and been beaten by a margin of three-to-one—not a bad showing since he had come into the campaign very late and with limited financial support. While Kenwood represented his political base, he had played no part in organizing these marches. He was engaged with many other responsibilities, increasingly being called upon to be a commentator rather than a planner and organizer.

As he spoke about the significance of the march, I reflected on his evolving role in the civil rights movement. Early on, he had advocated an activist approach to improving the school situation. He had helped organize voter registration drives; he had organized participation by Chicagoans in the March on Washington in 1963; he had served as president of the local NALC chapter for many years, and together we had taken on Motorola and the American Bar Association. Tim was not as much on the front lines as before but instead had chosen other roles in the unfolding civil rights scene. He certainly had not peaked! Instead, he was entering a new phase of his remarkable career, one increasingly devoted to scholarship and participation in a wide range of community and political activities.

As we left the scene and traveled home, we talked about this new emphasis on neighborhood rallies. Was this shifting of the focus away from Mayor Daley, away from City Hall, due to burnout? Or was community mobilization a necessary new strategy, an investment that would produce more soldiers for the next citywide campaign? Could it be that the shift away from confrontation mirrored what had been happening in the national scene for instance, in Selma, where the first march had been followed by a second, very peaceful demonstration? Then too, civil rights leaders across the country could take satisfaction that their programs of direct action had played an important role in convincing President Lyndon Johnson to do all that he could to ensure passage of the Civil Rights Act of 1964 and the Voting Rights Act of 1965. So possibly a phase of the civil rights revolution had been reached that required recalibration.

Perhaps the CCCO leadership had concluded that the Loop rallies were losing their impact, although they had to be continued to keep up the appearance of commitment and perseverance. It was becoming increasingly clear, however, that the deadlock between the city and the CCCO would be resolved only by a change in the political landscape. One step in this direction would be to loosen the Democratic machine's control of the black community. To that end, the rallies in these-inner city wards were very strategic—attacking Mayor Daley where he was most vulnerable by undercutting political support for the black aldermen he considered his.

Early in his stay with us during the summer of 1965, Al Pitcher mentioned one morning at breakfast that comedian Dick Gregory would be coming to our house that evening to huddle with several other leaders about his plan for leading nightly marches from Buckingham Fountain in Grant Park. I would have liked to have attended this meeting and observed Dick Gregory up close and to have tested the hypothesis that "comedians underneath are very *serious* people." But I was not invited.

The next morning I learned about Gregory's idea. He would be at Buckingham Fountain each afternoon about 5:00 P.M., and he would lead as many as joined him, initially to City Hall (the usual destination) and the offices of the board of education and eventually to the mayor's home in the Bridgeport section of Chicago. Since Gregory was on stage each evening at the Hungry Eye in San Francisco, this plan meant catching a flight to San Francisco after each march, performing his "gigs," then heading back to Chicago on the "red eye." Eventually, Gregory would lead more than forty of these nighttime marches.

In contrast to the marches from Grant Park that were planned by the CCCO leadership, the Gregory marches arose on a more spontaneous basis. Gregory and the individuals who showed up to participate chose the destinations and targets of these marches.

Gregory and his cadre of demonstrators decided on August 1, 1965, to extend their march beyond the Loop to Bridgeport. On August 2, the evening of the second march to Bridgeport, matters grew serious and confrontational. Before this episode was over, forty marchers would be arrested for disorderly conduct, and a resulting legal case would go all the way to the Supreme Court of the United States. The case garnered national attention since it highlighted a critical question: Could an angry mob (in this instance, residents assembled in Bridgeport) enjoy immunity while marchers who were demonstrating in a peaceful manner were arrested and fined? Over the years, this issue—the "hecklers' veto"—has been discussed extensively in the courts and law reviews. In his chronicle of the civil rights movement in Milwaukee, Patrick Jones describes a similar event when the marchers and not the out-of-control bystanders were arrested.[1]

The sequence of events and the high drama that ensued are captured in the testimony of the police lieutenant in charge,[2] who testified that on the evening

Dick Gregory being interviewed by phone, 1964. Library of Congress: LC-USZ62–121425, photograph by Herman Hiller.

in question he was leading a Chicago police department task force, and that his assignment for that day was to protect individuals who were going to march. About 4:00 P.M., he and his squad went to Buckingham Fountain in Grant Park on Chicago's lakefront just east of the Loop, where approximately 650 marchers had assembled. He observed Dick Gregory addressing the marchers and heard him say, "First we will go over to the snake pit [City Hall]. When we leave there, we will go out to the snake's house [the mayor's home]. And we will continue to go out to Mayor Daley's home until he fires Ben Willis."

About 4:30 P.M., the marchers, two abreast, walked out of the park and moved on to City Hall. The marchers then proceeded south on State Street to 35th Street and then west to Lowe Avenue, a distance of about five miles from City Hall. The mayor's home was at 3536 South Lowe Avenue. By this point, the number of demonstrators had increased to about 85, and they arrived at the mayor's home about 8:00 P.M. In addition to the police, their attorney and an assistant city counsel accompanied the marchers. At the suggestion of the assistant city counsel, Gregory had agreed that the group would quit singing at 8:30 P.M., but would continue marching.

Initially, about 35 bystanders stood on the corner and watched. When a group of 6 or 7 youngsters carrying a sign saying "We Love Mayor Daley" tried to join the marchers, the police stopped them. As the demonstrators started south into the 3500 block of Lowe Avenue, Gregory moved along the line telling everyone to keep singing and marching: "Don't stop and don't answer anyone back. Don't worry about anything that is going to be said to you. Just keep marching. If anyone hits you or anything, try to remember what he or she looks like, but above all, do not hit him or her back. Keep the line straight and keep it tight."

The demonstrators chanted: "Ben Willis must go. Snake Daley must go." "Ben Willis must go. When? Now." "We are going to the home of the snake. The snake pit is down the street." They carried signs that read: "Daley fire Willis" and "Ben Willis must go—now." They also sang the civil rights songs, *We Shall Overcome* and *We Shall Not Be Moved*.

The police ordered local taverns closed during the march. The police surrounded the block in which the mayor's home was located. There were about ten officers at each of the four intersections and about ten more spread along each of the four blocks. The rest of the one hundred police officers assigned to the march accompanied the demonstrators as they marched around the block. The police tried to keep all spectators across the street from the marchers. The police were equipped with walkie-talkie radios to relay reports of conditions to each other and a bullhorn with which they addressed the spectators and the demonstrators.

As the marchers started circling the block the first time, the neighbors began coming out of their homes. On the second time around the block, some of the residents had moved their lawn sprinklers onto the sidewalks and the demonstrators went into the street to get around the water. On the third trip around the block, the water sprinklers had been removed, presumably by order of the police. On their fourth trip around the block, marchers were met with the sound of people yelling out the windows, and the police asked spectators to close their doors and windows. About 8:30 P.M. the demonstrators quit singing and chanting and began to march quietly.

Between 8:00 and 9:00 P.M. the crowd increased steadily to a few hundred, but after 9:00 people just "seemed to come from everywhere" until the crowd grew to between 1,000 and 1,200. There was shouting and threats: "God-damned nigger, get the hell out of here." "Get out of here, niggers—go back where you belong or we will get you out of here." "Get the hell out of here or we will break your f—— heads open." Cars stopped in the street with their horns blowing. There were Ku Klux Klan signs and there was singing of the "Alabama Trooper" song. Rocks and eggs were also thrown at the marchers from the crowd.

About 9:30 P.M., the police commander in charge told Gregory the situation was dangerous and becoming riotous. He asked Gregory if he would cooperate and lead the marchers out of the area. Gregory responded that they had every right to continue marching. This request by the police for Gregory and the marchers to leave the area was made five times. The commander told the marchers that any of them who wished to leave the area would be given a police escort. Three of the marchers accepted this proposal and were escorted out of the area. The remaining demonstrators, refusing to leave, were arrested and taken away in two police vans.

Soon thereafter, Al Raby called a meeting of the CCCO in response to extensive public criticism of what had happened in Bridgeport. Indeed, several prominent citizens had called on the civil rights movement to suspend these evening marches. A well-known newspaper columnist, Irv Kupcinet, stated that several leaders of the CCCO were preparing a motion of censure and that the nightly marches were tearing the organization apart.

The Gregory marches had *not* been approved by the CCCO. They took place because a small group of committed activists supported Dick Gregory's decision to embarrass the mayor by marching in his neighborhood. So the purpose of the meeting was to close the gap between what was happening on the ground and the initiatives approved by the CCCO.

When I got to the meeting about an hour late, Al Pitcher was presiding. This development in itself was significant. I continued to be fascinated by the process by which a white man had moved to the center of power in the civil rights movement: from a place in the movement several months prior when he had spoken about his limited role of helping with long-range planning, to this meeting where he was actually chairing the session. And his new role had not been approved in any formal sense by the membership of the CCCO; in fact, he was not even a delegate to the CCCO since, as mentioned before, his fellow Baptists had not formed a citywide social responsibility committee. But who cared? Al was working twenty hours a day in behalf of the civil rights movement. He was writing all the important statements. He was the idea person in the inner leadership circle. Who, at a time of crisis, would worry about legalisms or insist on due process? The overriding need was to achieve consensus, and this CCCO meeting had been called for just that purpose. A *de facto* plan had been implemented to march to Bridgeport, and the agenda item at hand was to endorse the effort and to bring the thinking and support of delegates from the member organizations into alignment with this latest tactic.

Al Raby was not in attendance—at least for the first half of the meeting—but this did not really matter since agenda items early in the evening tended to be routine business matters involving reports and, in this case, a discussion regarding the organization of the office.

This meeting had been labeled by Irv Kupcinet as the "most important" in the history of the CCCO. While I doubted the meeting would repudiate the program of nightly marches, still I wondered about the direction the Chicago campaign was taking. Beyond Bridgeport, what? This was the big question running through my mind as I drove to the West Side church where the meeting was being held. By making the removal of Willis its sole demand, however, the civil rights movement had created a difficult bargaining situation for itself. It had formulated a demand that was not subject to compromise. You could not have half of Willis staying and half leaving. It was a situation that game theorists call a "win/lose" negotiation.From a strategic point of view, I wondered whether it would not have been smarter for the movement to have put forth a demand that was capable of compromise, or better yet, a proposal that was capable of being satisfied by several solutions. For example, if the civil rights movement had focused on the details of a transition in the leadership of the Chicago schools and not about Willis's departure "now," there might have been a basis for discussion. Could it just be possible for the mayor to give the superintendent "a trip around the world" as recognition for his service to the Chicago community or, more seriously, to retain him as a consultant when his contract ended? Such a solution would have enabled Mayor Daley to save face.

But the leaders of the movement were not interested in seeing Mayor Daley save face. They would rather have punched that face, or "walk all over it," and Pitcher had said as much in private conversations. One might have hoped for a more rational approach to negotiations, but the civil rights movement was an amorphous movement and not a finely tuned piece of machinery. If the leadership had become too sophisticated, too politically savvy in shaping a bargaining strategy, it might have lost the very genius of its existence—the support and dedication of its followers. From the viewpoint of the rank and file, it was necessary for the goal to be formulated in clear terms: "Willis must go—now." Any watered-down statement as to what constituted victory would not have kept faith with the feelings and sacrifices of those who had been putting their bodies on the line by marching each evening. Even if Al Raby and Al Pitcher had seen the possibility of a compromise, they could not have embraced it because of membership pressure for a big win. Consequently, they were on a course of action that had little chance of success because the militants within the movement would not accept anything short of complete victory.

In private discussions, Pitcher acknowledged this dilemma, and over breakfast one morning, he said, "What is more important to us now is not getting rid of Willis but maintaining the morale of the movement." He recognized that the civil rights leadership needed to manage expectations: on the one hand, they needed a big tangible goal ("Willis has got to go"), while on the other, they had to be careful not to risk the disintegration of the movement by settling for a gain that was not significant. The following episode illustrates this balancing act.

Shortly after the daily marches had begun, the mayor sought a meeting with the leaders of the civil rights movement. In planning for this meeting, Pitcher prepared a list of demands. He shaped the agenda in such a way that the mayor had to address the demand of getting rid of Willis. Pitcher's great fear was that the mayor would make some concessions regarding resources and educational policies to the end that some of the less militant leaders of the movement might feel a victory had been achieved. (For some in the civil rights movement, just meeting with the mayor might have been rewarding enough to create a feeling of achievement.)

The leaders of the movement knew that Mayor Daley had an image to preserve, namely, his long-held position of not interfering with the authority of the school board. It was true that his role was limited to appointing members of the school selection committee, but this committee recommended candidates for the board, and the board controlled the school system, particularly the tenure of the superintendent. Still, the mayor had invested considerable energy in building the image of someone who kept his hands off the running of schools.

By framing the list of demands with the removal of Willis as the number one demand, Pitcher structured the outcome of the meeting with the mayor, and it ran according to his predictions. The mayor said he could not do anything about their first demand (getting rid of Willis), but he would be willing to go to the board of education's next meeting and present their other "concerns." This response by the mayor was deemed not acceptable, and the leaders of the civil rights movement termed the meeting a failure—and support from the ranks remained solid.

While the strategy chosen by the leaders reckoned with the need for cohesion within the movement, it overlooked some important external problems. By stating their demands in extreme form and by continuing the protests for an extended period of time, the civil rights movement stretched the patience of the white community. Not many members of the white community were sympathetic with the tactics of the civil rights movement to begin with, and even those who were allies would tolerate the direct action tactics only for a limited period of time. As the marches continued, many white people concluded "the civil rights movement would rather be angry than win its demands."

The possibility was also emerging that Mayor Daley might seek injunctive action against the civil rights movement (as had been done as soon as the CCCO announced plans for a third boycott of the schools), and that a majority of the citizens might very well support such a move. Indeed, the movement found itself experiencing increased restrictions in its witness against Willis. Specifically, a marked contrast existed between the way the city earlier had policed the march on Good Friday and the new constraints being imposed on the daily marches.

Also the mayor's hand had been strengthened considerably as a result of the last elections when he had been returned to office for a third term with a margin of 140,000 votes. In these elections, all of the Daley "machine" aldermen (many of whom represented black wards) had been returned to office by large majorities.

The civil rights movement only possessed bargaining power if Mayor Daley could be assured that the possibility of future turmoil would be eliminated. If people acquired the idea that the civil rights movement was radical and beyond reason and that it was only doing damage to the reputation of Chicago, then there would be nothing gained by the mayor's making concessions to "end the disturbances." Rather, he might declare war on the demonstrators.

The new campaign also had shifted the focus away from just education. The marches in front of Mayor Daley's home spotlighted discrimination in housing. Bridgeport's residents were virtually all white, and the community strenuously resisted any spillover from adjacent black neighborhoods. By focusing attention on Mayor Daley, as Dick Gregory did by calling for daily marches to Bridgeport, the conflict had shifted from schools to a much broader agenda.

As I sat in the back of the room and waited for the CCCO meeting to reach the key agenda item (marches to Bridgeport), I concluded that the social dynamics of this confrontation were indeed highly complicated. My own thinking had taken many twists and turns. A few weeks earlier, I had predicted that the daily demonstrations against Willis would die out. I assumed that after people had marched, much of their hostility would fade away. (In fact, I hoped it would fade away so my own misgivings about the marches would be resolved.) But the demonstrations did not fade away—rather, they intensified. Some of this was due to the rough treatment given the demonstrators by the police, but the increased momentum also arose from the energy released by the symbolic acts of witnessing and their galvanizing force for the civil rights movement.

I also reflected on several developments that illustrated that the board of education did not enjoy a very high degree of internal coordination. For example, in an attempt to placate the civil rights movement, the chairman of the board had appointed a special selection committee to seek a successor to Willis. This action had been taken without consulting the board and as a result was severely criticized by members of the board.

Another example—probably caused by the rapid flow of events—came to light as a result of some field research conducted by one of my students. He had been investigating the extent of progress in desegregating unions and had been talking with a staff member at the board of education who was responsible for vocational education at the Washburne Trade School. The official complained that when leaders of the civil rights movement and representatives of the board of education held discussions about Washburne, he had not been included. In fact, when the board passed a resolution denying access to Washburne to any union that discriminated against blacks, the official was not even aware of the move until he read about it in the newspapers.

About 10:00 P.M., Al Raby finally arrived at the meeting, and things quickly came alive. He apologized for not having been there earlier but explained that he had been called to some important meetings and knew the chairing of the CCCO session was in good hands. Then he went on to say he was glad the opportunity had presented itself to pass the chair of the meeting over to other people. "I'm afraid this movement may become too dependent upon one person. The civil rights movement is not Al Raby. The civil rights movement is all of you." It was admirable how consistently he made the point of only being one member of the team.

When the subject of the Bridgeport marches was introduced, Al Raby asked Father Hogan to take the chair since Al wanted "to be free to speak his mind on the subject of Bridgeport." And indeed he did. To my mind, Al made a brilliant speech in support of the Bridgeport marches. He confessed that initially he had many misgivings about going into Daley's neighborhood, but that he had subsequently changed his mind.

Al outlined how events had unfolded over the previous several months, from the demonstrations against Willis, to the distributing of literature on subways, and now the marches on Bridgeport. He pointed out how this had been a logical, escalating sequence and described how the steering committee had analyzed all the possible strategies and decided on the best course of action at every turn. I wondered why he did not admit that this was a battle campaign and that the movement had to be opportunistic, that due to the fast pace of events some key people were not included in the decision-making process, and that some tactical mistakes had been made. Did the rank and file expect that everything would be handled so neatly during such a critical confrontation?

After he spoke, there was a round of applause, and a motion was immediately made to endorse the Bridgeport marches and to make Dick Gregory an honorary member of the CCCO. (Technically, to be a member, one had to be a representative of one of the member organizations and on that basis, Gregory did not qualify.) Hands shot up as many in the hall attempted to speak. I had not spoken at these meetings before, especially at a meeting as crucial as this one. I had hesitated in the past to say anything against the prevailing point of view for fear of losing all rapport with the leaders of the civil rights movement. However, I felt the time had come to express my reservations. How to say it without being misunderstood was the challenge.

But even more problematic was the task of getting recognized by the chair. Many people did not know me. The chairman called on people by name, and everyone who spoke was a familiar figure in CCCO gatherings. At one point, I was listed along with five or six others as slated to speak. The others were given their chance and I was ignored. Finally, Tim Black came to my rescue and said to the chairman that I had not been given the floor. If Tim knew what I was about to say, would he have intervened?

I opened by expressing my admiration for the commitment of the CCCO, in particular Dick Gregory, to march every evening and to keep attention focused on the issues, and I appreciated the potency of this tactic. At the same time, I felt uncomfortable with the "in-your-face" aspects of taking the campaign to the mayor's home.

I questioned the tactical focus of the Bridgeport marches, suggesting that the marches could only be successful if they focused on the kind of discrimination that was present in the Bridgeport neighborhood, namely, housing discrimination. But to do this would take the focus away from schools and Mayor Daley to that of housing discrimination. Voices from the audience immediately responded, "They're all wrapped up together." As the voting started, I whispered to Richard Nash (the other delegate from the Commission of

Chicago Liberal Churches) that I was going to vote against the motion. As it turned out, my small, weak voice was the only one raised in opposition.

As I left the meeting, I wondered what to do next. The votes of the two delegates from the SRC had been split. Richard Nash had voted in favor of the campaign, and I had voted against it. Consequently, I felt the need to explain my position. I even considered the idea of writing a letter to the newspapers. But this would be going too far. I already felt considerable discomfort over my position within the confines of the CCCO, but what would happen if I took my disagreement to the newspapers? I caught myself on this one—a tendency to grandstand. How could I, someone who had not really sacrificed for the cause, speak out and criticize the movement at this point? Such a role was reserved for those who had really put themselves on the line—for those who had helped shape the course of the civil rights movement.

And yet I needed to explain my views. One way of dealing with my dilemma would be to explain at the next meeting of the SRC why I had voted against the Bridgeport program. In some respects, I welcomed the opportunity to let loose at the SRC meeting since I had become quite disenchanted with this group. Perhaps it was a "lovers' quarrel"; perhaps the rift ran deeper.

As I thought about the work of the SRC and my own reaction to it, I reviewed several developments that had taken place earlier in the summer. In June an emergency meeting had been called for all the delegates from the Chicago-area liberal churches. The national chairman of the Social Responsibility arm of the Unitarian-Universalist Church, Homer Jack, had been invited, and he had flown in from Boston. (Subsequently, he pledged $250 from the national budget for work in Chicago.) Al Raby was on hand and gave a talk about the CCCO and the program for the upcoming summer.

I had gone to the SRC meeting wondering about the tactical wisdom of the daily marches to City Hall, which were already underway (the marches had not yet headed to Bridgeport)—not disagreeing with their legality or moral base, but wondering about the wisdom of expending energies on this strategy. However, I refrained from verbalizing my doubts and in fact found myself being swept along by the mood of the meeting, which was "let's back the CCCO."

When Al finished his speech, and Homer outlined several priorities, I made a motion to support the program. It would involve a good deal of effort, and I was mindful that I was committing myself to spending considerable time during the summer working with members of the SRC. But perhaps this was a way of helping without becoming overwhelmingly involved. I even took it upon myself to write to the members of the congregation at First Unitarian Church. In my letter, I observed that while polarization was unfortunate, perhaps it was a necessary prelude to any change in the situation. The power structure of Chicago needed to be confronted, and the civil rights movement was engaged in this strategy. I concluded by reporting that the SRC had passed unanimously a resolution supporting the CCCO's current program, and that all members of our congregation needed to support the program to the fullest extent possible.

About midway through the summer, another meeting of the SRC was held, at which various courses of action were debated. At this session, several participants pressed for less involvement in the CCCO. They wondered whether it was wise to be spending so much time on Willis. One of the delegates was an assistant principal. He admitted that the schools were weak and much could be done to improve them, but he wondered about the appropriateness of the Willis-must-go program. As these people spoke, I found myself getting more and more irritated. This was just the kind of rational and cautious approach I had often taken, but now I was much more involved than most of the delegates; I was impatient with what I saw as too much intellectualizing.

But then I had to cope with another bend in the road. At a subsequent meeting of the SRC, discussion focused on a recent statement by Mayor Daley about the leadership of the civil rights movement. In a vent of anger, he had suggested that some of the leaders were "communists" and that communist money was behind the daily marches in the Loop. A motion quickly passed to support the CCCO in its program of marches, including the round-the-clock vigil at City Hall. A subcommittee was formed and charged to prepare a press release while other items of business were being considered. About a half hour later, the committee returned and read its statement. The first part of it followed the consensus of the discussion quite closely, and then the committee read a sentence: "And we deplore the action of Mayor Daley in attacking the leadership of CCCO. By his actions he has placed himself in a class with George Wallace, the Ku Klux Klan, and the people of Mississippi." I immediately protested that this sentiment was not part of our discussion and urged that it be deleted. When a vote was taken on whether to delete this section, my objection was not supported.

I left the meeting feeling alienated. Was it wise to strike out at Mayor Daley and to use the same kind of intemperate language against him that he used against the civil rights movement? What was a church group becoming when it reached for the same kind of inflammatory language that it so often deplored being used by others?

Nash, who had been chairing the meeting and had refrained from commenting on the press release, expressed unhappiness about having his name added to it, but finally he consented. This tracked his role in the civil rights movement. While he may have harbored doubts, he ultimately supported the decision of the majority. This came from a desire to support and to serve and also from his leadership style. Nash's difficult task as chair was to seek consensus in a reasonably expeditious fashion in the context of a fast-moving situation. Some members of the SRC wanted to debate everything at length. These were the conservatives who wanted to do everything slowly and carefully. On the other side were the militants, like those who had prepared the press release and who wanted to "get Daley." One could understand Nash's style when he had so many viewpoints and emotions to reconcile.

So, to deal with the need to explain myself, I drafted a letter to Nash for the next meeting of the SRC that would be held shortly to discuss the Bridgeport situation. As it turned out, I could not attend the meeting—I was teaching that night—and in this letter, I attempted to explain my negative vote at the CCCO meeting to members of the SRC.

Also within my own church, I became silent. Rather than taking the initiative at the weekly Social Action Committee meeting, I stayed away. Under Tim Black, the new chair of the committee, a rump group had been formed to spearhead support for various CCCO activities. I begged off, saying I was leaving the country in the fall and was too involved with the citywide SRC. Part of this was true, but part of it was an excuse. Again, I felt very ambivalent and confused. I was at odds with the activists for wanting to support Bridgeport, but I was also disappointed with the church for not doing very much about race relations in Chicago.

Earlier in the summer, I had vented my feelings at a conference held at the Unitarian Church. My remarks were quite sharp. I reflected on the fact that we were indeed in some respects an integrated church, but we were not integrated socially or integrated across class lines. The church enjoyed the financial stability of a large endowment, and I felt it should be committed much more toward social action, rather than funding an associate minister. We should be doing other things, such as reaching out to Woodlawn to bring more people from that community into the church, and to face up to the idea of operating a Headstart school in the church during the summer. This proposal had been shelved because members of the church's board of trustees did not want to "mix church and state." I appealed for new ideas and a break with the past. I voiced the fear that the Protestant churches, not the Unitarian churches, were in the vanguard of liberal action. It was they who were talking with the Catholic Church about new partnerships. It was they who were cooperating with the board of education in running special nursery schools. And it was they who were most active in the civil rights movement.

Looking back on the crucial meeting of the CCCO that endorsed the Dick Gregory marches to the mayor's home and the ensuing reverberations for me, I realize now that I seemed to be at odds with every organization: with the CCCO, with the SRC, and with the Unitarian Church. The fault lines that had been thrown open in the city were being mirrored in my own ambivalence and discomfort: the status quo had to go, but was there an acceptable strategy to bring about the changes that needed to take place?

What might have been instituted as an alternative to the nightly marches? One idea would have been to work with community organizations to develop local school watchdog groups. Since the issues of the racial makeup of the schools, overcrowding, and quality of education were defined locally, efforts to involve parents and community leaders might have led to some productive engagement of local school officials.

Hindsight is always clearer than when making tough choices during the intense moments of mobilization. Local school councils eventually did come to Chicago. And if the emphasis had been on grass-roots mobilization rather than on getting rid of the person at the top, the ground might have been prepared sooner for constructive action in individual schools. To be fair, the hours contributed by marchers were not hours that could be redeployed into community organizing. Many who marched were rank-and-filers, foot soldiers, and they would not have been able to serve as tutors and other helpers in the school system.

Returning to the Bridgeport saga, on August 3 (the day after the near riot) the marchers were arraigned before two magistrates, and Gregory and four others who had served as leaders were fined $200, with the remaining 35 fined $25 each. Several public interest law firms, as well as the ACLU, immediately swung into action and initiated legal action to have the convictions set aside.

Marshall Patner served as lead counsel for the marchers. Marshall and I had developed a close relationship in many areas of professional interest. Since we lived on the same block in Hyde Park and our children played together, we saw each other frequently and enjoyed many early Sunday morning outings to the Maxwell Street flea market.

Marshall graduated from the University of Chicago Law School after completing his undergraduate education at the University of Wisconsin. Early in his career, he had worked as general counsel for the Illinois division of the ACLU. Throughout his career, he took cases in behalf of those who might be described as the under-privileged in society. He possessed incredible energy and many talents, a roaring appetite for anything edible, and a penchant for initiating exciting projects. He successfully pushed through an ordinance to make it possible for restaurants to open outdoor cafes (Marshall had brought to Chicago the idea of this pleasurable arrangement from his travels abroad). I also remember a campaign he spearheaded to protect Lake Michigan from a proposed third airport, using the memorable phrase "Don't do it in the lake."

Soon after Marshall and I became acquainted, he introduced me to Gordon Sherman, who had established a public-interest firm with which Marshall was associated, Businessmen in the Public Interest. My first brush with corporate infighting occurred when I agreed to be slated as a director in a proxy fight to gain control of Midas Muffler. Gordon's father, who had founded the company, led the opposition and of course we lost.

Marshall Patner, attorney who represented both Dick Gregory on charges stemming from the march to Bridgeport and Jeff Fort in his appearance before Sen. John McClellan and his committee investigating the Blackstone Rangers. Courtesy Mrs. Marshall (Irene) Patner.

Marshall will later reappear in this chronicle as the defender of Jeff Fort, leader of the Blackstone Rangers, when Fort was called before the McClellan Committee to talk about his activities on Chicago's South Side. Red Rooster, a store that came under attack by Operation Breadbasket, had employed Fort and members of his gang. Many years later, while I was serving as director of a large trucking company and needed a lawyer to represent a group of workers and stockholders to challenge a takeover of the company, I contacted Marshall, and he provided invaluable legal assistance. Marshall died suddenly in December 2000.

In the Dick Gregory case, Paul Goldstein, a member of the law firm of Ross and Hardy, joined Marshall. The time Goldstein spent on the case represented a *pro bono* contribution by his firm. The case moved slowly through lower levels of the legal system and reached a crucial level of review at the Illinois Supreme Court, which heard arguments in December 1967. Many years later, Goldstein recalled that he and Patner spent a great deal of time during 1965, 1966, and 1967 getting ready for their presentation before the Illinois Supreme Court, and eventually before the U.S. Supreme Court. He went on to say that he and Marshall would do their work while dining— "Marshall liked to eat"—either at the café in the Art Institute or at Jimmy's Tavern in Hyde Park, near where Marshall lived.[3]

In a decision handed down in January 1968, the Illinois Supreme Court unanimously affirmed the convictions of the 40 marchers, stating:

> Under circumstances of this case, defendants were not denied any right of free speech, free assembly, or freedom to petition for redress of grievances. The court had been persuaded by the facts of the situation, specifically, that the police experienced difficulty containing the crowd, and the looming possibility of a riot. The police asked Gregory five times to lead the marchers out of the area, and offered to escort any individuals who wanted to leave (three took this option) and consequently the police had no other alternative but to arrest the marchers, given the situation in front of them.[4]

The wheels of justice grind very slowly, but they do grind, and on December 10, 1968, Marshall Patner argued the case before the U.S. Supreme Court. The dream of every lawyer is to argue a case before the U.S. Supreme Court, and in recalling this high point of their work on the case, Goldstein related an amusing incident. He and Patner were surprised that Dick Gregory was not in the audience since other members of the Gregory family had traveled to Washington and were present during the proceedings. After the court adjourned, and they proceeded to the cafeteria, Gregory finally appeared. As everyone gathered for lunch of soup, sandwiches, or salad in the cafeteria of the Supreme Court building, Gregory, who was engaged in one of his fasting ordeals sat there with just a bottle of water. Patner's mother, Rose, demonstrating her motherly concern, leaned over to Gregory and said, "Aren't you going to have something to eat, Mr. Gregory? Please have a little soup. No one else will know."

In a unanimous decision, the U.S. Supreme Court, with Chief Justice Earl Warren writing the decision, overturned the convictions. The Court's thinking is best captured in the concurring comments of Justice Hugo Black:

> It must be remembered that only the tiniest bit of petitioners' conduct could possibly be thought illegal here—that is, what they did after the policeman's order to leave the area. The First Amendment specifically protects the right "peaceably to assemble, and to petition the Government for a redress of grievances." For the entire five-mile march, the walking by petitioners in a group, the language, and the chants and songs were all treated by the city's assistant attorney and its specially detailed policemen as lawful, not lawless, conduct.
>
> The so-called "diversion tending to a breach of the peace" here was limited entirely and exclusively to the fact that when the policeman in charge ordered Gregory and his demonstrators to leave, . . . Gregory— standing on what he deemed to be his constitutional rights—refused to do so. . . . Their guilt of "disorderly conduct" therefore turns out to be their refusal to obey instantly an individual policeman's command to leave the area of the Mayor's home. . . . To let a policeman's command become equivalent to a criminal statute comes dangerously near making our government one of men rather than of laws. There are ample ways to protect the domestic tranquility without subjecting First Amendment freedoms to such a clumsy and unwieldy weapon.[5]

How could the convictions be unanimously affirmed by the Illinois Supreme Court, and subsequently be unanimously set aside by the U.S. Supreme Court? Goldstein attributed the opinion of the Illinois court to the fact that "Mayor Daley had a lot of influence over the Supreme Court of Illinois," and its members were probably influenced by the harsh language used by the marchers, specifically phrases that referred to Mayor Daley as a "snake."

Irene Patner, Marshall's widow, recalled one moment in the proceedings before the Illinois Supreme Court that illustrates the tense nature of those proceedings, if not the inclination of the justices to be negatively disposed toward the defendants.[6] One justice, seeking to determine if the marchers were making as much noise as the hecklers, asked a question:

JUSTICE: *So, Mr. Patner, how much noise were the marchers making in Bridgeport?*

PATNER *(after a long period of silence)*: *You mean, Mr. Justice, could you hear them shuffling with their ankles tied together?*

The Gregory case caught the attention of the foremost theorist of First Amendment rights, Harry Kalven. In his definitive treatise, he commented, "The picketing of a private residence of a public official raised challenging counter values, and in this instance the speakers had in effect, 'invaded' the environment of the hostile audience. . . . The Court's ambivalent response is all the more striking because it is unanimous in upsetting the convictions."[7]

Not surprisingly, given my negative vote at the CCCO meetings, I too felt quite ambivalent about what had transpired when Gregory and his marchers had invaded Bridgeport. Later I will describe a similar situation when a hostile crowd gathered to confront the open-housing march to Chicago Lawn. In this instance, when the police offered to protect us, we readily accepted and we returned to the safety of the black residential community. We were glad for the safe retreat, and I wondered why Gregory and his marchers had not availed themselves of a similar safe exit instead of forcing the police to arrest them to avoid a major riot.

At the same time, I admired the decision of the U.S. Supreme Court to buttress the rights of free speech and *not* to allow police or municipal authorities to target and arrest marchers while ignoring the hostile actions of hecklers. Certainly, the right to protest and the right of free assembly are very much on our minds today, some five decades later.

Like spontaneous combustion, during the summer of 1965 riots flared in Los Angeles and Chicago at precisely the same time. In the large northern cities, tempers had reached the flashpoint by the middle of August; all that was required was a provoking incident to create the spark. Then too, the previous summer had witnessed ugly riots in a number of northern cities (but not Chicago) and everyone expected a repetition. In some respects, it all seemed like a self-fulfilling prophecy: the police department, under instructions from the mayor, prepared for trouble, and some elements in the black community helped them fulfill their expectations.

At first glance, there did not appear to be any pattern to the riots. In Los Angeles, the trouble started over a minor arrest and grew into the most serious race riots in the history of the United States to that point, with millions of dollars of property damage and scores of people killed and hurt. In Chicago, the precipitating event was much more serious: a black woman was killed by an undermanned fire truck—coming from a station that rostered an all-white crew in the face of continuing pressure from community groups for the fire department to integrate its crews. Fortunately, in Chicago the riots were brought under control with only a minor amount of property damage and no one seriously hurt.

How could the differences be explained? In the case of Chicago, some pointed to effective police work and the human relations training instituted by Superintendent Orlando Wilson. This forward-looking approach was in contrast to the narrow and tough-minded administration of Police Chief William Parker in Los Angeles. Others pointed to the contrasting roles of the Catholic Church in the two cities. In Chicago the church was actively involved in slum areas, helping to organize people into block groups, while in Los Angeles it remained relatively aloof from the problems of the black community; indeed, there church leaders voiced criticism of the civil rights movement.[8] But while there were differences, and Chicago seemed to be miles ahead of Los Angeles in race relations, still a flashpoint had been reached in Chicago, and a riot ensued. What brought it about?

For several months, a militant organization called ACT, led by Lawrence Landry, had been picketing a firehouse on the near West Side. The leaders demanded that blacks be assigned to the crew. Across the city, progress had been slow, and by the summer of 1965 only 10 percent of the city's firehouses had been integrated. By contrast, the police department was thoroughly integrated. The fire commissioner defended his record by noting that integrating a firehouse was a particularly difficult business since firemen lived together.

So when on August 12 a fire truck from this station killed a black woman, a large crowd quickly gathered. Members of ACT were present and attempted to calm the crowd, calling for a rally the next evening. At that rally, Lawrence Landry and Nahez Rogers delivered speeches, attacking the white community. When riots broke out soon thereafter, both Landry and Rogers denied responsibility.

This episode illustrates the role of rhetoric and how it can be used to escalate a crisis. Both men had been part of the CCCO and the organized civil rights movement in Chicago. Landry had been a delegate from SNCC and a key organizer of the school boycotts. He was a shrewd and tough-minded activist with a flare for making negative comments. Rogers was articulate and also adversarial. On several occasions, he had attempted to turn a CCCO meeting into a face-off of blacks versus whites. It was clear to me that both individuals wanted to provoke trouble in order to destabilize the status quo. Like Landry, Rogers had drifted away from the CCCO over disagreements about the tactics of direct action—they both desired more confrontation—and they channeled their energies into the new organization, ACT.

For his part, Al Raby played a dramatically different role. At the height of the riot, a police car was dispatched to the CCCO headquarters to bring Raby to the West Side. It was both poignant and ironic: Raby being rushed to the scene of trouble by the police—the very individuals he had confronted on so many occasions. Before the riot, the civil rights movement was held very much at arm's length from the mayor. With the outbreak of trouble, however, Raby found it necessary to use his influence to help stop the riot, and in so doing aligned himself with the establishment.

The riot hurt Raby's leadership and the civil rights movement in several ways. Inevitably, the turmoil provided an opportunity for white people to criticize black leaders. Many white businessmen who had been giving lip service to the cause of improved race relations openly attacked the civil rights movement for its "destructive" influence.

The nightly demonstrations outside Mayor Daley's home were called off and other direct-action programs were curtailed. In effect, the riot took the initiative away from the civil rights movement and gave it to the troublemakers in the black community and to police officers seeking to restore law and order.

As soon as the riot was over, Raby sought to reestablish his independence from the Daley administration by criticizing the mayor for "only reckoning with Negro grievances when there is disorder." He was referring to the fire commissioner's action in quickly integrating the firehouse after the riot had taken place. Raby sought to use the lesson of the riot to urge the mayor to take action on the schools and to meet CCCO demands. This argument struck many as persuasive since by contrast to the leadership of ACT, the leadership of the CCCO was constructive and moderate.

Another effect of the riot was that it pushed white influence within the CCCO into the background and accentuated the underlying schism between blacks and whites. It was, after all, the white firehouse that was the target of the ACT organization. It was the white police who came into the community and became the enemy. White ministers who ventured into the West Side were assailed with epithets. Al Pitcher volunteered to go to the West Side and help but was advised to stay clear because no one would realize that he was a supporter of the black cause; his white skin would be evidence that he was the "enemy."

On balance, it was hard to assess the long-run impact of the riot on the stature of the civil rights movement. Certainly, by comparison to the rioters, the civil rights movement had gained in respectability and had become a more desirable group with which to negotiate. On the other hand, the leadership of the civil rights movement within the black community, by the CCCO, had been weakened as other, more militant leaders had taken charge.

After the riot was over, commentators pondered a range of questions. Was this riot, as so many people asserted, the bitter fruits of the civil rights movement? Had the frequent resort to direct action and other forms of civil disobedience created the wrong example for the black community—transmitting the message that people had a license to do what they wanted? After all, the nightly marches led by Gregory, especially those to Bridgeport, had created considerable tension, and while in this case the troublemakers were white, achieving law and order on the streets of Chicago was becoming increasingly problematic.

Observers remembered that several years earlier, when students at the University of Chicago had occupied the president's office to protest the university's housing policies, soon thereafter a series of racial incidents occurred among local high school students. At the time, several black teenagers commented that they were "getting even" with the white kids from Hyde Park. Certainly, those who marched and those who rioted fell into two distinctly separate groups, and the demonstrations could *not* be seen as a training ground for the troublemakers. However, the dividing line between the two groups could become blurred when civil rights leaders held rallies and delivered speeches bristling with fiery rhetoric.

Al Pitcher, for one, interpreted the riots as symptomatic of deep social problems present in the black community. He used the calculus of expectations outrunning achievement: "We're no longer in a stable situation where the Negro is in his place and content with his lot. They have begun to see that it is possible to live like human beings. Unfortunately, results are much slower in coming than these aspirations. It is this gap that breeds anger and sows the seeds of violence." To the extent that people like Pitcher were right, the riots in Chicago and elsewhere were a call for massive programs to deal with the problems endemic in the black community: poor education, fractured family structure, and pervasive poverty. President Johnson's "Great Society" was desperately needed—and quickly.

Also, the riots made it abundantly clear that attention to the race relations question could no longer be exclusively focused in the South but needed as much to address the problems of large Northern cities. It was here that the disparities were most pronounced. While in the South many legal barriers remained after the Civil War, the social fabric had not been torn apart in the same way it had been in the North. Alienation from society appeared to be much more pronounced for many blacks living in the North.

However, other commentators differed, and this viewpoint was not just confined to the white community. They argued that the riots in Los Angeles and Chicago were the work of hooligans. "One should not engage in too much sociological analysis when acts of vandalism are involved. These rioters should be viewed as nothing more than outlaws and should be dealt with as such"—so went the analysis. When college students riot and conduct panty raids, editorials do not ascribe this behavior to frustration and alienation. As an undergraduate, I attended a university that frequently witnessed student riots, often occurring after football games. In the worst instances, traffic was halted and bonfires built to prevent trolley cars from operating. Individuals who could be identified were expelled. The disturbances did not lead to any soul-searching by university officials or any speculation that something was fundamentally wrong with the educational experience or conditions at the university.

Fortunately, many political leaders across the country took a balanced view. While they sought to quell the disturbances and to deal with the instigators as troublemakers, at the same time, they established committees to study the fundamental problems that were clearly present in the black community. President Johnson took the initiative and sought in the best traditions of our democratic society to respond to the grievances of a distressed minority. Specifically, during the summer of 1965, Congress passed the Voting Rights Act, and the previous July the Civil Rights Act of 1964 had been signed into law. The War on Poverty was on the drawing boards.

8. Looking Back on the Tumultuous Events of 1965

There is nothing wrong with power if it is used wisely and rightly.

—Edward Brooke, former U.S. senator from Massachusetts

In September 1965, as Nancy and I prepared to leave with our three small children to spend a sabbatical year at the London School of Economics, we looked back with a feeling of "Wow! What an amazing year!" It was indeed a watershed year. What started rather calmly with the Good Friday march had escalated into a program of nightly marches to City Hall and then to Mayor Daley's home neighborhood, culminating in the arrest of Dick Gregory and his fellow protestors. After a spring and summer of marches, Benjamin Willis was still the superintendent of schools for Chicago. In fact, he had been reappointed, which to many in the civil rights movement meant "They have really stuck it to us!" With the reappointment of Willis, the movement was reinvigorated, but this too ran its course, and by September and the end of another "long hot summer," the CCCO was about to hibernate and with it the campaign to oust Willis.

At the national level, the marches in Selma, with their high drama and confrontation, had occurred in March. Also on the positive side of the ledger was the passage of the Voting Rights Act in August.

However, the summer of 1965 had brought with it major riots in the Watts section of Los Angeles as well as other cities across the United States, including Chicago. While Chicago had been quiet during the previous summer, the outbreak of disturbances on the West Side presented serious challenges for the leadership of the CCCO. I felt the need to find time to talk about all of this with Al Pitcher and Alex Poinsett, my friend who was an editor at *Ebony*.

In many ways, I was looking forward to getting away from Chicago. Our lives had been filled to almost overflowing with demonstrations, marches, and meetings. And the riots certainly exerted a push. Living in another country for nine months would put some healthy distance between these momentous events and us. To be honest, I certainly had mixed emotions about leaving the Chicago scene and all the action that had been taking place in race relations. Martin Luther King's visit during the summer had crystallized the plan for SCLC to move its headquarters to Chicago and to undertake a major campaign in the North. So during the upcoming academic year, I would not be on the scene while planning was in full swing for a new campaign to take place during the summer of 1966. Nancy took one small step in dealing with our feelings by purchasing a record by Pete Seeger, featuring the key song of the movement, "We Shall Overcome."

In many respects, however, the timing for a big change was right. I had been promoted to associate professor; a major research project with Richard Walton had culminated in our book, *A Behavioral Theory of Labor Negotiations;* and because only one of our three children was in school, they could be uprooted without too much disruption to their education.

Thanks to Al Pitcher, we had benefited from an insider's view of the civil rights movement. I asked him shortly before we left town, "So Al, here it is August 1965. And after two years of school boycotts, marches, and many arrests, Benjamin Willis is still superintendent—has it all been worth it?" He replied, "Yes, it has. We have mobilized thousands of folks in this city to do more than just sit on the sidelines and discuss issues of race relations. We may not have forced any change in the leadership of the Chicago schools, but we certainly have focused attention on overcrowding in the schools and the extensive segregation by race."

I wondered out loud if the civil rights movement had focused on the right priority, remembering a statistic of how few black kids had opted to transfer to other schools even though the quality of education was likely to be better. Al said he could understand why parents might want to keep their children in neighborhood schools. He believed it took time for the changes to occur that would make a big difference for education. Most important was the need for open occupancy—something Martin Luther King and his SCLC team certainly would address when they came to Chicago.

But still I pondered whether the focus on "Ben must go" hadn't stiffened the resistance of the board of education to making changes outlined in the Hauser and Havighurst reports. Al thought that Ben Willis had been a perfect target. While the Urban League and many civic organizations had been working on the improvement agenda, their efforts had only created minimal change. The civil rights movement needed to go for big changes and the way to do this was to start at the top. He was convinced that replacing Ben Willis would make a big difference.

Changing the subject, I said, "With the SCLC coming to town, what's going to happen to the CCCO and Al Raby? It would be too bad if the CCCO loses its role."

Al responded, "I doubt that will happen, Bob. Remember that King and his lieutenants chose Chicago for their first base in the North, precisely because they saw in CCCO a broad-based consortium of religious and community organizations and in Al Raby a dedicated and hardworking leader."

"Yes," I agreed. "Al has really matured. I couldn't believe what Mayor Daley said after one of the mass demonstrations: 'Who is this man, Raby? He doesn't represent the people of Chicago.'"

"Right on, Bob," Al said. "In my mind, there is no doubt that Al Raby is 'The Leader.' Did you know that he is *not* going back to his teaching job this fall? He has quit so he can devote himself full time to the civil rights movement."

Al Raby himself helped provide closure for the summer of 1965 with an address at a CCCO conference in late August. He reminded the participants that over the past summer 72 marches had taken place and 400 people had been arrested while occupying Chicago streets, all in an effort to convince Mayor Daley that Ben Willis had to go. Some progress had been made; several city leaders had endorsed the concept of quality, integrated education, and urged the school board to make changes. A resolution had been passed by the board to integrate Washburne Trade School, and a superintendent for integration had been appointed. However, within the ghetto community, the smoldering roots had ignited, and the violence of the summer represented a tragedy that could have been prevented. The facts had been ignored, and those who brought them to public attention had been attacked and slandered.

Raby emphasized that just talking about the problem would not do much. The mayor and the city would only be moved to the extent that mobilization and organization continued, and this meant doing the real work on the ground in the neighborhoods.

In conclusion, Raby said, "We must get to work. We must get to work now, not only to meet the challenge of Chicago but to meet the challenge of achieving victory in Chicago. It is the challenge of Harlem and Birmingham, Jackson and Detroit, Selma and Los Angeles. It is the challenge of America."

So, facing up to the break from Chicago, I assembled all my notes and papers relating to the movement, packed them in a trunk, and took them to Navy Pier for shipment to London on the Cunard Line. More to the point, I made a pact with myself that I would record the chronology and details of as much of the movement as I had witnessed during the preceding several years. I dictated furiously for several weeks after arriving in England and sent the tapes back for transcribing by my secretary at the University of Chicago.

I continued to wrestle with separation remorse and asked Alex Poinsett if we could stay in touch by mail. Since first meeting Alex in the early 1960s in the adult discussion group of our church, our friendship had steadily developed as one of great potential, if not fully realized. Both of us could be classified as liberals and enjoyed sharing our social concerns with each other. But I also revealed my feelings to Alex, in contrast to the way I interacted with leaders of the civil rights movement. With them, the conversation centered on specific tasks, like planning for negotiations with Motorola or drafting letters.

The back-and-forth with Alex even turned to occasional needling, although he confessed to feeling a bit uncomfortable about being kidded by a white person. I ribbed Alex on several occasions—with mixed results. One evening he was telling a group of friends about his adventures while traveling to Fort Wayne. He had missed the scheduled flight and found himself forced to charter an airplane in order to reach the Unitarian Church in time to deliver a sermon at the 11:00 service. With great glee, he told about the baffled expression of the two pilots when he chartered their plane and laid $140 on the line. At this point, I interjected: "They must have thought you were Martin Luther King." He took the comment in stride, but I could sense discomfort.

He freely admitted to practicing the art of gamesmanship with his black friends. In fact, he described a favorite pastime of blacks—playing a game called "the Dozens." It is a game in which each person seeks to out-disparage the opponent (today the word would be *diss*). For example: "Yo mama is so dumb she got hit by a parked car."

I wished our friendship were closer—perhaps even to the point of being able to do some kidding and have it be taken as an act of affection. Such was the approach I used with white friends—"You old SOB, you . . ." But such freedom was not possible with Alex. The relationship remained at the level of "We should get together more often."

One turning point in our association came with a visit by Alex and his family to our home on a Sunday afternoon. Along with his wife and two children, he stopped by to have a cup of coffee after church. Our son, Billy, played with Alex's two children, Pierre and Perrette, as naturally as he did with kids from our immediate neighborhood. After Alex and his family left, Billy remarked: "Negroes are smart, aren't they?" Asked what he meant by that, he said that the little Poinsett girl could tie her own shoes (for several months Billy had been urged to learn how to tie his own shoes but had not mastered the technique). Then he went on to make some strange remarks about "Negroes having warmer blood and having different colors." Clearly, the race question had entered his thinking in a new way and he was beginning to sort out his impressions.

As I talked about this event with Nancy, she related a moment of great potential embarrassment during the visit. At one point, Billy had gone up to Alex as if to kiss him, although not drawing any closer than several inches. I had noticed the overture and indeed had been puzzled by it. "He was smelling Alex," Nancy said, "and I was about to go through the floor." Then the picture became clear. Several weeks earlier in a swim class, Billy's instructor had been an African American. On coming home, he had remarked to Nancy, "Why do Negroes smell different?" Nancy had hastened to assure him that there was no difference. But a little boy is not easily persuaded by arguments; he has to experience the truth himself. And this was the basis for his exploratory sniff of Alex. Billy never talked about this aspect of his racial feelings; no doubt his parents' strong convictions made open discussion of such a subject difficult.

While African Americans were very much in evidence in our neighborhood, mainly as passersby, as letter carriers, and as cleaning ladies, relatively few came into the area as guests. Nancy and I hoped that our children would gain a balanced view of African Americans, reflecting our family values. But this did not happen, at least initially. Several teenage boys on our block exerted a questionable influence on our oldest. One day, Billy (then age six) came home and asked, "Why do we have to lock up our bikes?" When I asked why he was thinking about this, he answered, "Jimmy and the fellas down the street said that Negroes are no good and that they steal everything." Try as I might, I was unable to modify this idea that had been placed in the head of an impressionable boy. Indeed, Billy frequently voiced antiblack feelings, not on the basis of experience but merely on the basis of emotions that had been conveyed to him by the older boys on the block. So this episode with Alex and his family was helping provide some new data for Billy—new feelings and attitudes were taking shape in him. For this we were thankful.

As I got to know Alex better, I made a point of buying copies of *Ebony*. As a staff writer for Johnson Publications (the publisher of *Ebony*), Alex was asked to write stories about "the Negro problem." In fact, *Ebony* made a business of publicizing black successes and failures. He tackled these assignments with great relish. Early in our friendship, Alex offered to take me on a tour of their publishing facilities. He extended the courtesy after learning about my research project comparing the labor and civil rights movements. In his characteristically helpful way, he had offered files of newspaper clippings at the magazine so I could gain a quick overview of direct-action programs in other cities.

As we walked through the various offices, I wondered about several things. Was *Ebony* really interested in the civil rights movement? Wasn't its coverage of the civil rights movement just good business? If the civil rights movement really succeeded, wouldn't the magazine be out of business?

These questions were on my mind when a few weeks later I attended at a large meeting sponsored by the Illinois Chamber of Commerce. In an effort to close the gap between the fast-moving civil rights movement and a business community that seemed to be dragging its heels, the Chamber of Commerce had organized an all-day conference on the subject of race relations. On the program was the president of Johnson Publications, the company that published *Ebony*. But his speech served only one purpose: the business interests of *Ebony*. In optimistic terms, he described the growing Negro market; he documented how ineffective white businessmen were in reaching this market. The only thing he did not do was to fill in the blanks, namely, that *Ebony* was the vehicle for tapping this great potential. *"What a shame,"* I thought, as I left the meeting. Here was a gathering of businessmen interested in understanding the civil rights movement, and the president of *Ebony* delivers a self-serving message.

Clearly, Alex felt deeply about the "Negro problem," but I wondered whether he would put his body on the line. Alex could write, no denying that. But would he march? Early in June 1965, the whole person of Alex Poinsett was revealed. By coincidence, the CCCO had scheduled a major demonstration in the Loop for the same time and place as the official celebration and parade for two astronauts was due to take place. The CCCO was under tremendous pressure to cancel this march for fear the civil rights movement in Chicago would be discredited. As a result, the leadership of the civil rights movement faced a serious dilemma.

The decision whether or not to march was not made until the last minute. As usual, a group of potential marchers had gathered at Buckingham Fountain: the militants, moderates, and curious. The discussion about whether to confront the city (meaning, in effect, the police) ranged over a number of arguments: the country will be watching Chicago; what better time to dramatize the civil rights struggle? Or, a disturbance on this day of celebration would provoke the wrath and hostility of the crowd! Ultimately, the decision was made not to march. Another demonstration seeking the removal of Ben Willis was not as important as avoiding bad press.

To the side of the spectators watching the parade stood Alex Poinsett. He carried a sign that read: "WHAT HAPPENED TO THE NEGRO ASTRONAUT?" His statement made a very relevant point. As of 1965, only one black astronaut was in training but no blacks were on deck for a flight.

So it was against this background that an opportunity presented itself in late summer of 1965 to go at it with Alex. He stopped by the house one evening about 6:00 to return some materials I had loaned him for a talk on poverty. After some coaxing, he agreed to stay long enough to chat about developments in the civil rights movement, even consenting to a small drink despite a restricted diet owing to a heart condition.

As we entered the living room, the first thing he spied was the August issue of *Ebony* with the cover story entitled "The White Problem in America." He autographed the article he had written, an elaboration of the sermon he had delivered at the First Unitarian Church: "Who Speaks for the Poor?" I offered a toast to *"Ebony* and the White Man" to which Alex laughed and then raised his glass.

I began to share my concerns about the marches to Bridgeport. I opined that, to my way of thinking, the marches lacked a tactical focus. The objective of the CCCO was the removal of the superintendent of the schools. So how did the marches into Bridgeport connect to this objective? Nothing was being said about discrimination in housing, which was actively practiced by the residents of that community. He responded: "Bob, I think you are making an artificial distinction. To me, housing, jobs, education, and all forms of discrimination are tied up in one ball of wax. You cannot separate them."

I was troubled about the excursions into Daley's ward because they were a form of "dirty pool." Yes, they were legal, but they were hitting below the belt. I thought the mayor had a point when he said that they were invading his privacy. Mayor Daley was not mayor of Bridgeport, he was mayor of the city; he only happened to live in Bridgeport. Alex countered: "For myself, I would like to march right through Daley's house. Did you read that article by Mike Royko with that delightful parody about Al Raby and Dick Gregory living in Daley's house? I feel just that way and would like to march all over him." He thought the kind of reaction we had seen from the whites who lived in that neighborhood illustrated the problem blacks faced in the city. "We have to keep the spotlight on Daley and on the kind of discrimination he tolerates. In fact, the kind of discrimination that is rampant in his neighborhood."

I wasn't giving up. "Just the same, these marches do not have the same noble quality as those conducted by King in the South," I said. "They strike me as being too vindictive and too provocative. The country accepts Martin

Luther King because he embodies the ethic of love and nonviolence; the marches over at the Bridgeport have been done to 'get even' with Daley."

Quite seriously, he said, "Listen, Bob, don't think we're going to get any change until some people get their heads bashed in. I almost got killed covering three race-conflict stories in the South. We've been trying the strategy of gradualism for a hundred years and not very much has happened. You can't tell me to be righteous in my choice of tactics when the rest of society holds a club over my head."

I argued that permanent change could never take place until the majority became an ally of the civil rights movement. "Take President Johnson—he is not responding to the civil rights movement just because the civil rights movement is making his life uncomfortable. For him, it has become a moral issue, and he is reflecting the feelings of many people in this country."

As Alex was leaving, he said, "Don't get me wrong about some of the things I said. We all have problems. Last weekend when I was on my way over to the King rally, I passed all my neighbors, out watering their lawns. You'd think they would walk a couple of blocks to hear Martin Luther King. There must have been 6,000 people at that rally but very few of them were from my neighborhood. One of my close friends was at a tea. This block group had scheduled a meeting—they went right ahead with the tea and none of them went to hear Martin Luther King."

After reaching England, I shared an early draft of my notes for this chapter with Alex. He responded with a letter:

What does a professor know about being poverty-stricken before they even invented the word? It's not kosher, not neat to invade Mayor Daley's privacy. Does he know our privacy has been trampled on for more than 300 years? Did he ever see a little black girl crying because she's hungry or a woman dying because a white hospital won't accept her? What does he know about coming from a broken family and being shuttled from foster home to foster home and having a sister with illegitimate children and a father who is a drunkard and a wife beater and being ashamed to pick up welfare rations at a neighborhood collection station and eating beans three times a day and rats, roaches, and razors and winter-sleeping in houses that were never warm enough, and wearing shoe soles that swell up and flap like a bell clapper when they get wet? What does he know, what can he ever know about being colored?

"Your tactics might alienate larger sections of the white community," he says. "You will need the aid of whites before the problem can be solved."

Yeah, but at what cost, at what terrible cost? Can white people give freedom, and if so, can they dole it out based on the smiles or frowns of Negroes? Can they tell Negroes how to frame their posture of protest, how to scream, and how to cry or, indeed, whether they should cry at all? Here it is, we're fighting a barroom brawler who knees in the clinches and gouges between rounds, but Bob stands on the edge of the ring, holding us to Roberts Rules of Order. If it alienates whites to have Negroes given rights that whites have always enjoyed, then we say: "Tough! They'll just have to be alienated." Maybe I expect more of Bob than I would myself. What apple carts does he not want to upset? His family . . . his friends . . . his University of Chicago professorship? He did not get these overnight. Can you really expect him to jeopardize his lifetime of hard work and achievement?

How far are you really willing to go for the sake of racial justice, indeed, for the sake of your own manhood? How dear are family, friends, and career to you? Are you willing to go over the brink and would others follow?

The correspondence continued, and in the final chapter, I will draw on Alex's brilliant and highly charged analysis of the conditions facing African Americans.

9. The Campaign for Open Housing, Summer 1966

Chicago is America's most segregated city.

—*Chicagoist*, October 31, 2010

When Nancy and I returned to Chicago in June 1966, Martin Luther King and his team were very much on the scene. King had taken up residence in an apartment on the West Side, and plans were well underway for the open housing campaign that was soon to regalvanize Chicago's civil rights movement and mark an important turning point in the history of race relations in Chicago. By 1966 King's stature was without parallel in the United States. Readers today may not be familiar with the series of pivotal events and experiences that took King from his leadership of a church congregation in Birmingham, Alabama, to a position of national prominence. Anyone following events in the South during the late 1950s and early 1960s would have been aware of Martin Luther King and his position as leader of the Southern Christian Leadership Conference (SCLC). The news media were filled with reports of sit-ins aimed at desegregating lunch counters, of boycotts such as the one in Birmingham to desegregate seating on busses, and of the violence carried out against protest leaders. The timeline provided in appendix C highlights many of these pivotal events.

During the early 1960s, I developed a growing appreciation of the singularly important role that King was playing in the civil rights movement. In a conversation I had with Harvey Cox, he remarked, "Dr. King is someone to watch." Harvey, a close friend from college days, had, upon completion of his studies at Yale Divinity School, accepted the position as chaplain of Oberlin College. He invited King to speak to a campus gathering and found himself stunned by the eloquence and power of this person.

My own first opportunity to hear King speak occurred during the fall of 1961 when he preached at a Sunday worship service held at Rockefeller Chapel at the University of Chicago. I remember the date even now, since my in-laws were in town to celebrate the birth of our second child in November 1961, and Bessie and Pete Crosier (my in-laws) joined me at the service. The sanctuary was packed, and King did not disappoint the audience.

Then came the March on Washington in August 1963, and King's "I have a dream" speech, which still gives me a rush whenever I hear it broadcast, usually in conjunction with the celebration of Martin Luther King Day each year on or around January 15. During the years 1963 to 1966, King visited Chicago regularly to lead rallies, usually during the summer and usually at Soldier Field. Increasingly, his presence was sought from all quarters of the United States, and Chicago's civil rights leaders had to compete with many other activist groups around the country for a day or two of his time.

The fact that King selected Chicago as the first northern city for a campaign came about because SCLC leaders were impressed with the CCCO organization and its execution of school boycotts, marches, and rallies. Another indication that SCLC viewed Chicago as a good "test bed" for expanding outside of the South occurred in early 1966 when the SCLC granted Jesse Jackson the first northern "franchise" to launch Operation Breadbasket in Chicago.

So it came as no surprise when Al Pitcher announced one morning at breakfast during the summer of 1965 that King was coming to Chicago for a short visit to test the feasibility of launching a major campaign to confront housing segregation. Al found himself in charge of organizing the schedule for King's visit, including what was to be a large rally in the Loop. To illustrate King's larger-than-life role, Al discussed with Nancy and me some of the problems associated with planning a breakfast for King with local labor leaders.

Shortly after the newspapers announced that King planned to spend several days in Chicago, the CCCO office received a call from Robert Johnston, district director of the UAW, offering his services. He asked if he could recruit a group of labor leaders from Chicago who would meet with King to discuss matters of mutual interest. The idea sounded good and Pitcher was given the job of working out the details. Al related what happened next: sharp disagreement soon developed over who should be invited to the breakfast. The United Auto Workers (UAW) director could claim no "good works" on his part regarding the civil rights movement in Chicago. In fact, for the most part, the labor movement had remained aloof from any of the demonstrations, except for several black locals and a few "fringe" unions, such as the

United Electrical Workers (UE) and the Packinghouse Workers, which had participated in the Good Friday demonstration.

As a subordinate to Walter Reuther, president of the UAW, Johnston was obliged to show hospitality to Martin Luther King. Reuther had vigorously supported the SCLC, had marched in Selma, and often appeared with King on platforms throughout the country. At the same time, Johnson—along with most of the labor movement in Chicago—supported the Daley machine. Mayor Daley could not be elected mayor of the City of Chicago without strong support from the union movement, including the industrial and the craft unions. Leaders of the industrial unions, such as Johnston, found themselves facing an especially tough dilemma: on the one hand, they were anxious to support the movement; on the other hand, they were closely aligned with the Democratic political establishment that the movement was confronting. For this reason Johnson had remained in the background during the confrontations between the civil rights movement and the mayor.

This same lack of involvement described other key labor leaders in Chicago. Also, the names Johnson had submitted to Pitcher as potential invitees were those from the "establishment." How unfair, Pitcher thought, to invite the labor "brass" so that they could bask in King's presence.

Which labor leaders were most deserving? Tim Black had submitted his own list—all active members of the NALC. They had worked hard in behalf of the civil rights movement, and while they were all members of labor unions, they were not "important" people. Many of them were members of unions, like the UE, not affiliated with the AFL-CIO, or with unions like the Packinghouse Workers who were known to be radical in orientation.

As the issue was debated, it became clear that the dilemma would not be easily resolved. The Chicago Labor Council, an affiliate of the national AFL-CIO, would object if too many people were invited from the "maverick" unions. On the other hand, individuals like Tim Black and his colleagues from the NALC, who had been working actively to bring about a fusion of the civil rights and labor movements, would be offended if only the "big wigs" were invited. Like Solomon, Al decided to invite an equal number from both lists.

Why was the relationship between the established labor movement and the arm of the civil rights movement represented by Tim Black (NALC) so tense and complex? There were many reasons for common cause. To mention the most salient: both arose out of deeply felt grievances and the need to mobilize power in order to redress these grievances. At the same time, there were realities that pulled the two movements apart. Recall the earlier discussion about Washburne and limited entry for blacks into apprentice programs, and the considerable distance that had always existed between the civil rights movement and the craft unions.

While in town, King spoke at a large rally in Soldier Field, followed by a march with several thousand followers to City Hall. Since the march occurred during a weekend and with full cooperation from the police, little disruption in the Loop occurred and no arrests were made. Most observers judged the long weekend visit of King a success, thereby setting the stage for the SCLC to turn to Chicago for its first major effort in the North.

The SCLC advance team arrived in Chicago during the fall of 1965 and started planning for what would become the Open Housing campaign to be launched the following summer. This shift in emphasis away from schools was noteworthy. Significantly, an announcement in late May 1966 by Superintendent Benjamin Willis, that he would retire early, for the most part went unnoticed; SCLC was in town with a new agenda.

The targeting of housing as the focus for the summer campaign of 1966 reflected the reality that housing segregation was seen as the root cause of so many other pathologies facing the African American community. The fact that housing segregation was much more pronounced in the North than in the South[1] must have influenced the decision of the SCLC leadership. The crowding of African Americans on the West Side and the South Side of the city led to segregation in the schools and many other social problems. Research showed that poor white neighborhoods received more public services than comparable black neighborhoods. Because Chicago had the dubious distinction of being the most segregated city in the nation in terms of housing,[2] the selection of open housing as the theme and Chicago as the scene made eminent sense from a strategic point of view.

During the summer of 1966, I was back in the classroom with a full teaching schedule, so most of my hours each week were committed. To the extent time was available, I volunteered to work with Operation Breadbasket, an organization that was rapidly becoming a centerpiece of the civil rights scene in Chicago (chronicled in the next chapter).

The time demands required to represent the liberal churches of Chicago at meetings of the CCCO had vanished since Al Raby and his small leadership team had merged with the larger staff of the SCLC under the banner of the Chicago Freedom Movement. While the arrival of the SCLC promised more dollars and leadership talent (and these resources did indeed arrive), the grass-roots, town-meeting quality of the CCCO was replaced by a small leadership group from the combined SCLC/CCCO that took over the planning and execution of all direct-action activities. As a result, regular meetings of the CCCO ceased. One clue to the shift in decision making could be found in the whereabouts of Al Pitcher. He had shifted his attention and talents away from the CCCO to working with Jesse Jackson and Operation Breadbasket.

The centralization of planning and execution just described for the Chicago Freedom Movement also occurred within other civil rights organizations. Mary King observed that as SNCC matured it needed a strong central organization. Not exactly the "iron law of bureaucracy" but the "iron law" of control and coordination.[3] So I remained a follower with respect to the new priority of "open occupancy" in housing, and I was not involved in any decision making. Nevertheless, two engagements occurred during the summer of 1966 that proved memorable and in one case quite traumatic. As part of the campaign to break down the barriers that blacks faced in finding housing in the city, the leaders of the SCLC and the CCCO staged a rally at Soldier Field on Sunday, July 10. About 30,000 people—by other estimates as many as 60,000—attended.[4]

For the first time, I asked our oldest son, Billy, who was almost seven, if he would like to join me at the civil rights event, and he readily agreed. The spectacle at Soldier Field, a large stadium capable of holding 70,000 to 80,000 people, the festivities, especially the music, clearly awed Billy. And the most impressive part of the afternoon was a concluding march from the field to City Hall, with King leading the parade.

Unlike what was soon to develop in the weeks ahead, no hostile crowds greeted us as we marched up Michigan Avenue past stores closed for the

Al Raby shaking hands with people in the crowd at 1966 rally at Soldier Field. Courtesy Chicago Urban League records, University of Illinois at Chicago Library, Special Collections

Sabbath and along the streets of the business district. At the conclusion of the march, King posted on the doors of City Hall the demands of the civil rights movement for open housing for all ethnic groups. The symbolism harking to the posting of a credo by Martin Luther centuries earlier was not lost on any of us.

In the weeks after the Soldier Field rally, King led several marches into various white neighborhoods. These marches were different in purpose from the daily marches of the previous summer, which Dick Gregory had organized and led to the mayor's residence to protest the continued presence of Willis as head of the Chicago school system. These demonstrations involved many more participants, numbering almost 500 in one case to be described shortly, and the bystanders grew increasingly hostile and violent as the marches moved into more and more sensitive areas of the city.

Earlier in the summer, the marches had ended at City Hall—similar to the route followed after the rally at Soldier Field that Billy and I attended. But fairly soon the leadership concluded that the open housing campaign, with daily marches in the Loop and in black neighborhoods, was not generating sufficient traction to force the city's political leaders to pay attention.

The *modus operandi* of the SCLC had always been to mobilize large numbers of people to march with the expectation that the white community would hit back, thereby escalating matters to the point where the authorities would have to intervene in an effort to reach some accommodation, usually a compromise between maintaining the status quo and the demands of the civil rights movement.

As the SCLC and CCCO leadership reviewed the status of the open housing campaign in late July, they recognized that some progress had been made. King had moved into a "slum" neighborhood on the West Side. Marches and demonstrations had taken place on a regular basis following the rally at Soldiers Field, but they were no closer to opening the housing market to African Americans beyond existing areas. It was against this background that King and his lieutenants decided to launch a series of marches into white neighborhoods on July 30 and 31, to be followed by another on August 5, which King himself would lead.

I agreed to join the march on Sunday, July 31, which was led by Al Raby, to an area called Chicago Lawn. I drove our brown Chevy, which I had bought as a used car from the local Hyde Park dealership, and parked it in Marquette Park near the target area of Chicago Lawn. The park served as a buffer between adjoining all-black residential areas and Chicago Lawn, which at the time was all white. We assembled in New Friendship Baptist Church in Englewood. My position in the line of march, which started after an initial prayer service, was toward the rear. As we approached the end of the park and neared the white community, I could hear loud jeers and commotion toward the front of the line. Matters turned ugly and to put it mildly, I was scared. Fairly soon, I saw bottles and rocks being thrown at the leaders and before I knew it, these missiles were coming at us.

We marched two to four abreast and young black teenagers flanked us, probably members of gangs who had been recruited from the black neighborhoods by the leaders of the march to offer us "protection." And indeed, they did, for in some instances they reached up with baseball gloves and with basketball skill caught flying objects before they hit any of us.

While some of the young blacks grew visibly angry, I did not see any of them "return the fire." In fact, the doctrine of Martin Luther King and the civil rights movement, which had been drilled into all of us, embraced the spirit of Gandhi—to turn the other cheek, remain nonviolent, and just keep walking. The crowd of onlookers and hecklers, which must have numbered in the thousands (or so it seemed), appeared especially incensed to see nuns and priests in the line of march. The residents of Chicago Lawn, with its strong Polish/Slavic population, clearly viewed the Catholic Church, or at least some of its clergy, as having betrayed their community.

About an hour into the march, the line stopped and then started to move in a different direction. Police officers had intervened and were heading us back to a nearby black community. The missiles continued to fly as we slowly retreated. We certainly wondered whether we would make it back to the safety of the ghetto. I thought, "How strange to be visualizing the black community as a haven."

Eventually we made it back, and I can remember as we reached Ashland and crossed into the ghetto where black children were playing in the streets, how comforting was the calm that descended over all of us. For a moment I felt like crying, happy and relieved to be safe but saddened by the near riot and a display of such intense hostility by elements of the white community.

The Chicago Lawn march affected me deeply. My earlier involvements—teaching in a freedom school during the boycott, marching to the Loop, attending rallies—had engaged my mind and feet. But now I realized that placing my body on the line and exposing myself to taunts, bricks, and arrest was shaping my commitment in a very different and deeply fundamental way.

We were told that we could *not* return to Marquette Park to retrieve our autos. It was not safe—the angry crowd had damaged many of the cars and special transportation was provided to return us to our communities. So the next day I traveled to a tow lot on the far southwest side of Chicago to see if I could find my car. I was not optimistic because the newspapers reported that many cars had been set on fire and vandalized. Well, much to my surprise, my car had not been touched—and therein rests another irony.

My car carried no bumper stickers proclaiming support for the civil rights movement, as was the case for many of the cars owned by the marchers. No doubt those intent on destroying the vehicles of the marchers must have assumed that the owner of this "junky" machine was not one of those liberal whites but someone like themselves, a working-class guy.

Racial confrontation on Chicago's West Side during the drive for open occupancy in housing, August 7, 1966. Library of Congress, Prints and Photographs Division, LC-USZ62–135693.

At the time of the Chicago Lawn march, I found it hard to understand the hostility of the residents into whose neighborhood we had marched. As with violence in the South, this turn of events provided a helpful wedge for the civil rights movement in its campaign to engage the power structure of the city. As I have reflected over the years about this episode that proved very traumatic for me, I have become more appreciative of the economic impact of housing desegregation on white residents and why it was, and continues to be, so difficult to create stable interracial communities.

During the decades following World War II, the perimeter of the black ghetto had been steadily expanding on Chicago's South Side and West Side. Residents of white neighborhoods that stood adjacent to black areas faced the possibility that, like a forest fire, the spread of black residences would jump Marquette Park and soon be in their neighborhood. The sad history of housing in Chicago and many northern cities has followed a familiar pattern. As soon as one black family moves into a new area, it is only a matter of time before the whole community "turns" all black. One exception has been Hyde Park, where I lived. There, special factors have helped stabilize the interracial character of the community, especially the presence of the University of Chicago, and the practice of a form of discrimination, not racial but financial—the number of blacks who can afford to live in the relatively expensive housing has been limited.

At the time the bottles and epithets were flying, I could not understand the extent of the hate and violence toward us. Was it racism and dislike for another race, in this case blacks? Or was something else possibly involved? With hindsight I can see that our push into their community and the campaign that was taking place across the city to open up housing for blacks in communities like Chicago Lawn raised the specter of big losses in housing values for these residents. But thoughts about the deep fears that must have been driving the whites into such a rage were not on my mind as the violence flared that Sunday afternoon during the summer of 1966.

The crisis created by Chicago Lawn and similar marches into white neighborhoods prompted calls from many quarters for negotiations. Newspapers were filled with pictures of white residents throwing objects and shouting epithets at marchers.

While Mayor Daley did not want to be seen to be giving in to pressure, certainly the neighborhood marches, as well as a riot that had taken place on the West Side earlier in July, had set the stage for face-to-face talks. Once the summit meetings started in August between the SCLC/CCCO, representatives of the city, and real estate agencies, the civil rights leadership agreed to suspend marches into white neighborhoods, but vowed to continue marches in the Loop, observing a limit of 500 participants.

The summit negotiations have been well told by many participants.[5] In one account, Garrow recounts a memorable moment from the negotiations, demonstrating King's inspirational power:

> Let me say that if you are tired of demonstrations, I am tired of demonstrating. I am tired of the threats of death. I want to live. I don't want to be a martyr, and there are moments when I doubt if am going to make it through. . . . I hope that we are here to discuss how to make Chicago a great open city and not how to end marches. We've got to have massive changes. We don't have much money, we don't really have much education, and we don't have political power. We have only our bodies. We want to be visible. We are not trying to overthrow you. We're trying to get in. We're trying to make justice a reality.[6]

So at a critical point in the summit negotiations, King had effectively changed the mood from one of distrust and adversarial dealing to one embracing a larger vision.

After several weeks of talks, a settlement was reached on August 26, which committed the city, its agencies, and the real estate board to promote housing integration, and most observers (with a few significant exceptions) hailed the agreement as a breakthrough. Some expressed reservations, however. King later told his followers, "We should have gone back to the members and voted on whether to accept the accord."[7] Later, when I interviewed Al Pitcher's widow, Sara Pitcher, she said, "Al thought the housing agreement was a sham."[8]

The agreement emerging from the summit negotiations committed various agencies to lend their best efforts to achieving open housing. The civil rights movement did not possess the resources to monitor conformance to open housing. So the task of finding and introducing blacks into white neighborhoods was left to signatory organizations such as the Urban League, the UAW, and other nonprofits. As a result, Chicago continued to rank as one of the most segregated cities in the United States.

If the SCLC had not come to Chicago, would the high-level negotiations have occurred? The answer is not clear, but certainly King's national stature must have been a factor. Daley could say of Raby: "Who is this man, does he speak for the black community?" However, he could not challenge the authority or leadership of King in the same way.

And what about Al Raby and the CCCO? During the summer of 1966, he remained at the center of deliberations, and he marched side by side with King. However, during the winter of 1967, when the SCLC phased out of its Chicago commitment, it was only a matter of time before Al Raby announced that he too was phasing out. Barbara Reynolds noted, "After the summit on the housing agreement in the summer of 1966 and into 1967, King continued turning his attention more toward other national concerns and long-time activist Al Raby resigned, supposedly to write a paper on black power."[9] James Ralph noted that Raby stepped down citing "battle fatigue."[10]

Although Bill Berry of the Urban League and John McDermott from the Catholic Interracial Council announced that they would assume the leadership reins of the CCCO, no more meetings of that organization took place, and for all practical purposes, it ceased to function. The CCCO had been on the scene for almost five years, and except for a period at the outset when Arthur Brazier of TWO had presided, Al Raby had served as its convener and hardworking chair.

The summer of 1966 represented a pivotal period in the civil rights struggle in Chicago. As King expressed the strategy, "We have only our bodies," and when the leadership took the marchers (and their bodies) into white neighborhoods with the expected reaction of violence, Mayor Daley was forced to convene negotiations with the SCLC/CCCO leadership. While the long-run value of the agreement reached over housing was unclear, nevertheless the

Bill Berry and Martin Luther King Jr. Courtesy Chicago Urban League records, CULR_04_0120_1392_002, University of Illinois at Chicago Library, Special Collections.

summit negotiations achieved for housing what had eluded the civil rights movement in their campaign to oust Willis; namely, face-to-face meetings resulting in some type of agreement. Certainly face-to-face negotiations and an agreement in 1966 were better outcomes than the "nothing" that emerged from the protests between 1963 and 1965 over schools. King and the SCLC were able to leave Chicago with some sense of success as they moved on to other campaigns.

At the national level, President Lyndon Johnson urged Congress to pass an Open Housing bill. However, on September 19 the Senate was unable to stop a filibuster and the bill was shelved. It was not until 1968, one week after King was assassinated, that Congress passed and President Johnson signed into law an open housing statute.

Mayor Daley fared well. In April 1967, he was reelected with the largest plurality ever—half a million votes.

10. Jesse Jackson, Operation Breadbasket, and Minority Enterprise

*Small businesses are the backbone of our economy
and the cornerstones of our communities.*

—President Barack Obama, May 12, 2010

After returning from England, I called Al Pitcher to get his update on what had transpired during the preceding academic year. With great enthusiasm, Al described a new effort of the civil rights movement in Chicago called "Operation Breadbasket." The SCLC had formally established the program in September 1962, after a successful pilot test by Leon Sullivan in Philadelphia. Expanding the program to Chicago in February 1966 provided another major test of the concept: mobilizing the patronage power of the black community to leverage more business for struggling black entrepreneurs.

Al described a young divinity student in the Chicago Theological Seminary (CTS) by the name of Jesse Jackson who was holding weekly breakfast meetings in the cafeteria of the CTS with a group of black ministers and ten to fifteen black businessmen. He mentioned some of the retail products that were manufactured and distributed by these concerns: wax, drain cleaner, barbecue sauce, and milk. Jackson and his team of ministers were negotiating with the major retail food chains, and Al predicted that settlements would soon be in place.

Several years prior to enrolling in CTS, Jackson had demonstrated his leadership skills in organizing a 1963 march in Greensboro, North Carolina, where he was a student at North Carolina A&T. Ignoring an order by the school's president that students stay on campus, Jackson, a twenty-one-year-old junior, led the march in support of the boycott of downtown businesses that had been organized by the local ministerial alliance. Illustrating his rhetorical skills, Jackson came up with a memorable phrase: "When a police dog bites us in Birmingham, people of color bleed all over America."

Before describing Operation Breadbasket (OB) and how I connected with this organization, I need to put this initiative into the historical context of what came to be called "Black Capitalism." The strategy of encouraging black people to patronize businesses operated by blacks can be traced back to earlier movements (e.g., Marcus Garvey and W. E. B. Du Bois) that sought to galvanize the black community to engage in self-help efforts and not to rely on "handouts from the white community." St. Clair Drake and Horace Cayton provide an excellent account of the business economy within the African American community in Chicago.[1] While the data for their study are taken from the time period just preceding and during World War II, the same patterns predominated when Jesse Jackson assumed the leadership of the Chicago chapter of OB several decades later.

Most businesses owned and operated by blacks relied on what some called the "double-duty dollar"—blacks directing their purchases of goods and services to minority businesses in order to keep the purchasing power within the community. The lines of business that were helped in this way included undertakers, barber/beauty shops, and insurance agencies. Very few black-owned enterprises served the larger white community due to the lack of capital, lack of training, and know-how.

While Jesse Jackson and the originators of OB did not ignore the tradition of "double-duty dollars," their strategy aimed at enhancing the economic development of the black community by expanding opportunities for black businesses to sell products and services in major retail food chains. Rual Bolles, who had been manufacturing and selling wax products under the label of Diamond Star, was a case in point. His struggling business had only sold products in the ghetto. Jackson reasoned that with some "urging," large retail chains in Chicago could be persuaded to provide shelf space for Diamond Star products, and as a result sales would increase dramatically. In the spirit of reciprocity, Bolles would be expected to make a financial contribution out of his increased profits to help defray the overhead expenses of OB. The same sequence of mutual gains would be possible for other companies producing products such as sausage, drain cleaner, and milk.

By the end of 1966 and early into the next year, OB successfully signed agreements with Hawthorne-Melody Farms, High-Low, A&P, Jewel Tea, and National Tea, to expand employment of minorities and, most important, to

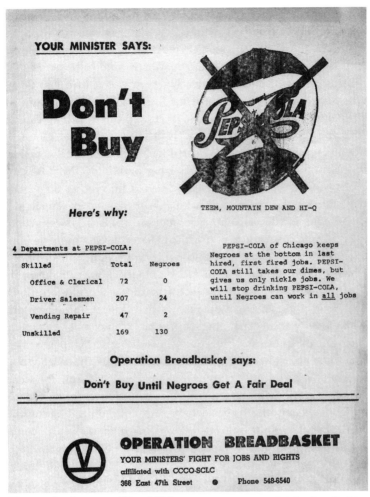

YOUR MINISTER SAYS:

Don't Buy

Here's why:

TEEM, MOUNTAIN DEW AND HI-Q

4 Departments at PEPSI-COLA:

Skilled	Total	Negroes
Office & Clerical	72	0
Driver Salesmen	207	24
Vending Repair	47	2
Unskilled	169	130

PEPSI-COLA of Chicago keeps Negroes at the bottom in last hired, first fired jobs. PEPSI-COLA still takes our dimes, but gives us only nickle jobs. We will stop drinking PEPSI-COLA, until Negroes can work in <u>all</u> jobs

Operation Breadbasket says:

Don't Buy Until Negroes Get A Fair Deal

OPERATION BREADBASKET
YOUR MINISTERS' FIGHT FOR JOBS AND RIGHTS
affiliated with CCCO-SCLC
366 East 47th Street • Phone 548-6540

Flyer urging boycott of Pepsi Cola. Courtesy Operation PUSH, Rainbow Coalition archives.

gain access and shelf space for products produced by its member companies. Jackson had developed an effective strategy that used power (the threat of a patronage strike) with incentives (expanding opportunities would be "good for your business") and moral suasion ("it's the right thing to do"). These elements represented a powerful methodology and a well-integrated system. The "troops" were customers of the retail chains that were on the target list of OB. These buyers could be mobilized to boycott a target store through Jesse's exhortations at his Saturday morning rallies as well as by the distribution of handbills and other information in the community. In the background, the scavenger companies, the banks, the manufacturers of food, cleaning, and other products, stood ready to exploit these new business opportunities resulting from the covenants signed between OB and the retail chains.

Years later, I interviewed Rev. Calvin Morris, who had served as an executive director of OB and subsequently served as executive director of the Chicago Renewal Society. Summarizing the impact of the program, he said that it enjoyed considerable success in its attempts to recruit ministers and black business people who had relatively little experience interacting with each other except as preachers and parishioners. He recalled that both sides were pleasantly surprised to see how well they worked together; for example, churches pooling their funds to benefit black banks rather than utilizing white banks. For their part, the black banks responded by supporting the ministers' efforts to develop outreach programs to black businessmen.[2]

By creating a consortium of black suppliers, Jackson improved on the "virtuous cycle" that had been pioneered by Sullivan in Philadelphia. Sullivan had organized a group of 400 black ministers who, from their pulpits, urged their members to engage in selective patronage, initially targeting baking companies and then ice cream makers, newspapers, and supermarkets. Sullivan's focus was on expanding jobs for blacks in companies producing products bought by blacks. When Sullivan launched the Opportunities Industrial Center to train and refer black workers to jobs in the labor market more generally, his selective patronage campaigns faded from the scene.[3]

Not all the retail chains targeted by Jackson and OB readily agreed to sign the covenants; some offered considerable resistance. When first confronted by OB, the initial response from High-Low Foods was negative. The company ran a notice in the local newspaper:

Remember! There Are Two Sides to a Story!!

Do not be misled by the incorrect information issued by "Operation Breadbasket."

You should be aware that High Low Foods, Inc. does hire Negroes fairly and has in fact hired many Negroes as new employees and is constantly advancing those who qualify to better jobs.

There is in fact a great shortage of Negro butchers and every effort is being made to fill the need. As many apprentices as can be trained are being hired by High Low and every effort is being made to acquire competent applicants to meet Union qualifications.

We suggest that you ask our Negro employees how they feel about the treatment they receive from High Low. If you will do this, we are sure you will continue to shop at High Low.

Eventually, High-Low agreed to negotiate and signed an agreement in November 1966.

Long after Jewel Tea had joined forces with OB and Jesse Jackson, I talked with Donald Perkins, who was CEO at that time.[4] When he became president and CEO of Jewel in January 1965, he received many letters from minority suppliers making sure he was aware of them. In the midst of one pile was a telegram from Jesse Jackson. While Perkins could not remember the specifics of the message, he knew the intent of the words, "You're next!" Being targeted was no surprise to Perkins, since he had heard much about OB and the covenants that had been signed with soft drink, milk, and ice cream companies. He knew it was just a matter of time before the supermarkets, including Jewel Tea, would be approached.

Perkins agreed to meet with Jackson, who came with more than 30 people, while Perkins brought only one person as a witness. Jackson talked for 40 minutes. Perkins remained silent until finally Jackson said, "Don't you have anything to say?" Perkins responded, "Well, I wanted to hear you out."

Jackson made the incorrect assumption that Perkins had inherited his position. Perkins then told Jackson, "Well, now you have to understand me so you know who you're dealing with. I was born on the other side of the tracks. We didn't know to call it a ghetto. I had scholarships to Yale and Harvard Business School, so that's why I'm here. I want to make sure that you know I have a lot of sympathy for what you're trying to do. And I think Jewel should have more black employees." Clearly, Perkins wanted to keep control of the situation. He indicated to Jackson that his organization would be surveyed to determine how many additional employees could be hired and how many products could be put on its shelves. He said quite directly that he did not want to overpromise, and he was committed to making good on any commitment. He went on to say, "I would rather have you picket us now because we didn't promise enough than to picket us a year from now because we didn't do what we promised. You can be sure that we will do what we promised." He said they could not just place a product in the stores without knowing more about it. So he offered the company's lab in Barrington to test any product that Jackson wanted to bring in, and Jewel would test it and decide whether it warranted being on the shelf. One of the first products sent for testing was a bowl cleaner that was pure lye, and Jewel would not put it on their shelves.

Perkins also offered one other thing that he later said would not have been done if Jewel were not trying to help OB. He offered Jewel buyers as marketing and distribution advisers for any product that it decided was worth putting on their store shelves. He told Jackson that the real problem was not getting a product on the shelf; the problem was getting it *off* the shelf, that is, packaging, promoting, and filling orders. In this regard, Jewel could help.

Jackson requested that Jewel deposit money in black banks, and Perkins agreed. But when Jackson wanted to know how much Jewel would put in, Perkins replied that Jewel would put in enough dollars to service the account and then something beyond that to be of help to the bank. However, he was not about to say exactly how much that would be, observing that any bank that would supply such information to OB would not be a bank he would ever use.

Soon after meeting with Pitcher, I started attending Jackson's breakfast meetings and was fascinated by the mixture of religious service, pep talk, and business seminar. Many of these businesses were in the early stages of developing their brand images and needed help designing merchandising strategies. The idea quickly crystallized to recruit MBA students who could provide technical assistance to these business people who needed help developing business plans, preparing loan applications, and improving operations. The black MBA students enrolled in the special program within the business school (described earlier) would be ideal consultants to provide this technical assistance. Being realistic, however, I knew that given the busy schedules of most MBA students, I would have little success recruiting them merely by

Rev. Jesse L. Jackson signing an agreement with Jewel Tea Co. that would open job opportunities to African Americans and create shelf space for products made by member companies of Operation Breadbasket. *Left to right*: Rev. Story Freeman; Donald S. Perkins, president of Jewel Tea Co.; Rev. Clay Evans; Rev. Martin Luther King Jr.; Jackson; Rev. Claude Wyatt; and Jewel Tea personnel Mrs. Mary Harris and Allan Dean. Courtesy Operation PUSH, Rainbow Coalition archives.

saying, "Let's do a helpful thing for Negro businessmen on the South Side of Chicago." It would be necessary for the students to receive course credit for their work in the field. Since I had been teaching a course in business policy, dealing with the broad functions of business, it was not much of a stretch to put together a series of cases and readings on small business management and to offer a seminar on the subject.

Thereafter, I offered the small business course on a regular basis. Another faculty member, Harry Davis, offered a course that combined his interests in marketing with entrepreneurship, and his students also worked with several of the black businessmen. On one occasion, I offered the seminar jointly with Robert Hamada, who later became dean of the school. Drawing on Hamada's expertise in finance, we constructed a cost-benefit analysis of the economic consequences of increasing the size and profitability of these small, struggling businesses. We encountered immense challenges in collecting the right data, and while we were able to show some positive impact, the results were not overwhelmingly positive. Even so, for individual businessmen, the students and faculty added value. Two of the firms that our students assisted—Parker House Sausage and Grove Fresh Orange Juice—expanded, and by the end of the decade, sales for each of them exceeded one million dollars.

Those of us from the university found it necessary to walk a fine line in providing technical assistance to the member companies of OB. Our role needed to be supportive, yet not directive in our advice to the staff of OB and to the black businessmen. Donald Benedict, the tireless and inspired leader of the Chicago Missionary Society (later renamed the Chicago Renewal Society), describes in a memoir a meeting he had with Jesse Jackson in which he succumbed to the temptation "to tell [Jackson] how to run his organization." Regretfully, he recalled, "I had exhibited the white racism that so often lurks below the surface in all of us."[5]

During the academic year 1966–67, I continued to attend the Saturday morning OB breakfast meetings, now held in a large church. While Jesse Jackson's upbeat talks remained central to the meetings, these events increasingly became the "place to be" for politicians. Big names appeared frequently. On one occasion, Joe Louis greeted the assembly because one of the milk companies used his name in marketing its products. At the time, I recalled with some discomfort how, in the late 1930s, I had rooted for Billy Conn in the big heavyweight-boxing match with Joe Louis. All of the kids on my block were white. In fact, in the graduation photo from grammar school, only one black student, Adrian Evans, can be seen, and he lived in a different part of town, so he was not part of our gang that hung out together on the block. So it was inevitable that we identified with Billy Conn, also white. Wanting to be one of the boys, I went along and hoped Conn would beat the "Bronx Bomber." But that did not happen. Little did I know in June 1967 that I would see Joe Louis up close as a guest of Jesse Jackson at one of the regular Saturday morning meetings of Operation Breadbasket.

Attendance at Jackson's meetings grew steadily, and on one Saturday, Martin Luther King attended and gave a stirring talk. (On another occasion some months later, I vividly remember Reverend King speaking against the war in Vietnam and how troubled I was at hearing this talk. Being a veteran and believing—naively—that the administration in Washington knew what it was doing, yet at the same time having the deepest respect for Reverend King, I found myself in a quandary.)

By far the most interesting aspect of my work with OB was participating in what came to be called the Attunement Committee. I first joined this group in the summer of 1967 and continued participating through early 1969. Initially it was called the Membership Committee, and its chair was Cirilo McSween, a highly successful insurance salesman well known in the region, especially in the black community, for having been an Olympic star in the early 1950s.

The committee's primary purpose was to screen applications from black businessmen for membership in OB. The term "Attunement" was chosen to reflect what the leadership of OB saw as the defining qualification for being enrolled in the organization. The committee's minutes reveal this emphasis:

> *January 23, 1968*: It is clear that the important attribute for membership is attitude, and not whether the business has a track record of achievement.

> *March 12, 1968:* The Chair emphasized that Operation Breadbasket was not as much interested in dollars as in attitude.

> *March 19, 1968:* Breadbasket is anxious to create new values and build new men, and not focus as much on money.

This theme was stressed in a subcommittee report dealing with membership criteria: "Since very few products will fail to qualify in terms of the basic business and quality standards, membership is based on attunement."

To underscore the difference between OB and the *modus operandi* of a local Chamber of Commerce or other business development groups, each meeting of the Attunement Committee opened with a prayer. This practice seemed natural since at least three members of the committee were ministers. In fact, the core leaders of OB were all divinity students, including Gary Massoni, who served as an aide to Jackson, and several others who were fellow students of Jesse Jackson's at the Chicago Theological Seminary.

Left to right: Rev. Jesse Jackson, Martin Luther King Jr., and Cirilo McSween, planning an Operation Breadbasket event. Courtesy McSween family.

The Attunement Committee faced some tough decisions about which businesses to bring on board. Given the leverage that OB was beginning to enjoy with supermarket chains, many fledgling companies wanted to become part of OB and have a case made to the big food retailers that their products be displayed. Some members of the Attunement Committee, especially some of the more established businessmen, were concerned that the admission of companies that had not yet met the market test would tarnish the image of OB.

I found myself on the other side of the argument, thinking that we should be much more inclusive. In weighing whether the standard for admission should be that of an organization emphasizing business viability, or that of a grass-roots organization open for all—especially for new and struggling businesses—I supported the concept of an open community. For example, at one meeting, I supported membership for a company that manufactured barbeque sauce, observing that the criteria of sales volume and adequate production facilities would be relevant at a later stage when the product was

Rev. Gary Massoni (*right*), key lieutenant for Jesse Jackson. On left is Rev. Andrew Juvenall, Gary's pastor while Gary was in high school. Courtesy Gary Massoni.

presented to a supermarket. However, it was important to admit this individual and his company into the OB family to provide assistance during the development phase, even though when analyzed in terms of the criteria a banker would use, the long-term outlook for the firm might be uncertain.

By December 1967, admission standards had been crystallized to include "spiritual participation, organizing a consumer club, use of Negro products, especially Negro banks, participation in Breadbasket advertising, contributions to SCLC, and enrollment of children in Operation Breadbasket schools." Clearly, these represented community rather than business standards, and they were very much in line with what the leadership of OB meant by being "attuned" to the program.

Early in the committee's work (December 1966), the number of businesses that had been certified for membership stood at 10. By the April 1968 meeting, however, 33 new applications had been completed and distributed to the committee. Membership was growing rapidly, and at one meeting Cirilo proposed a "group therapy" session to help the leadership more efficiently explain the principles of OB to the large number of applicants. By October 1968, when the committee was debating whether to create a directory of black businesses, over 100 businesses had qualified for membership. Clearly, OB had become the "game in town" that many black businesses wanted to join.

As the number of businesses within OB grew, the leadership found it necessary to group them into "spokes"; for example, those selling food products, manufactured cleaning supplies, construction companies, exterminators, and scavengers. This last spoke generated some tough issues for the Attunement Committee. By the nature of their work—traveling around the city and seeing each other as their routes crisscrossed—as well as their being "tough and savvy"—the scavengers naturally banded together to form a tight-knit group.

At one point, the scavenger spoke rejected a membership application for a new business that had been approved by the Attunement Committee. The reason given: when this individual suffered an equipment breakdown, other scavengers had stepped in and covered his stops, but subsequently he failed to show any appreciation or reciprocity. On another occasion, the scavenger spoke "admitted" a business that had not been vetted by the Attunement Committee.

Other issues surfaced that illustrated the difficult terrain being traversed by this "community" approach to business development. When a white scavenger realized that black scavengers had replaced him at one of the major food chains, he threatened to go to the IRS to "finger" several black scavengers who had not been filing income tax reports. (How he came by this suspicion was not clear.) At another meeting, a report was received that several scavengers had used arm-twisting tactics to collect money from their members and had sent checks directly to the SCLC in Atlanta. The Attunement Committee reminded them that financial contributions to SCLC had to be voluntary. But scavengers who knew the way the "game" worked—favor for favor—were quite ready to contribute and to "urge" other drivers to contribute.

Despite attempts by the scavenger spoke to assert their autonomy, the leadership of OB maintained firm control over business development. In the March 19, 1968, minutes, the chair observed: "Breadbasket is responsible for getting stops [number of scavenger pickups] to distribute them, and if necessary, to take them away. Distribution is based on attunement, on total participation in the Breadbasket program."

Fairly early in its work, the Attunement Committee recognized that it needed to play a bigger role than solely that of a gatekeeper. This led to the development of a marketing plan aimed at helping these growing businesses expand into new outlets. I served as an adviser for this work.

Furthering this goal, Jesse Jackson and the leaders of Breadbasket decided to create a merchandising-consulting organization named HIC (the initials of the principals). However, the establishment of HIC created new issues. When the Attunement Committee mandated that all member companies must use HIC, several businessmen who had been using other vendors objected strongly. The committee also debated (to no conclusion) the question whether HIC should be allowed to work with companies outside of OB (presumably white-owned and managed).

Throughout 1968 and into 1969, the Attunement Committee focused on helping member businesses become better managed. Professors Davis and Hamada, as well as several of our black MBA students who were providing technical assistance to the members of Breadbasket, attended these meetings and contributed to the discussions. As part of my role in providing technical assistance, I invited Mitchell Watkins from the Real Estate Research Corporation to make a presentation to the Attunement Committee. In his talk, he identified promising areas for business development for black entrepreneurs.

When I was asked to offer several seminars, I used my small-business course as a vehicle for responding to this need. I also offered to have the business game that we used in our business policy course serve as the basis for a workshop.

During the fall of 1968, several faculty members from Marion Business College presented a comprehensive plan for providing technical assistance and business development and indicated that they were interested in working with the Attunement Committee in a similar capacity as the faculty from the University of Chicago. Their comprehensive report proposed seminars and marketing studies that would help these businesses realize their potential.

On several occasions, major trade expositions were held in conjunction with Operation Breadbasket conferences, and considerable publicity was given throughout Chicago to these events. At these expositions, the black businessmen displayed their products.

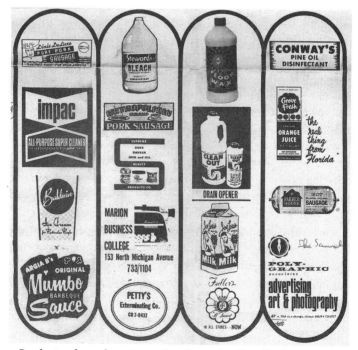

Products of member companies, Operation Breadbasket. Courtesy Operation PUSH, Rainbow Coalition archives.

The Attunement Committee and OB navigated an uncharted terrain containing many dilemmas and challenges. For example, the Attunement Committee debated whether a type of "Good Housekeeping Seal of Approval" would be applied to products. In a letter to the committee, I argued that while "OB did not want to endorse products that were clearly hazards or frauds, at the same time they could not embargo products that violated some of our explicit values. For example, the practice of straightening hair might be something that some thought not socially appropriate, but the Attunement Committee could not get in the way of precluding cosmetic companies that had a role to fulfill in the marketplace for African Americans. The same would be true with the drain cleaner, Outclean, which many thought was a very "potent" product. If used properly, it did the job.

I also tried to focus efforts on increasing the size of the "pie" and not just allocating the pie among existing entrepreneurs. In meetings, I expressed concern that OB was devoting too much attention to distributing the new shelf space in the retail food stores to member companies rather than generating marketing programs to expand sales for member companies. In some ways, it was operating like a cartel, and such arrangements never serve the interests of the consumer. I argued that OB should be "opening new markets, creating new businesses, and challenging the community with the need to support Negro entrepreneurship." If OB placed too much emphasis on allocating gains among its member companies, it would tear the organization apart.

At one meeting, the committee entertained a request from a prospective member that he be allowed to continue banking with his usual bank, rather than shifting to a black-owned bank (one of the requirements for membership). The request was granted. Other members found it difficult to organize consumer clubs. Organizing a consumer club took time away from the necessary activities of running a growing business. These clubs, which were the brainchild of Jesse Jackson, sought to create awareness within the black community regarding products being produced by black businesses, so that when members shopped they would make their purchases in the "right way."

At another point, it was reported that some black businessmen were visiting retail stores that had signed covenants with OB announcing that they were members of the organization when in actuality they had not been certified. This led to a proposal for creating a membership card that could be shown by members to the retailers. Again, I was concerned about the control aspects of OB. I did not think it was a good use of the staff's energy to "police memberships."

What exactly constituted a black business also presented a major dilemma. For example, when the Wanzer Milk Company—white-owned but employing many black managers—was awarded contracts as a result of OB's negotiations with major retail chains, the Joe Louis Milk Company filed a complaint with the committee. At another time, the Committee debated the question whether a particular trucking company-seeking membership could be eligible if the ownership was white even though all of its drivers were black.

After the assassination of Martin Luther King in the spring of 1968, rivalry arose between Ralph Abernathy and Jesse Jackson over who would become the heir to King. It was inevitable that Jackson would break with the leadership of the SCLC and convert OB (a franchised program of SCLC) into his own "brand"—Operation PUSH, which eventually evolved into the Rainbow Coalition-Operation PUSH. By this time I was no longer involved with Operation Breadbasket. I still taught the small business course, and my students were working in the field with many OB companies. The Attunement Committee had been disbanded and a small leadership cadre governed Operation PUSH.

As I look back on the activities of OB and especially the work of the Attunement Committee, it is clear that some significant gains were achieved. The strategy of expanding outlets for these black businesses was successful. In some cases, however, the progress resembled "two steps forward, one step back." As mentioned, High-Low signed one of the first agreements in November 1966. However, when High-Low failed to employ the additional black workers envisioned in the agreement, OB placed pickets at the stores. In turn, High-Low sought an injunction and only after protracted negotiations did the parties reach a second agreement in July 1967.

How successful was Operation Breadbasket in expanding black business? It is clear that for a number of years during the late 1960s and early 1970s, many of the black businesses expanded and even thrived as a result of the political and economic "muscle" that Jackson and OB used to secure covenants with many large retail food stores in Chicago.

As an incubator, OB served as a launch pad for projects that were then passed on to other organizations. For example, during the late 1960s, OB sponsored a series of black expositions to showcase the products and services of its member companies in an effort to help them develop and expand connections. This program was then spun off to another organization.

On the other hand, when I visited Chicago several decades later, curious to learn what had happened to the black businesses that my students had worked with as consultants, I learned that the wax company had gone out of business, as had the orange juice company. In the case of the barbeque sauce company, management had been passed to the granddaughter of the founder. One of the exterminator businesses was doing well, and an advertising agency that started in the 1960s was also doing well. Many enterprises in the banking and scavenger services remained going concerns.

To the extent that more could have been done, especially by the Attunement Committee, to help the struggling businesses survive and grow, Gary Massoni, one of Jesse's lieutenants, commented, "We probably tried too hard to get the black businessmen to relate to the community with our priorities, such as banking with black institutions, forming consumer clubs, and contributing money back to the community [as well as to Operation Breadbasket]. We probably should have spent more time helping them with business fundamentals."[6]

The fact that many of the businesses supported by OB have disappeared is not surprising. In general, small businesses tend to have a high mortality rate, but for a period of time in the 1960s and 1970s, many of these businesses realized major benefits from the support and work of OB. Calvin Morris, former chief of staff, offered his analysis of the demise of many black businesses: "One of the things we know a lot more about today is this whole issue of capacity. You have to have the capacity to advertise. You have to have the capacity to give the product a name brand. And we're talking about fledgling operations that were going up against multi-hundred-million-dollar corporations. It was a time when white corporations were more and more aware of the African American market. Today you've got these mammoth corporations using their machinery to appeal to the black consumer. So this lessened the attentiveness of the black community toward these new products of the black businesses, less known, less marketed."[7]

Remember that another priority for OB was expansion of jobs for blacks, and on this dimension the balance sheet is positive. Donald Perkins made the point succinctly: "I think we would have done much of what we did without Jesse Jackson, but the impetus of Jesse Jackson focusing attention on shelf space and employment—I have to give him credit. He got us moving earlier and faster than we might otherwise have done."

The pressure for change exerted by OB provided many business leaders like Perkins with a rationale for transforming their organizations. Perkins affirmed this point. As a result of the challenge made to Jewel Tea by OB, he surveyed his organization and asked his staff for a plan to address the problem. Often he received considerable push back from his team, some of whom asked, "What about our kids?" Would there still be reserved slots for the children of white employees? Because Perkins had signed an agreement, the organization had to honor the commitment. Perkins observed "some of the very individuals who were following through on the covenant may have been some of the same people who were probably throwing rocks at the marchers in Marquette Park."

In his classic analysis of the civil rights movement in the North, Thomas Sugrue identified three distinct strategies: (1) engaging black elites, (2) fostering black self-help, and (3) appealing to interracialism.[8] To Jackson's credit, he combined elements of all three approaches in the way he structured Operation Breadbasket. The elites were represented on his Steering Committee (for example, Cirilo McSween, former Olympic running star and successful insurance agent), as well as the many dignitaries who appeared on the weekly program for the Saturday morning meetings. The emphasis on black self-help was embodied in various OB programs that challenged the member companies to grow beyond "mom and pop" businesses to become viable enterprises that could compete outside the ghetto. Finally, Jackson recruited fellow divinity students and professors—for the most part whites—to his team and relied on them for advice and execution of the many OB initiatives.

Leon Sullivan in Philadelphia did not utilize this last strategy in his selective patronage program, which may explain its early demise. Matthew Countryman observed, "Sullivan rejected appeals from white liberal supporters in favor of building racial solidarity within the city's black communities."[9]

In many ways, the *modus operandi* of OB resembled a theocracy. Much of what was done aimed at creating a business cooperative, and whether some of the activities of the organization, in retrospect, should be viewed as "restraint of trade," I leave it to others to decide. Like many innovations, a "reversion to the mean" gradually occurred. As OB grew from a small meeting in a cafeteria at CTS to a large weekly event held in a spacious auditorium on the South Side, the emphasis on business development gave way to an expanded agenda: inspirational talks, politicking, and entertainment. Jesse Jackson's vision expanded, and he proved adept at developing a large following for his concerns and interests in the fields of education, housing, and eventually for himself and his family in politics.

Before leaving the subject of retail food stores and black business development, I want to describe an episode that tangled together the work of students I was supervising, a company that OB had to target, and a street gang called the Blackstone Rangers. At some point in late 1967 or early 1968, an MBA student of mine, knowing of my interest in inner-city economic development, introduced me to Bernie Hahn, CEO of a chain of food stores called Red Rooster and the business model he had developed for success in the inner city. The student was related to Bernie, and he wrote a report on Red Rooster to fulfill a course requirement.

At the time, several big food chains like A&P (not Jewel Tea) were pulling out of the ghetto, providing Hahn with an opportunity to expand his operations. He owned and operated four supermarkets on the South Side of Chicago and employed 300 workers, almost all African American. His formula for success was straightforward: he offered credit on food purchases, hired blacks as store managers, and charged high prices, so when the risks of doing business in the ghetto, bad debts and theft, were tabulated, his stores were still profitable.

From the viewpoint of OB, Red Rooster's operation raised many obvious issues, such as "higher prices, lower quality products, spoiled meat, and continued errors in overcharging at the cash register."[10]

When Bernie and I first met, I asked him where he got the name "Red Rooster." He had obviously been asked the question many times, and his answer came quickly: "My parents came from Germany and in that country *hahn* means chicken or rooster. So I was really naming the store after myself."

Initially, my involvement with Bernie Hahn consisted of recruiting several students to analyze the feasibility of expanding his operations on Chicago's South Side. At this point, his chain only numbered four stores, and he was anxious to expand in order to gain the advantages coming from larger-volume purchases from his suppliers.

Bernie knew how to return a favor with a favor. One evening just before Christmas (after the students and I had presented our recommendations to Hahn), the doorbell rang and voila! we were presented with a large box of steaks and roasts. The provider was not the meat department of Red Rooster but an upscale butcher shop specializing in gift packages. My first reaction was: "I can't keep this. It must be returned." (I was being compromised, or so I thought.) The issue of gifts and favors had received considerable press during the Eisenhower years (1950s) with questions such as: At what size or weight does a gift of a ham cease being insignificant and become a bribe? The saga of the vicuña coat and the resignation of Sherman Adams that had embarrassed the Eisenhower administration were vivid images in my mind.

I called Bernie and said we could not keep the meat, but he said that was impossible. So we kept the gift, and then wrestled with the next dilemma— whether to throw it out, give it away, or use it ourselves. I am sure you can guess the outcome, given the fact that a true Scot never throws anything away. We did give several of the steaks away but kept the rest and found we had been given some of the best meat we had ever tasted.

During the spring of 1968, as part of its campaign to develop more business for black-owned companies, Operation Breadbasket turned its sights on Red Rooster—again, using the leverage of its consumer clubs to mount a boycott of Bernie's stores. In addition to placing pickets outside the stores and as part of its campaign of pressure on Red Rooster, OB filed complaints with several city agencies seeking to revoke Red Rooster's licenses. Thus began the second phase of my relationship with Bernie Hahn.

Ever ready to practice my third-party skills, I offered to serve as a mediator as soon as it became clear that Red Rooster had become a high-priority target for OB. On October 9, 1968, I sent a letter to Rev. Calvin Morris in which I volunteered the opinion that Red Rooster was not as bad as its reputation. In retrospect, I wonder whether my evaluation was influenced by the gift and whether I also was returning favor for favor.

My offer came on the heels of a tense meeting between OB leaders and Hahn and his black president, Richard Kay. The meeting produced little in the way of agreement but unleashed many accusations, with Hahn labeling OB's tactics as blackmail. In turn, the OB representatives labeled Kay an "Uncle Tom."

My efforts to intervene got nowhere, and the next thing I knew, Hahn was on the phone calling me from his lawyer's office somewhere in the Loop. "Professor, you've got to help me. It's a matter of life or death. A contract is out on me." At the time, I was so inexperienced that I did not know the meaning of the term "contract." Apparently, what had happened was that Jeff Fort, the extremely effective leader of the Blackstone Rangers, a large gang based on the South Side of Chicago and with connections to the Mafia, felt—or the Mob felt—that they had been double-crossed, and Bernie was now in their crosshairs.

I said I did not know how I could help. Bernie replied: "The only people who can protect me are the Feds, and you know George Shultz, so would you please get in touch with him?" Now I felt on the spot, thinking of all those delicious steaks. But I was not about to call George, who at the time (early 1969) had just taken over as secretary of labor, on leave from the dean's job at the University of Chicago Graduate School of Business. So I agreed to meet with Bernie face to face.

He had moved out of his home and was living in an apartment hotel somewhere on the near North Side. A twenty-four-hour police guard had been posted at the door. The meeting was inconclusive; I was not able to suggest anything that he had not thought of already. My explanation for not calling Shultz was that the Department of Labor was far removed from the Justice Department and the FBI.

Bernie related that when Breadbasket started its campaign against Red Rooster, he contacted a person "high up" in the Daley administration to get "the revocation of his license thing" stopped. The contact turned out to be Alderman Ralph Metcalfe, one of the black political leaders loyal to Mayor Daley. From his contacts with Metcalfe, Bernie reported that the mayor's office was determined that Jesse Jackson "must be stopped."

Bernie ended up selling Red Rooster and leaving town. I wondered at the time whether a "squeeze play" had been administered in order to get him to sell at a bargain price. Eventually Red Rooster folded, probably due to the high costs of doing business in the inner city and also due to the falloff in patronage as a result of the boycott by OB. At the time, I puzzled over what had gone wrong for Bernie. I speculated that in an effort to get OB off his back, Bernie had reached out to Jeff Fort, gang leader of the Blackstone Rangers. Jeff demanded compensation, Hahn paid him $15,000, and Hahn's black president, Richard Kay, joined the Rangers. Hahn then contacted the syndicate and asked for a "favor": that they protect Kay. When Hahn revealed to Fort that he had contacted the syndicate, Fort was furious. This started the backfire stage of the saga. By casting his lot with Jeff Fort and his connections, Bernie Hahn had gotten in over his head.

A more likely scenario, buttressed by the work of several investigative reporters, is the following: In his negotiation with Hahn, Jackson demanded that Red Rooster hire members of the Blackstone Rangers. When Hahn failed to follow through ("welched on his commitment"), the Rangers, with their connections to the syndicate, put out a contract on him.

Barbara Reynolds, a reporter, has this to say about the saga of Red Rooster: "The concessions won from Red Rooster turned into a hollow victory [for OB]. By September, the new owners were hauled off to federal court on tax delinquency charges and soon afterwards filed for bankruptcy. Another factor contributing to the firm's demise was the padding of salaries for 22 members of the Blackstone Rangers street gang, which forced their way into the company under the auspices of the Coalition for United Community Action and Breadbasket."[11]

What about Jeff Fort, the Rangers' leader? Marshall Patner knew him and had represented him in court, and anyone living in Hyde Park was well aware of the gang. In fact, a University of Chicago student had been murdered just a few feet from our front door when a young male, carrying out the initiation to become a gang member by mugging someone, escalated matters to the point that an innocent person was killed.

It is intriguing how Jeff Fort's career connected to two of my heroes: Tim Black and Marshall Patner. Tim Black knew Jeff Fort very well since he was Tim's student at Hyde Park High School. Tim characterized Fort as very smart but certainly not interested in the books. Tim attempted to work with Jeff and some of his friends, but that ended when the principal of the school expelled them for unruly behavior. To Tim's view, this was the event that pushed Jeff into another career and channeled his leadership skills into organizing a gang.

Marshall Patner and William Brackett represented Fort in hearings before the McClellan Committee in the U.S. Congress. Some background is required, and for this, I draw heavily on an interview with Bill Brackett.

Rev. John Fry, minister of Hyde Park Presbyterian Church, had gained the confidence of Jeff Fort and the other leaders of the Blackstone Rangers. This occurred early in the 1960s. With funds from Chuck Kettering, Fry was attempting to turn the talents of the Blackstone Rangers to peaceful, lawful, and productive pursuits. Chuck Kettering was the son of the Kettering who played a key role in establishing General Motors, and through the wealth that resulted, he created a foundation aimed at scientific research. However, the younger Kettering was more interested in financing social activism.

At some point in the mid-1960s, Fry approached the law firm of Ross, Hardie, and McGowan to see if they would be interested in helping the Rangers "get the cops off their backs"—specifically by providing criminal case representation, business law services, as well as business counseling to the Rangers, who were in the process of creating small businesses on the South Side. The law firm agreed, and put Bill Brackett on the project who in turn recruited Patner. The project, supported by funds from Kettering, did not last long since Kettering's interest waned quickly. However, a few small businesses were started, and Patner and Brackett worked with the gang to handle some of the criminal charges that were brought against them.

Subsequently, Senator McClellan, who chaired the Senate Investigative Committee (the same one that Senator Joseph McCarthy previously had headed), decided to investigate the Office of Economic Opportunity and the War on Poverty, claiming that the Rangers had used some of the federal grant funds improperly. Brackett viewed the work of the McClellan Committee as somewhat problematic. They were looking for publicity, and he felt that they tried to bully John Fry, claiming it was "immoral that he was encouraging the lawless Blackstone Rangers." The committee ignored Fry's efforts to head Jeff Fort and the Rangers in a new direction. While the committee called many witnesses and issued many statements, nothing substantive resulted from the investigation.

Ultimately, Senator McClellan called Jeff Fort as a witness. Marshall Patner and Bill Brackett represented Fort before the committee. Fort refused to testify, saying that he refused to "talk to those whores." He also refused to use the Fifth Amendment protection, saying that to do so would make it seem like "we committed crimes." Patner and Brackett warned Jeff that if he insisted on that course of action he would be charged with contempt of Congress, and indeed he was, and Judge John Siricca convicted him. However, Patner and Brackett were successful in having Fort sentenced under the Youth Act, thereby cutting the period of time he served in prison. Brackett found the process fascinating but it also increased his cynicism, as he saw the "racism, dishonesty, and cynical publicity-grabbing of McClellan and his staff up close." Brackett praised the efforts of John Fry and Patner, and while he wondered whether any overall, lasting benefit would ever materialize, he also believed that fundamental principles for future cases had been put in place.[12]

While Senator McClellan may have had the Blackstone Rangers on his blacklist, others including President Richard Nixon were intrigued by the potential to turn these street leaders in a different direction:

> The inclusion of the street gangs in the [civil rights] movement was indicative of the times. In the late 1960s, it was in vogue to attribute the gang bloodletting to the fact that the gang members were culturally deprived. Gang leaders often addressed audiences from the Breadbasket pulpit. The Rangers were held in such high esteem, police records notwithstanding, that former Pres. Nixon invited two top members to his first-term Inaugural Ball. There they were, resplendent in black tie and tails, while many more "deserving" blacks did not receive an invitation. Among these not invited was Rev. Jackson. In appreciation of the recognition, the Rangers invited Nixon to the opening of their new carwash. He declined.[13]

Fort's fortunes took a turn for the worse when in 1972 he entered a federal prison for accepting a bribe from Libya's Muammar Gaddafi, and as of 2012 he is still incarcerated.

11. The Movement and the Decade Wind Down

I see tremendous entrances and exits, new

combinations, the solidarity of races.

—Walt Whitman, *Years of the Modern*

With Martin Luther King moving on to projects outside Chicago and the demise of the CCCO in 1966, the civil rights movement in Chicago effectively passed from the scene, at least the direct-action phase of the "revolution" that was seeking significant change in the lives of African Americans. A similar diminution or cessation of activity occurred in other cities in the North that had witnessed civil rights campaigns during the 1960s, including New York City[1] and Milwaukee.[2] The exact moment when the direct-action phase ended differed, but Thomas J. Sugrue concluded that by the early 1970s "pessimists found plenty of evidence that the movement was over," that America had entered a "post–civil rights era."[3]

Some analysts have applied the concept of a life cycle—an onset, then expansion, and, ultimately, decline—to the marches, demonstrations, and riots during the decade. For example, Countryman notes this dynamic for Philadelphia: "By the 1970s, movement organizers found themselves increasingly unable to demonstrate to most black Philadelphians that the payoff from social movement strategies was worth either the risk or the effort."[4]

In Chicago, several organizations, in addition to the CCCO, that had employed direct action such as boycotts, demonstrations, and marches left the scene or shifted their focus to less confrontational measures and programs. The NACL, under the leadership of Tim Black, which had forced Motorola into negotiations seeking to increase employment of minorities, had, at the national level, morphed into a research and educational institute, and Bayard Rustin succeeded A. Philip Randolph as national head of the organization.[5] Operation Breadbasket, having used consumer boycotts to force retail stores to provide shelf space for minority-owned suppliers, turned its attention to providing technical assistance to those firms. TWO, which successfully used demonstrations to get the attention of the University of Chicago, shifted its focus, joining with the university in initiating a series of partnership programs. The next chapter describes these developments.

Several questions about the direct-action programs of the civil rights movement of Chicago remain:

- What did the civil rights movement accomplish in Chicago? Or stated differently, were any of the strategic objectives realized? Did any change take place for African Americans as a result of the direct-action programs?

- Given the variety of direct action tactics that had been employed during the 1960s, what can be said about their relative effectiveness? Did the strikes, marches, and demonstrations have any impact?

- Specifically, did the negotiations (or "discussions," as some of the target organizations preferred to describe them) produce any concrete results?

The short answer to these questions has to be a qualified "yes." In two cases, written documents emerged: the Covenant Agreements between Operation Breadbasket and the major food chains, and the summit agreement signed by the City of Chicago and the Chicago Freedom Movement. In the case of Motorola, the understandings were never formalized into a document, but did involve assurances by a key executive that the company would actively search for and hire more black employees.

At the time, the negotiated agreements were hailed as important "breakthroughs," but did these signed pieces of paper and verbal assurances produce any significant change? Did Motorola hire more blacks? Were minority suppliers to retail food stores better off? Were blacks able to find housing in areas of Chicago that were previously "off limits"?

While the overall impact of the direct-action campaigns is difficult to gauge, several failures are easy to identify. Specifically, the civil rights movement was unsuccessful in achieving two key objectives: forcing Superintendent Benjamin Willis to retire early, and unionizing workers in the hospital industry.

Given the number of organizations involved in the CCCO, combined with the orchestration and drumbeat of school boycotts, frequent marches, and demonstrations, the inability of the movement to expedite the departure of

Benjamin Willis was regarded by everyone as a major failure. The unsuccessful union organizing campaign and accompanying strike at Mt. Sinai Hospital and the Home for Incurables was not unexpected, given the fact that hospitals in the 1960s were not covered by any legislation mandating union representation elections. Certainly, strikes were a weak tool: management could readily hire replacements, and low-income workers with limited economic resources were unable to hold out for more than a few weeks. In contrast, the campaign for open housing, which led to face-to-face negotiations and an agreement in 1966, produced a better outcome than the "nothing" that emerged from the school protests in 1965. King and the SCLC left Chicago with some sense of success when the team moved on to other campaigns.

What is probably the major accomplishment of the civil rights movement in Chicago was the creation of the nerve and command center for the civil rights movement, the CCCO. The ability of Arthur Brazier and Al Raby to pull together numerous community, church, and direct-action groups into a functioning body that organized and deployed thousands of participants over a five-year period must be judged as a major achievement. The necessary ingredients for this mobilization were present: longstanding grievances over schools, employment, and housing; and a strong moral imperative that the time had come to address these grievances. Local leadership was needed to rally the forces and direct their energies in a series of direct-action initiatives, and the CCCO was fortunate to have Brazier, Raby, and Pitcher at the helm.

Various tactics, especially school boycotts, played an important role in the development of the CCCO during the 1960s. The marchers, teachers in the freedom schools, and parents who coped with two "no-school" days all became recruits and supporters of the movement. These well-publicized, direct-action programs in Chicago paralleled similar programs in many other cities and can be viewed as part of the broader strategy of sustained and symbolic pressure to sensitize the larger community to the need for changes in civil rights and race relations. The intransigence of the school board in the face of large-scale protests, backed by the unyielding posture of Daley, also energized the movement and encouraged more supporters to join the campaign. In his account of the civil rights movement in Milwaukee, Patrick Jones observed the same galvanizing result when the city initially refused to enact an open housing ordinance.[6] When public interest was waning just before the second Chicago public school boycott, the reappointment of Superintendent Willis reinvigorated the movement, and a new chapter unfolded: nightly marches from Buckingham Fountain, first to City Hall, and then to Mayor Daley's own neighborhood. Dramatic campaigns were needed to capture the attention of people and organizations that were not yet targets. The indirect benefits of direct action can be substantial as others watch, learn, and act to avoid becoming the next targets.

The CCCO was a unique organization. With a large number of community, religious, and direct-action organizations in its fold, it exerted tremendous influence throughout the city of Chicago during the 1960s. From my vantage point as a delegate from the liberal churches of Chicago, I witnessed the impact of the various initiatives of the CCCO on the congregation of First Unitarian Church. If the discussions and resulting participation by church members in the CCCO programs that I observed in one locale were duplicated in other member organizations, then the citywide impact of CCCO was monumental.

The *modus operandi* of the CCCO represented a mix of a parliamentary-type organization with that of a command center. This latter role characterized the way decisions were made during the campaign for open housing. The challenge posed by Dick Gregory and his program of nightly marches—first to the Loop and then on a regular basis to Mayor Daley's home community—illustrated another reality for the CCCO. In this case, authority went to individuals who could generate a following, and even though the marches were not initially authorized by the CCCO, ultimately the organization found it necessary to bless Gregory and his campaign.

Ironically, the arrival of the SCLC and its partnership with the CCCO under the banner of the Chicago Freedom Movement during the summer of 1966 served to diminish the need to develop "backup" leadership within the CCCO. In effect, Al Raby was incorporated (*co-opted* might be more accurate) into the SCLC leadership team, and regular CCCO meetings ceased. Then when the SCLC left town, Raby was ready to resign (citing burnout and indicating he was stepping aside to "write his memoir"), and there was no one with his energy and capacity to continue the leadership of the organization.

It is interesting to speculate about the time frame for what can be termed the life cycle of direct-action, grass-roots organizations. Mary King notes that SNCC's rise and demise also occurred over a five-year period of time. Whether it is "mission accomplished," internal divisions, or leadership burnout, there seems to be a limit to how long momentum can be sustained.[7]

Significantly, the confrontation tactics of the CCCO strengthened the hand of the Urban League, which had been working behind the scenes, for example, by providing Motorola with training programs and other forms of technical assistance. In a type of "good-cop/bad-cop" scenario, Bill Berry, executive director of the Urban League, was able to say (behind the scenes—and

I am paraphrasing here): "Look, even if Willis stays—because you cannot be seen as giving in to pressure—other changes need to be instituted."

In many respects, the CCCO set the pace for comparable direct-action programs and organizations in other northern cities. For example, school boycotts first took place in October 1963 and February 1964 in Chicago; followed in May 1964 and October 1965 in Milwaukee, and in February 1964 in New York City. A similar sequence took place with open housing campaigns, first during the summer of 1966 in Chicago and subsequently during the summer and fall of 1967 in Milwaukee.[8]

Another positive outcome stemming from the civil rights movement could be labeled "leadership development." In Chicago, hundreds of African Americans acquired experience and understanding in how to run a campaign, how to raise funds, how to handle themselves in public—attributes of what can be called "human capital." I am reminded of the young men who served as our escorts in the march to Gage Park, and Nancy recalled with admiration the talent of the young black men who accompanied the Chicago delegates after they arrived in Selma.

It is important to reflect on the point that many leadership opportunities fell to or were seized by young black men. Interestingly, black women remained in the background. Against the historical reality that black men have faced major challenges in establishing their manhood and footing in society, in this very significant way the civil rights movement must be seen as instrumental in developing the human capacity of individuals who had faced closed doors.

It is important to observe that the leadership of the NALC, the CCCO, and Operation Breadbasket, at least initially, resembled a "male only" club. Reviewing the roster of names involved in the summit negotiations leading to the 1966 agreement on housing also shows a male-only profile. At that point (late 1960s) in the history of civil rights in the United States, the focus for equal rights had not yet turned to the status of women and the need to address their exclusion from important leadership roles.

What happened to the thousands of individuals who participated in the movement? David Halberstam has chronicled the life stories of the group of activists who integrated the lunch counters in Nashville, Tennessee,[9] and Doug McAdam has described the subsequent careers of a large group of northern students who participated in the Mississippi summer programs.[10] Considerably more longitudinal research is needed.

Reviewing the direct action campaigns in Chicago provides a number of interesting insights and prompts several questions regarding the relative effectiveness of various strategies and tactics.

- Why was the NALC able to engage Motorola with only a threatened demonstration (and the same could be said for Operation Breadbasket vis-à-vis Jewel Tea), while it took the SCLC a summer of tumultuous marches before negotiations leading to a summit agreement occurred?

- Why was TWO successful in getting the attention of the University of Chicago by mounting demonstrations that focused on the university's "failing" role in responding to the needs of the community? (To be discussed in the next chapter.)

- Why was it that the CCCO, after three years of agitation, including two boycotts and countless marches aimed at Willis, was not able to produce any discernible results for the civil rights movement?

Certainly, the sensitivity of the target organization to the publicity accompanying a boycott or demonstration explains much of what happened. Both Motorola and the food retailers came to the negotiation table with the NALC and OB, respectively, because they needed to minimize unfavorable publicity. In some cases, the *threat* of demonstration can be as effective as the real thing. This was illustrated by the NALC's success in getting the attention of the American Bar Association, as well as inducing Motorola to discuss its employment practices.

In many respects, the lack of success in forcing the resignation of Willis—the primary objective of the CCCO—serves as a counterpoint to the more apparent successes of the other campaigns just summarized. While the school boycotts, which withdrew children from school on two separate occasions, did impose some economic cost on the board of education (the system lost per capita support from the state), this tactic has to be seen more as mobilization aimed at enlisting parents in the campaign and, most important, as demonstrating to the board that the civil rights movement needed to be taken seriously.

In the aftermath of the first boycott, meetings did take place between representatives of the CCCO and members of the board of education. These meetings in no way could be characterized as formal negotiations; the board was willing to receive presentations from the CCCO, as it would from any group of parents or other stakeholders with concerns about the schools. Possibly, something approaching tacit negotiations did take place. Al Pitcher was convinced that assurances were given to the leadership of the CCCO that efforts were underway to enable Willis to depart "gracefully" when his contract expired at the end of August 1965—so everyone could "save face."

Given the reality that a majority of the board of education strongly supported Superintendent Willis and that the number one demand of CCCO required Willis to step down, there was no way that anything resembling formal talks could take place. And even if Willis were to go, his departure could not be seen as giving in to the coercive tactics of the civil rights movement. This unyielding stance of the board (and indirectly of Mayor Daley) continued in the face of the second boycott and the Good Friday mobilization.

Enter Dick Gregory to lead nightly marches during the summer of 1965—initially to City Hall and then to the mayor's home district of Bridgeport. This tactic was triggered by the reappointment of Willis to another term. With the decision to take the marches into Bridgeport, Gregory and the leaders of the CCCO knew that their presence in that community would inflame the situation. By refusing to leave and insisting on their rights of assembly, they hoped to precipitate an ugly situation. Gregory did what any platoon captain would do: he flushed out the "enemy." He needed to provoke a confrontation so that many white residents would be revealed as racist. After several weeks of marches from Grant Park only to the Loop, the actions of the civil rights movement were no longer on the front pages, so Gregory needed a way to escalate the campaign to unseat Benjamin Willis.

The dynamics of a union picket line present an interesting parallel. Early in a strike, the presence of pickets telegraphs the fact that a dispute is at hand, along with leaflets that present the rationale and justification for the work stoppage. As the strike drags on, tactics usually become more aggressive: cars are stopped, and drivers crossing the picket line are likely to be harassed. Strikers grow restive and increasingly frustrated that nothing is happening. Violence makes news, and the campaign underway may need the assist that comes from this publicity, especially if strikers get arrested.

Certainly the near-riot and the arrest of Gregory and his group of marchers in Bridgeport put the civil rights movement back in the news. But negotiations with the board of education or City Hall never occurred. Benjamin Willis stayed, and Gregory and his lieutenants were arrested. And while the arrests were later found to be without justification, the decision did not occur until a long time later, not until the U.S. Supreme Court heard Gregory's case in 1968.

Why did the direct-action campaign, orchestrated by the SCLC, produce face-to-face negotiations while the Gregory marches failed to do so? With Martin Luther King in town and leading marches that summer, and with thousands rather than hundreds of marchers participating, Mayor Daley could no longer ignore the developing crisis. When violence flared as the marchers headed for the all-white, working-class neighborhood of Chicago Lawn and civil rights leadership promised more of the same, Daley had no recourse but to orchestrate negotiations between representatives of the city, real estate brokers, and the civil rights movement. As soon as talks started, the SCLC and the CCCO agreed to limit marches and demonstrations—similar to Tim Black's decision to call off a demonstration against Motorola when Ken Piper agreed to meet.

Even though negotiations occurred and a summit agreement was reached, there has been considerable skepticism about the ultimate significance of Martin Luther King's campaign in Chicago during the summer of 1966. While King and the civil rights movement in the South had brought about changes in overt discrimination at lunch counters, on buses, and in public accommodations, changes in the North, where discrimination was much more subtle, proved much harder to eliminate.[11]

Certainly the visible victories for the movement in Chicago were not large, but there were major developments at a level above the local fray in Chicago; namely, passage of federal civil rights legislation in 1964, the Voting Rights Act in 1965, and the Open Housing Act in 1968. The decade of the 1960s can be seen as one of the unique periods in American history when alignment of the necessary ingredients for fundamental change produced legislation with far-reaching impact.

Can the civil rights movement of Chicago be given credit for the passage of these pieces of legislation? My answer is that these pieces of legislation would never have passed without the "awakening" of the country that resulted from the local actions of the civil rights movement. Consider Chicago as a case in point. The direct-action programs of the NALC on the employment front in 1963 preceded the passage of the Civil Rights Act of 1964, which established the Equal Employment Opportunity Commission (EEOC) to deal with employment discrimination. Similarly, the open housing campaign of the SCLC/CCCO during the summer of 1966 foreshadowed the passage of the Civil Rights Act of 1968 aimed at ending discrimination in housing.

Stories from many parts of the country were much the same: whites joining the campaigns to eliminate racial discrimination—a cause to which numerous black leaders had devoted their lives for many decades. But more was needed before legislation could be passed. The larger population needed to be drawn in. What made the decade of the 1960s so profound was that the "silent majority" became advocates for change. John Davis noted: "The realization that America's racial problems could not be solved by Negroes or by Whites, but by concerted efforts of the American people, was a long step towards the eventual resolution of the matter."[12]

The "contagion effect" of all the demonstrations and marches that had taken place earlier in the decade also affected the 1968 Democratic National

Convention. The object lesson—that Chicago could be an arena for mobilization—was not lost on those opposed to the Vietnam War, who saw the convention as a ready-made opportunity for protest and disruption. Given Martin Luther King's increasingly harsh assessment of the Vietnam War and the disproportionate sacrifice of the black community in lives damaged and lost to that conflict as well as the tragedy of King's assassination in April that year, the stars were in alignment for what would become a major confrontation between militant activists and the Daley administration during the Democratic Convention in the summer of 1968.

In drawing up a balance sheet for the Chicago civil rights movement, another reality during the decade needs to be accounted for: riots. Many commentators lumped together the riots and the peaceful demonstrations of the civil rights movement. While some members of the African American community seeing leaders like Al Raby being arrested for engaging in civil disobedience might have concluded that they had license to break the law by looting stores, I think such a connection is not plausible.

The Kerner Commission Report provides a more tenable explanation for the riots.[13] The commission on civil disobedience was convened in July 1967, and its 600-page report was issued in March 1968. The commission concluded: "White racism is essentially responsible for the explosive mixture which has been accumulating in our cities since the end of World War II." It also observed, "The continuing exclusion of great numbers of Negroes from the benefits of economic progress through discrimination in employment and education, and their enforced confinement in segregated housing and schools, [has been] the source of the deepest bitterness and at the center of the problem of racial disorder."[14] Most significantly, the commission recommended, "The only possible course for a sensible and humane nation [is] a policy which combines ghetto enrichment with programs designed to encourage integration of substantial numbers of Negroes into society outside the ghetto."[15]

Certainly the riots stemmed from the same underlying conditions that motivated the civil rights movement: limited opportunities resulting in poverty afflicting successive generations of African Americans across the country. They could be seen as "undisciplined" direct action. So in this sense, the riots were as much a part of the change equation as the demands of the civil rights movement, and they served to underscore the message of the movement that the African American community was "hurting." And while no policy makers would want the riots to be given credit for the various legislative initiatives passed during the 1960s, nevertheless the stark reality of the violence was a reminder that fundamental problems needed to be addressed.

How severe were the Chicago riots compared to others that occurred around the country? The Kerner Commission's answer was, "Nowhere near as bad." For instance, no riots occurred in Chicago during the summer of 1964 when riots occurred elsewhere in the country, nor did any occur in Chicago in 1967 when serious riots occurred in Detroit and Newark.

The riots that did occur during the summers of 1965 and 1966 in Chicago must be put in perspective. For example, in 1965 the riots in the Watts district of Los Angeles killed 31 people and injured scores more. By comparison, no one was killed in Chicago that same summer, although 80 were injured. The more serious riot in Chicago occurred in 1966 when three blacks were killed (from sniper fire) and five policemen were injured.[16] The Kerner Commission highlighted New York City (Harlem), Los Angeles (Watts), Newark, and Detroit; Chicago was not mentioned. Some credit must go to the leadership of the civil rights movement in Chicago for keeping the scope of the riots much more limited than was the case in other cities.

Woodlawn remained quiet during the summers of 1965 and 1966, but after the assassination of Martin Luther King in 1968, showed signs of exploding, especially in the business district along 63rd Street. Fortunately, the Blackstone Rangers, the youth gang led by Jeff Fort and discussed in chapter 10, instituted effective measures for discouraging violence by posting gang members at strategic points. Whether they also extracted protection money from merchants in exchange for "security" could not be verified, although such rumors persisted.

Donald Perkins of Jewel Tea provided another example of the positive social dynamics that were operating during the riots following King's assassination. During an interview, he observed, "Martin Luther King was assassinated and the fires happened in Chicago, and it may have just been sheer luck—but I always thought it was more than that because by then we had changed our reputation—not a single Jewel store was damaged. In fact, one story I love was that somewhere in the middle of Southside Chicago, we had a good-sized store with a mixture of white and black employees. As it was described to me, when the riots started, the black employees got the whites to their cars and said, 'Get out of here, we can't control things.' The affection that existed was obvious."[17]

Mayor Daley blamed the 1966 summer riots on the civil rights movement and put the onus on King, who had led many demonstrations that summer. And there were words in the Kerner Report that were interpreted by some to support the mayor: "We think it is clear that the intolerable and unconscionable encouragement of violence heightened tension, creating a mood of acceptance and an expectation of violence, and thus contributed to the eruption of the disorders."[18]

So how should we assess Chicago's civil rights movement of the 1960s? I would give it a passing grade. Others such as Anderson and Pickering give it a failing grade—a lot of effort and not much to show for it.[19] I see the glass being at least half full, laying the groundwork for national legislation, leadership development, the birth and growth of Operation Breadbasket, and significant changes occurring in two established institutions—the University of Chicago and the Unitarian Church.

12. Initiatives Continue within the University and the Unitarian Church

The days of recompense are come.

—Hosea 9:7

After key leaders of the civil rights movement left the Chicago scene in 1966–67, taking with them their programs of direct action, the initiative shifted to other institutions, especially two organizations that anchored my life, the Unitarian Church and the university.

The assassination of Martin Luther King in the spring of 1968 hit members of the Unitarian Church very hard. We were devastated. As James Baldwin expressed the change: "Since Martin's death, something has altered in me. Something has gone away."[1] King embodied all the qualities and values embraced by the congregation. He was a minister, he spoke and wrote as an intellectual, and he insisted that whites be welcomed into the civil rights revolution (in contrast to the fast-developing Black Power movement).

A memorial service at the Unitarian Church to honor the memory of the fallen leader left me quite agitated. While at a few points I wanted to exclaim "Amen," for the most part I wanted to shout out about what seemed to me the absolute sterility of the service. To ask an African American to lead a tribute to Martin Luther King in an essentially white church was to ask that person to assume an impossible burden. The African American cannot "tell it like it is"—he is forced to be reasonably polite and to practice the moderation that is the hallmark of an integrated group. In effect, he must say the things that everyone expects to hear, namely, that we all are guilty of racism.

But to ask a white person to deal with the evil that produced King's death was to ask that person to assume an equally impossible and heavy burden. Without question, racism existed. I had been on the receiving end of it on several occasions, starting in the 1950s with experiences at the interracial camp for city kids, where I experienced extreme viciousness on the part of several white parents, and continuing through the tumultuous marches into white Chicago neighborhoods during the summer of 1966.

The only resolution for whites was to alter their behavior, and it was by this crucial test that I saw little change taking place during that Sunday morning service. Where was the program? Where was any mention of Operation Breadbasket? Where was the pledging of additional money to the civil rights movement? Where was the pledging of time? My notes from that time concluded: "I remember the words of the Quaker with whom I worked at the interracial camp in Pennsylvania. He used to tell a story of the visitor who, upon seeing everyone sitting quietly, inquired at a Friends meeting house, "When does the service start?" The answer came simply and directly: "The service starts when the worship ends." I had the feeling that when 12:00 arrived on this Sunday morning, nothing new had begun.

While the First Unitarian Church of Chicago welcomed blacks, very few had become church members. Was this a reflection of the fact that few blacks had reached middle-class status? Could it be that the cerebral approach to religion that characterized Unitarianism did not resonate with folks coming from a tradition of gospel music and expressive worship? The Saturday morning "services" conducted by Jesse Jackson pulsated with warmth and emotion. By contrast, our services at First Church were orderly and intellectual.

I have reported on how members of the congregation debated and wrestled with choices thrust upon them by developments in the civil rights struggle. While out of the country, I received a letter from Alex Poinsett in March 1966. He reported that his efforts to persuade the Unitarian Church to become involved as an institution in supporting the movement was bearing fruit. Happily, the board of trustees had voted to take $9,000 from the endowment and split it between the SCLC and the CCCO. While this action had to be approved by the congregation, Alex felt that given other steps that had been taken, it would be approved quite easily. Rev. Andrew Young had preached at the church, and a series of photographs taken during the Selma march were on exhibition. Alex concluded, "So the ball is rolling, finally, and I think it will brush aside any opposition."

Soon after Martin Luther King's death in 1968, a group of blacks within the Unitarian denomination decided to assert themselves. During the mid-1960s, they had formed the Black Unitarian Universalist Caucus (BUUC).

The BUUC proceeded to petition the Unitarian Universalist Association (UUA) to establish a Black Affairs Council (BAC) "as a vehicle to express the interests, feelings and aspirations of Black Unitarian Universalists for power within the denomination." The BAC would become an affiliate agency with a clear majority of blacks on its board. The BUUC also called for increased representation of blacks on all of the UUA's policy-making boards and committees and urged it to "make a real financial commitment to black people" by releasing $250,000 each year to BAC for four years to fund community and economic development projects in "Black America." Soon thereafter, another group formed: FULLBAC (comprised of white individuals recruited by Rev. Jack Mendelsohn, minister of Arlington Street Unitarian Church in Boston and later minister of the Chicago Unitarian Church) committed to full funding for BAC. At the same time, an integration-oriented group, BAWA (Black and White Action), emerged to compete with BUUC. At the 1968 UUA General Assembly in Cleveland, the UUA board and President Dana Greeley urged delegates to substitute voluntarily raised funds for the million dollars demanded by BUUC and to accept both BAC and BAWA as affiliate members. However, the General Assembly delegates voted 836 to 326 to form and fund BAC, while BAWA received neither funding nor affiliate status.

Rev. Jack Mendelsohn, minister of First Unitarian Church of Chicago and adviser to Jesse Jackson. Courtesy Jack Mendelsohn.

Then in November 1969, the UUA board, facing a substantial deficit, cut one-third of its budget and voted to reduce the BAC allocation by $500,000 and to stretch its obligation to BAC to five years rather than four. As a result of this action, the BAC voted to disaffiliate with UUA in order to raise its own money, since affiliate groups had to be funded solely by the UUA. Finally, at the 1970 General Assembly held in Seattle, a motion to restore full funding to BAC was defeated. As a result, Alex Poinsett and more than a thousand other African Americans left the denomination.

At the same time, fallout occurred on the other side of the aisle. When word got out that George Sikes (a white person who had marched in Selma in 1965) was told he was not welcome at a BUUC meeting, many in the congregation were upset. Bob Moore and his wife, both African American, decided to leave the church, saying that they believed in integration and objected to the race-conscious direction that BUUC was going.

This development of the Black Power theme proved very disquieting to many of us. I understood the need for blacks to assert their leadership; however, carried too far it could amount to reverse discrimination. Alex made the case for Black Power quite eloquently. Using the words *empowerment* and *self-determination*, he argued that black people should take charge of affairs affecting black people so that white people could no longer tell blacks what their values should be and what was good for their communities. "Because we face racism daily, in both North and South, we are experts," he said.[2]

The dilemmas the church faced were similar to those emerging for the university and, by extension, for me. These were highlighted at various times in my association with Operation Breadbasket when I found myself on the

Black Power movement at Chicago Freedom rally, Soldier Field, 1966. Courtesy Chicago Urban League Records, CULR_04_0092_0966_001, University of Illinois at Chicago Library, Special Collections.

defensive about my employer. Members of the Attunement Committee asked: "The University of Chicago is probably the largest employer and purchaser of services on the South Side of Chicago, so why is it not 'buying black'?" And from my faculty colleagues, a more pointed question: "So, McKersie, wouldn't your energies be better spent getting the university to change its policies than marching around Chicago and acting like some kind of do-gooder?" I never saw it as an either/or choice except to the extent that the reality of only so many hours in the day inevitably created some tradeoffs.

I agreed that getting the university to play a leadership role with respect to its purchases, and getting the faculty to volunteer their technical expertise, would pay big dividends. So I urged the university to consider shifting its business purchases to companies who were part of Operation Breadbasket. In this connection, I contacted Robert Heidrich, the director of purchasing and auxiliary services at the university, and engaged in several rounds of correspondence and conversations with him, identifying companies that the university could consider rostering as preferred providers. As it turned out, one of them, Rual Bolles, already supplied his product, Diamond Sparkle Wax, and Heidrich reported that the university's experience had been positive. He also mentioned that "Part of the problem we must overcome is the feeling by the black businessmen that they are not acceptable or cannot make a direct approach to the university. I think enough word-of-mouth is out now that this stigma is probably beginning to break down, and we will see possibilities where we can work with other black businessmen." At the same time, Heidrich expressed a concern: How to expand the number of black suppliers without raising expectations, only to have some of the applicants turned down.

As another way to leverage the resources of the university, specifically those of the faculty, Al Pitcher and I drafted a letter to all faculty members urging them to consider shifting their checking accounts to banks owned and operated by African Americans. One faculty member, Rand Lincoln, took the time to draft a thoughtful note about the importance of not just calling for deposits into black banks but also changing the policies of white-owned and managed banks:

> Thank you for your letter of March 31 urging me to transfer my checking account to a Negro bank. (My savings are currently deposited in the Hyde Park Bank and Trust Company)
> I am sympathetic to your concern; but before I would consider withdrawing my account from the Hyde Park Bank, I would want to offer that institution an opportunity to provide evidence of its current policies

concerning the financing of Negro-owned enterprises. I assume that your goal in urging people to increase the prosperity of two Negro banks is not the welfare of those institutions per se, but rather is based on the assumption that they will, if resources are available to them, do a better job of financing Negro enterprises than white banks have done. This assumption may well be correct, but should not, I think, be accepted without question. If your current effort has the effect of encouraging white banks to make more sound loans to Negroes, that will also contribute to your goals. I am sending a copy of this letter to the president of the Hyde Park Bank and Trust Company for his information.

Ron Grzywinski, president of the Hyde Park Bank and Trust Company, who received a copy of the letter, subsequently developed a national and international reputation for a program of lending to black homeowners on the South Side of Chicago using loan officers who understood the local community.

Working with the purchasing office and alerting faculty were steps in the right direction, but the potential role the university could play in the economic development of South Side Chicago was huge, and I wanted the institution to embrace this vision. So I drafted a memorandum outlining a program that would expand the function of the university beyond teaching and research. I urged that the staff in the purchasing office of the university be expanded and that purchasing, which had been decentralized, be given strong oversight so people making purchasing decisions would be sensitive to the need to place orders as much as possible in the developing minority business community. I went further and asked that the board of trustees issue a policy statement that would commit the university to doing all it could to help with economic development on the South Side. To this end, it would be desirable to create an arm that would work with community groups like TWO in Woodlawn.

The concept of community development corporations had worked in other regions of the country, and there was a great opportunity to do the same for the pressing needs on Chicago's South Side. Such an organization might receive loan funds from the university's investment portfolio, as well as tapping in to other institutions such as Michael Reese Hospital, and it might also be possible to receive foundation support.

Clearly, I was pressing the university to go far beyond its normal academic role. And while the university had helped create the Southeast Chicago Commission (an organization primarily concerned with the physical development of the South Side and assuring safety on the streets), I was asking for a much more proactive role. While the university did not initiate programs on a scale envisioned in this letter, it did move step by step to connect resources, both financial aid and faculty, to the Woodlawn community.

By the late 1960s, relations between TWO and the university had changed for the better. They were no longer characterized by conflict and contentiousness but instead exhibited elements of accommodation. Leon (Len) Despres best summed up the history of that evolution between the university and its neighbor to the south. He observed that at some point in 1955, soon after he was elected alderman, the then-president of the University of Chicago, Larry Kimpton, invited him to lunch. "The university wants to know what it can do to be of help to you, Mr. Despres." He answered, "You can do something for Woodlawn, because it is a neglected area." Despres commented that Kimpton was not especially responsive to this suggestion.[3]

The low point in the university's relationship with Woodlawn came in 1960 when the university sought to build a submerged expressway down 60th Street from Stony Island to the Midway. This would have created a barrier between the university and Woodlawn. As a result, protesters from the Woodlawn community marched down 63rd Street carrying signs that said, "Woodlawn, Sí; University, No!"

Soon thereafter, Despres and Arthur Brazier attended a meeting in the mayor's office. The university, realizing it had made a mistake, agreed to abandon the highway proposal and expressed interest in developing low-cost housing along Cottage Grove. This represented a change in direction: the university was no longer going to neglect the community. As a result, Brazier and the university began to work together on an important urban renewal program.

Following the federal Model Cities legislation enacted in 1968, cities across the country eagerly responded to the call for applications for funds to cover a wide range of urban improvement projects. The Chicago Department of Housing and Urban Development had designated Woodlawn as the target area for the Mid-South Model Neighborhood Area. Realizing that the city of Chicago was preparing a proposal with little input from the Woodlawn community, TWO asked for help in preparing its own Model City proposal, and a faculty team under the direction of Jack Meltzer, director of the Urban Studies Center, was mobilized to provide technical assistance.

While the university provided substantial manpower (over 40 faculty and students were involved), TWO maintained control and exercised final approval of the plan. Professor Morris Janowitz, who served on the steering committee for the university, articulated this caveat: "The Woodlawn Organization does not believe that experts should determine policy. Although faculty and students have participated in drafting every section of analysis

Bishop Arthur Brazier with the Woodlawn Organization (TWO) members Rosa Scott and Mary Booth, outside TWO headquarters, April 1963. Bishop Brazier cofounded TWO in 1960. Courtesy Chicago History Museum, ICHi-37486

and documentation, every product is the end product of various committees of The Woodlawn Organization and its ruling bodies."[4]

Working groups from the university were organized by subject areas: education, finance, consumer practices, health, social welfare, civil rights, housing, ways and means, employment, and commercial development (the committee I chaired), welfare and family planning, legal rights, and housing and environmental planning.

All the faculty members served in their capacity as individuals; the university did not participate officially as an institution. All our work was done on a *pro bono* basis, and the faculty and graduate students contributed many hours during 1968 and into 1969.

Woodlawn was a community that had experienced rapid changes during the preceding decade. Between 1950 and 1960, the racial composition had flipped from predominantly white to predominantly black, as shown in the table. The economic implications of this transition were profound. In 1966 Woodlawn ranked as one of the ten poorest communities in Chicago, with a median family income of $5,508, compared to the citywide figure of $8,100.[5] In 1968, more than half of the residents of this community lived in poverty, and females headed almost 60 percent of the families.

Census changes, 1950 to 1960

	1950	1960
Whites	48,000	8,000
Blacks	6,000	51,000

Source: Woodlawn Organization (1970), 15.

The analysis and documentation that we assembled went well beyond statistics, concluding that Woodlawn was indeed a community that was "hurting." Julian Levi who, in addition to being a professor of urban studies, chaired the Southeast Chicago Commission offered a poignant description of this reality. "Woodlawn," he said, "is a community where one out of every ten men cannot find a job; where six out of ten high school students drop out; where one out of three children born is illegitimate; and where one-quarter of its population is on welfare. Its infant mortality rates, venereal disease rates, and premarital birth rates are among the highest in the city."[6]

The task force prioritized several goals:

- Education of the young, including new opportunities for education outside of school

- Employment and long-range economic development to help the large number of unemployed young adults

- Income maintenance and the provision of social services needed by many members of the community

- Decent housing and a suitable living environment for every family in Woodlawn.

The proposal provided for the creation of a core corporation with spokes or "pads." The organizational structure included a community board for urban education, a housing and economic development corporation, and a health division. Procedures for community control were specified and seen as key to the governance system. The report emphasized community responsibility with the creation of networks to involve citizens in Woodlawn in the provision and receipt of vital services.

From one perspective, all the work came to naught, as the co-chairs, Leon Finney of TWO and Jack Meltzer of the university, stated in the preface to the proposal: "This TWO Model Cities plan was not accepted by the City of Chicago. Rather, the city and federal government, in the spring of 1969 approved the plan approved by the city's agencies."[7] But even though the version of the model cities plan developed by TWO with the assistance of university staff did not move forward, other joint efforts occurred during the 1960s. Consequently, despite the defeat, TWO used the expertise gained in the planning process, leveraging many features of the plan to establish and administer a series of health, housing, and social services programs.[8]

After TWO failed to win federal approval for its plan, it negotiated a compromise with the city of Chicago and participated in a number of the city's programs. TWO counted over 30 individuals employed in its various initiatives. It is important to note that TWO did not participate in the open housing campaign launched by the SCLC in 1966, preferring to concentrate its attention on improving living conditions in the immediate community and not be seen as working at cross purposes with the city of Chicago.

According to my diary, during the 1960s most of my involvement could be labeled technical assistance. While I marched and participated in demonstrations organized by the NALC and the CCCO, I devoted considerable time to preparing a report using data from the EEOC on the status of minorities in the Chicago labor market and developing a target selection system for the Office of Federal Contract Compliance. In offering the small business seminar that sent students into the field to work with minority-owned businesses, I fulfilled my teaching role while at the same time extending technical assistance. I also became involved with the local Small Business Administration (SBA) center sponsoring a range of programs to help black businessmen, eventually leading to another opportunity for frequent travel to Washington, D.C.

Toward the end of the 1960s, the efforts of organizations like Operation Breadbasket to stimulate business development within the black community took on a more political tone. What could be more attractive to politicians seeking office than advocating programs that fostered entrepreneurship among African Americans? Whites in general were nervous about initiatives that appeared to emphasize the racial divide echoing in the rallying cry of "black power" and black self-determination. So what could be more American than assisting blacks in their desire to start new businesses and to expand existing ones?

Richard Nixon, in the lead-up to the 1968 elections, embraced the concept of black capitalism and a flood of articles appeared touting the possibility of an "achieving ghetto."[9] Several prominent black leaders, such as Floyd McKissick and Ray Innis (both associated with CORE), urged their followers to vote Republican in large part because of Nixon's support for black capitalism.

On the other side of the picture, Andrew Brimmer, a respected economist, a member of the Federal Reserve Board, and an African American, referred to black capitalism as a "cruel hoax" and urged African Americans to work for economic integration.[10] Others saw the idea as a throwback to the Back to Africa Campaign led by Marcus Garvey many decades earlier. Several policy analysts joined the debate, and a series of studies emerged.[11] While no consensus emerged, I felt that black capitalism could be seen as a transition strategy in the same way that affirmative action could jumpstart employment and provide better careers for African Americans.

This perspective informed my own decision to accept a presidential appointment to the Advisory Council for the newly formed Office of Minority Business Enterprise (OMBE) in early 1969. How did this come about? Not because I had voted for President Nixon. I voted for his opponent, Hubert Humphrey. Nor was it due to the influence of George Shultz, the new secretary of labor. When I asked him about this possibility, he commented: "Bob, you got here on your own." I attributed the appointment to my work with the Chicago Economic Development Corporation, an agency supported by the SBA. Both SBA and the new OMBE were housed in the Department of Commerce.

No doubt a contributing influence was the wide dissemination of an article I wrote for the *Harvard Business Review* entitled, "Vitalize Black Enterprises," based on my work with Operation Breadbasket as well as insights gained from my students who provided technical assistance to struggling black businesses on the South Side of Chicago.[12]

Before accepting the appointment, I met with Jesse Jackson, and while he thought I should accept the assignment, he expressed some concerns, which I conveyed to Secretary of Commerce Maurice Stans. I reported that some black leaders like Jackson were very suspicious of "black capitalism" and "minority enterprise" for fear they represented only a token response to the circumstances facing the African American community. The leaders with whom I had talked would rather that the emphasis be on fundamental economic development.

Serving on OMBE and chairing the Business Opportunities Task Force brought me to Washington on a regular basis. President Nixon had appointed as chairman a generous campaign contributor, Sam Wyly, a successful entrepreneur in the new field of computers and data storage. The staff of OMBE was comprised of talented black professionals. The person supporting the Business Opportunities Task Force, Tony Stadeker, had previously worked for the Chicago Economic Development Corporation. I knew Tony well and working with him and OMBE meant working with my head and not just with heart and feet (when marching and demonstrating).

Members of the academic community, especially in the social sciences, love to be called upon to offer advice. It was heartening to be asked for ideas about how to improve minority enterprise and the employment position of blacks. At the same time, it was a good change of pace to have an alternative to the front lines of the civil rights movement. It coincided with my desire to spend more time writing about the strategies and tactics of the movement, as they unfolded, and conducting research on the employment of blacks in the Chicago labor market.

I needed to pursue a research agenda that would help my case for tenure. A major opportunity for obtaining important data came my way when, in 1965, the assistant research director for the Equal Employment Opportunity Commission (EEOC) in Washington, Phyllis Wallace, called and asked if I would be interested in analyzing the first year's data being assembled under the requirements of the recently enacted Civil Rights Act. Phyllis assembled a cadre of scholars from around the country, including Orley Ashenfelter (Princeton), Lester Thurow (MIT), and James Heckman (Columbia, then University of Chicago). We met several times in Washington to discuss our research findings.

I assembled a team of research assistants, and we analyzed the data (stored on computer tapes) to identify patterns in the employment of minorities in the Chicago Standard Metropolitan Statistical Area (SMSA). Gauging the impact of housing segregation on the employment position of African Americans proved to be an important line of analysis. Before concluding that a company might be discriminating in its hiring, it was necessary to account for the time and cost of commuting to its location from the black residential areas on the West Side and the South Side. Our team completed a detailed report—and then came the surprise. The EEOC printed hundreds of copies but declined to be identified with the report, and the copies remained in the commission's warehouse. I never understood the reason for such a bizarre outcome. Was our report shelved because of our findings?

> Twenty-nine percent of all employers in Chicago counted no African Americans on the payroll.

> Only 6 percent employed African Americans in both clerical and blue-collar occupations.

> Most African Americans were employed in low-level occupations.

However, I was not deterred by the inaction of the EEOC. Rather, I embarked on a project for the Office of Federal Contract Compliance and

Programs (OFCCP) in the U.S. Department of Labor. The OFCCP had been created by an executive order issued by President Johnson in the early 1960s as the civil rights movement was gathering momentum. The office was charged with leveraging the purchasing power of the federal government to enhance the employment position of minorities throughout the economy. To fulfill this mission, each supplier or contractor to the federal government was required to develop a plan of action (eventually called "affirmative action") that committed the firm to increase the number and occupational position of underrepresented minorities, defined as black, Hispanic, Native American, and Asian Americans. Rather than using a guideline that each business should "do its best," the OFCCP needed yardsticks that would help it evaluate and decide whether to approve a submitted plan. This is where I came into the picture.

Using EEOC data, several research assistants and I constructed a target selection system that compared the density of (referred to as *penetration*) and occupational level for black employees in a specific firm against the numbers for other firms in the same SMSA. This system, which carried my name, served as a tool for identifying companies that OFCCP could then select as targets, directing them to submit revised affirmative action plans that hopefully would improve the employment position of blacks. The system also was used to justify budget requests and allocate resources for the affirmative action offices of various government agencies.[13]

Eventually there were complaints from government contractors that they were being targeted on the basis of "statistics" without any evidence of discrimination or deliberate exclusion of African Americans. The issue came to a head in a case that reached the Supreme Court. Mississippi Power and Light[14] argued that as a government contractor it was not covered since its only involvement with the federal government was to supply power to federal agencies, a role about which it had no choice. The Supreme Court ruled against the company but told the lower court to review the company's charge that if it was a contractor, it had been arbitrarily selected for review by OFCCP. In the lower court review, the OFCCP argued that the use of the McKersie selection system was proof that its actions were not arbitrary. The target selection system was abandoned when the director of research for the OFCCP, George Travers (who happened to be a PhD from the University of Chicago) moved to another civil service position in the federal government.

So what began with involvement in the work of Operation Breadbasket evolved into activities more typical of those pursued by an academic. A Republican administration had seen political advantage in embracing minority enterprise and from my base in a business school, engaging in research and policy prescription seemed very appropriate to everyone, especially and quite importantly, to my dean.

Although at times I felt vulnerable at the university because I spent time on "outside" activities while colleagues urged me to concentrate on my research agenda, at no time did I feel that my right to engage in activist work was not supported. When the issue arose with Motorola over my attack on their actions to unseat the chair of the state Fair Employment Practices Commission, Dean Shultz protected me. With respect to issues facing nearby communities, the university responded in a variety of ways: with technical assistance to TWO in developing a plan for model cities, with purchasing commitments to minority suppliers, and by instituting the Black MBA program.

Students benefitted from the many learning opportunities available in the Model Cities and Operation Breadbasket programs. Early in the 1960s, without waiting for faculty to take the initiative, a group of students created a clearinghouse for matching requests from black businessmen seeking technical assistance with students anxious to be helpful and relevant. In another instance, twenty students responded to a request from the consulting firm Booz Allen to create an economic development plan for the Kenwood-Oakland community. During this project, several of our students challenged representatives from this community about the goals they had set. These experiences were cited by the students as extremely valuable in preparing for careers in business and government.

Although during the 1960s I had misgivings about the responses of the First Unitarian Church to events in the civil rights arena as those were playing out, my involvement with the church was essential to my development as a person. The best way to characterize the congregation would be the metaphor of "family"—a place where kindred spirits meet and share concerns, with only a subset of the congregation participating in direct action.

From the beginning, churches were at the center of the civil rights movement. Without the leadership of ministers and without the organizational capacity of the denominations to rally members to march and to attend rallies, the push for civil rights would never have become a movement. The early 1960s was a time of fast-moving developments, and members of the Unitarian Church and its minister spent many hours deliberating on the choices to be made. But in terms of follow-through from deliberation to action, too often (to my taste) the congregation never moved beyond the talking stage. However, Unitarians do put their pocketbooks behind social causes: the church, both locally and nationally, committed substantial resources to many socially useful projects. To its credit, the board of trustees, while generally more conservative than the congregation, did allocate resources on several occasions to the civil rights movement and agreed to support a freedom school during the second school boycott.

For me, as a discussion leader and facilitator of discourse, my work with the Adult Discussion Group proved to be the highlight of my association with the church. I enjoyed the experience, assembling background materials and keeping participants with disparate views communicating with each other. The unfolding actions of the CCCO created great material for the group to discuss and certainly threw "hot potatoes" into the lap of the Social Action Committee.

Today the congregation is very much integrated, and the Social Action Committee continues to have a full agenda. In fact, while I was in Hyde Park early in the new century (May 2003), I witnessed a march that brought intense feelings of déjà vu. As my wife and I returned to our former neighbor's home on Sunday afternoon about 3:00, there ahead of us, stretching several blocks, loomed a line of marchers en route from the Unitarian Church, proceeding north to 53rd Street, and over to a park near Lake Michigan. The day was cold, and the marchers moved vigorously to keep warm. Then I recalled seeing a flyer at the church that morning announcing a march to protest the war in Iraq organized by the church's Social Action Committee. So, while the agenda had progressed from marching for civil rights to other, newer issues, the energy and enthusiasm of the members of the church had remained vigorous—perhaps even more so, given the hesitant moves of the Social Action Committee during the 1960s.

While during the 1960s I may have often been impatient with what I saw as too much talk and not enough participation in the direct-action programs of the civil rights movement, nevertheless the church provided a gateway for members of the congregation to become involved in the cause. It also served as a multiracial meeting ground, allowing members to examine the moral dimensions of complex and entrenched social issues and problems. By helping me focus on the values that informed and framed the complex world of race relations, the church community provided a good undergirding for the "rational-analytic" debates that infused (and continue to infuse) my social science research.

13. Race Relations and the Personal Equation

One lives by hope. It's not merely my middle
name. It's my life. I live by hope.

—John Hope Franklin

Although the historical assessments of gains for African Americans emanating from the civil rights struggles of the 1960s are inconclusive, I would count my involvement in the civil rights movement as the most important chapter in my several careers as an academic, a practitioner, and a cheerleader for social change. Ultimately, how I feel about events of that period can be reduced to a personal equation. While this story is about a movement and the institutions involved in that movement, it is more importantly a story about leaders, about individuals I observed at close range who, in varying degrees, I came to know as friends and close associates.

Daniel Thompson, in his probing study of black leaders, describes a spectrum of approaches ranging from Uncle Toms, to diplomats, to race men.[1] During the 1960s, the Uncle Toms on the scene would have been the black aldermen who were beholden to Mayor Daley and took no part in the civil rights movement. One racial diplomat clearly was Bill Berry who, as head of the Urban League, was well connected to the power structure of the city while at the same time he played an influential role within the CCCO—even becoming the co-convener when Al Raby retired. Tim Black, Alex Poinsett, and Jesse Jackson were race men whom I came to know and admire. Before paying my respects to these three individuals, there is one other hero I would like to salute.

The civil rights leader I got to know best was Al Pitcher. He lived with our family for a summer, and we were both faculty members at the University of Chicago. He exuded warmth, compassion, selflessness, and a self-effacing and supportive style of leadership. Pitcher is someone I would call a "master": someone with conviction, yet a willingness to take on any chore that needed attention. He wrote press releases, developed strategic plans, chaired meetings (only when the requisite black talent was not present), and advised key leaders (especially the more zealous individuals) about the necessity to address political realities.

Pitcher's career illustrates the important point that effective leadership does not have to be charismatic. Staff support is crucial, and dedicated individuals like Al Pitcher made a huge difference in the CCCO's ability to get itself organized and to function as well and as long as it did.

A eulogy published in the *University of Chicago Record* captures the essence of Al Pitcher: "Most of all, however, Al is a warm human being who has a capacity to listen deeply to people. He manages to act in small, nitty-gritty, concrete ways in people's lives while at the same time thinking and acting globally."[2]

Turning to the person who was my entrée into the movement, Tim Black had more influence on me than anyone else. With Tim, I never had the feeling that I was pushing my way into the movement. On the contrary, at times I failed to meet his expectations for my getting involved more deeply. On one occasion, Tim called the house when I was out of town. He told Nancy, "You know he has to keep involved."

To Tim's credit, he orchestrated my participation with considerable skill—recall the episode when I was the only white person attending a planning meeting held by the NALC leadership team, and Tim offered a gracious hint to leave: "Bob, we know you are busy, so don't feel you have to stay." I look back on that moment with some amusement and admiration for his ability to tap my energies and at the same time to deal with his colleagues' desires to have their organization directed solely by African Americans.

Paula Pfeffer, in her biography of A. Philip Randolph, reports that most members of the national NALC governing group wanted their organization to be run exclusively by blacks. Likewise, Tim found himself managing the same sort of tensions in Chicago as Randolph, who as a vice president of the national AFL-CIO could not close the door to involvement by interested whites.[3]

Mary King describes the soul searching she experienced when in 1964 SNCC decided to "expel" whites.[4] By contrast, the activist organizations NALC, CCCO and Operation Breadbasket with which I worked sent "messages" for whites to stay in the background in supportive roles but never closed the door to our participation.

Tim and I have kept in touch, and during one of my trips to Chicago for a board meeting, we agreed to meet for breakfast at the famous interracial meeting ground on 53rd Street, the Valois Restaurant. A graduate student at the University of Chicago, writing his dissertation in the spirit of *Street Corner Society*, turned it into a book called *Slim's Table*, which observed the social dynamics of this establishment.[5] Actually, another book could be written entitled "Tim's Table," since it seemed like half the restaurant knew Tim, greeting him with "Hello! How ya' doing? Fine, fine!" as they passed by.

I wanted Tim to help me fill in some gaps, primarily names, in several episodes in this memoir. Tim, now in his early nineties, had the recall ability of a young man. In many ways, Tim Black reminds me of Adlai Stevenson. Both leaders sought, without success, election to a high office. Stevenson, of course, wanted to be president. Tim Black started to campaign for a seat in the state assembly, but it was aborted by a behind-the-scenes deal orchestrated by Bill Berry of the Urban League. Like Stevenson, Tim always took the high road: an example of this was his decision to call off the demonstration against Motorola when the company agreed to meet, despite the fact that it angered many of his supporters. Stevenson became an elder statesman and adviser to several presidents. In his own right, Tim Black has served just as well.

He has no peer in his grasp of the civil rights scene. As a teacher, as the leader of the former Chicago branch of the NALC, and as a writer and commentator on race relations and the social agenda facing our country, Tim continues to be an incomparable resource. Despite his age, he maintains a full schedule and is completing a major writing project that presents the life stories of two generations of blacks, starting with those who grew up in the South and moved to Chicago, to the present generation that is moving ahead on a wide range of professional and business opportunities.[6]

Tim's life tracks how far we have come in race relations. In an oral history project, he recounts this event: "During World War II, I was on a bus in Richmond, Virginia, in uniform, on my way to Camp Butner to see my brother. This white fellow, not in uniform, gets on the bus with his girlfriend. He comes up to me and says, 'You will have to go to the back of the bus.' I said, 'What do you mean?' He said, 'That's the law.' I responded, 'you mean I am going overseas to lose my life for you? I'm not going to move.' At that moment in my life I was prepared to die."[7] Fortunately, the white fellow backed down and Tim did not die.

Jesse Jackson, who like Tim Black is a race man, had a powerful influence on me. To be honest, I was "swept off my feet" during the early days of

Operation Breadbasket. Attending Saturday morning breakfast meetings at the Chicago Theological Seminary and watching Jesse in action—building a community, motivating struggling black businessmen to raise their sights, and preaching to many admiring gatherers—this weekly event was a wonderful tonic for a young assistant professor questioning the social utility of his teaching and research.

As Operation Breadbasket thrived, I came into closer contact with Jesse, serving on the Attunement Committee and conducting seminars for students who were assisting member companies with business development. While involvement in the Attunement Committee created some dilemmas for me, since its *modus operandi* at times resembled a cartel, on balance I found my involvement in Operation Breadbasket extremely worthwhile and my interactions with Jesse in many behind-the-scenes meetings very engaging and inspiring.

After leaving Chicago in 1971, I followed Jesse's career in the newspapers. In many respects, it unfolded in spectacular fashion: two runs for president of the United States in 1984 and 1988, missions to several countries as a troubleshooter and peacemaker, and father to former U.S. Congressman Jesse Jackson Jr. I sometimes turned to him for advice. Given the expectation that I would be joining the Nixon Administration in 1969 (I had been asked to head up the Office of Minority Business Enterprise), I wanted to elicit his reactions and, truth be told, receive his blessing. Ultimately, I did not go to Washington on a full-time basis—but not due to any advice against it from Jesse. In fact, he supported the move and saw some advantages for Operation Breadbasket.

Jesse's genius rests with his keen sense of how to mobilize and deploy power—presumably for good ends. While the nonconfrontational and more deliberate approach of organizations like the Urban League had been utilized for decades, truth be told, progress in race relations had been painfully slow. It was time for new strategies and tactics, and Jesse saw the opportunities.

Certainly many businesses targeted by Jesse considered him and Operation Breadbasket coercive, always asking for more. By urging customers to stop making purchases from stores that did not provide shelf space and services for black businesses, Operation Breadbasket was following a long U.S. tradition of groups organizing to promote their own advancement. Despite his youth and inexperience, Jesse had the ability to create a practical vision of economic development and growth for struggling black businesses. He understood their operating needs and the multiplier effect for the larger black community in obtaining outlets for their products.

Was Jesse an opportunist when he convinced the SCLC to create a franchise for Operation Breadbasket in Chicago and then, after the death of

Martin Luther King, establishing an independent operation under the banner of Operation Push and eventually merging it with his political organization, the Rainbow Coalition? Possibly so. But without his strong leadership, it is unlikely that the civil rights movement in Chicago would have been as effective as it was during the late 1960s and into the early 1970s.

I know of no person on the national scene who is more available to speak and champion the interests of the disenfranchised. In my own field of industrial relations, Jesse has been very effective. Early in the new century, he went to Los Angeles and mediated a settlement between the transportation authority and striking drivers. In other instances, he has championed workers who were seeking representation and collective bargaining rights.

How is he viewed by people whose opinion I respect? I know how Al Pitcher felt about him: "A man for all seasons." When I interviewed Harold Baron, former research director for the Urban League, he commented, "Jesse Jackson is the most skilled media communicator I have ever seen—and I've lived with a few: Bill Berry, Martin Luther King, and Harold Washington. His sheer capacity is amazing. I've seen Jesse in 30 seconds think of things that would take me three days to think up."[8]

When I met with Jack Mendelsohn, who had been minister of First Unitarian Church from the late 1960s through the early 1980s, he described his trip to Syria with Jesse Jackson, which took place in an effort to secure the release of a downed American flyer who happened to be African American. Jesse took several ministers with him on this "unofficial" trip. Mendelsohn attended all the meetings, including the final and crucial one when President Assad agreed to release Lt. Robert Goodwin. "Jesse was eloquent, respectful, and most importantly, persuasive." Mendelsohn related what happened next, when word came to the delegation that Goodwin would be released: "He grabbed me around the waist, lifted me up. And we spun around in a victory dance! The only problem is that I ended up with a cracked rib. Jesse's prowess at football, executing a good tackle, left me hurting for several weeks."[9]

Having watched Jesse for much of his career, from a young divinity school student mobilizing struggling black businessmen into a functioning community, to a presidential candidate with a penchant for always finding the limelight, several adjectives come to mind: inspired preacher, consummate negotiator, organization builder, counselor to the powerful, and ambitious. Jesse is the most prominent surviving representative of the leadership group from the Chicago civil rights movement of the 1960s. His longevity is a testament to his organizational skills and resourcefulness.

Why haven't other leaders cut from this cloth emerged? The answer is that direct-action organizations of the type that were prominent in the 1960s are not as prominent today, at least for racial issues. Today, black leaders are much more likely to emerge in education, business, and government.[10]

On one of my regular trips to Chicago early in the new century (October 2003), I decided to stay over and attend the weekly Saturday morning meeting of Operation Push. The meeting was scheduled to start at 10:00 A.M., and I arrived at approximately 10:45 A.M. (past experience told me that not much of significance would happen during the first half-hour). Upon entering the sanctuary of what had formerly been the KAM Temple, I experienced a flashback to the time when I had visited and attended a Jewish service in this building. Now, instead of the Torah at the front of the sanctuary, there was a large picture of Martin Luther King. The stage also held a choir (all but two members were African American) and a four-piece band.

The session was well underway, and Jesse, with his usual fervor and dynamic presence, was speaking to the "flock." People had been directed to sit on one side of the sanctuary, so this section was filled from front to back. This created the picture of a very full house since the meeting was televised on a community cable channel operated by his organization, as well as being videotaped for future streaming on the Web. Jesse had been talking for ten to fifteen minutes, and he would talk for another forty-five minutes. During this time, he dealt with a wide range of subjects, including many of the political issues of the day, such as the possible bankruptcy of United Airlines and what this would mean for employment in Chicago. He called on the Bush administration to approve a loan for United and to give this company the same consideration that earlier administrations had given to Chrysler and to Continental Bank. He asked for volunteers to be trained for work in a lead removal program. He sought volunteers to perform a variety of social services for folks who lived by themselves and could not prepare meals without help or just needed someone to talk to. Since it was October, he had some things to say about the upcoming winter, using the example of the squirrel that prepares for the winter ahead. "No squirrels go hungry!" This was a lead-in to an event that was to happen after the meeting—the distribution of several hundred bags of food to needy folks in nearby neighborhoods. He focused on the alarming statistic that 14,000 homes in Illinois were without heat.

He then moved into high gear, describing a program that his organization had worked out with Governor Ryan and utility companies to release funds so that people with delinquent accounts could have their gas and electricity turned on again. He introduced representatives from the administrations of both the outgoing and incoming governors who spoke and answered questions from reporters in attendance about his efforts to provide heat to the distressed.

As Jesse neared the end of his talk, the band sensed its opportunity and started to play. The "congregation" rose to its feet with clapping and many gestures of "We are with you, Jesse." In fact, throughout his talk, members of the choir would stand and clap, and the whole proceeding exhibited high involvement on the part of the audience. As the talk progressed, he periodically pulled a handkerchief from his pocket and wiped his brow—all of this attesting to the intensity of his preaching.

Before adjourning, Jesse asked for those who could contribute $100 to come forward, and he then proceeded to read 50 or 60 names. Then he moved to the $50 level, then to $25. The meeting could be described as part church service, part political rally, and certainly a fund-raising event.

When the session ended at approximately noon, one of Jesse's associates, Gary Massoni, took me on a tour of the premises. The offices are numerous, as more than forty individuals work for the organization. An addition has been built at the back of the synagogue to house a new office for Jesse and to provide space for a telephone center and a complete broadcasting unit. As we left the building for lunch, I observed scores of people lining up to receive the food bundles that had been assembled by the staff.

I pondered the juxtaposition of two pieces of my life coming together. As guests of our friends and neighbors the Patners, Nancy and I had attended a worship service at KAM during the 1960s. Aside from the fascination of an ecumenical experience, I had wanted to meet the rabbi, Jacob Weinstein, who was well known in my field of labor relations for his work as a mediator. Now this building served as the headquarters for Jesse's many initiatives and in a symbolic way as a type of bridge between Jews and blacks—two communities with a very complicated joint history.

My fourth hero is Alex Poinsett, a frequent sparring partner. Alex and I have been friends for over forty years. At times I am certain that I have been boring, given the number of times I used him to get race-related thoughts off my chest. Fortunately, our friendship has continued. He is a consummate thinker and writer,[11] and the two of us have engaged in many spirited discussions. I have been the beneficiary of these sessions, and a major motivation for this book has been to return the favor and to provide another outlet for his wisdom and passionate convictions.

Early in my sabbatical leave during the 1960s, I used a letter to Alex to vent my feelings about the predicament of the white liberal. I opened the letter with the point that "the white liberal is damned if he does and damned if he doesn't." I reflected on the assumption held by many of us that if we approached the minority question by eliminating attention to race (e.g., removing it from employment applications), then discrimination would go away and members of the minority and majority populations would be treated equally. This did not happen. As a consequence, an important emphasis of the civil rights revolution has been to bring attention back to race in an explicit way. But this has forced us to always be talking about "race relations." Blacks may appreciate this concern, but on the other hand, this attention can be suffocating and degrading.

I pinpointed the core of the dilemma: it may be easier for blacks to assert their manhood in opposition to someone who is racist than to engage in friendship with a white liberal. I observed that perhaps blacks would prefer that white liberals come out and reveal their hidden, perhaps unconscious racist attitudes, since then it would be easier for blacks to know who they were really up against.

Closing my letter, I wondered whether the typical black would have any concern for this predicament of the white liberal. The black may experience an inability to really express his manhood, but at the same time the white liberal feels an inadequacy in expressing his ambivalence about black power. I said that frank dialogue was the only solution. Ignoring race would not be honest, and since it is clearly on the minds of blacks and liberals, it needed to be brought out into the open. At the same time we could not return to ignoring race; we have to move beyond viewing each other as "aroused" blacks and white liberals.

Alex responded:

I agree with your lament that the white liberal is damned if he does and damned if he doesn't. Paradoxically, his dilemma arises out of the very fact that he is a liberal rather than relevant—which is to say, radical. Generally, he is content to accommodate himself—and hence the Negro—to existing socio-political arrangements rather than fighting to transform them at their very core. Where order and justice collide, he prefers order because it satisfies his rationalistic sense of things. He wants results without risks, freedom without danger, and love without hate. Thus, for example, the liberal will pass a voting rights bill. People like myself and the members of SNCC refuse to say "thank you" because we know the major problem—enforcement—is still unsolved partially because its solution may in fact cause temporary disorder. Instead, we would urge liberals to do what they don't seem to have the courage to do: unseat the Mississippi delegation, send Federal voting registrars to all of the diehard counties of the South—not just a token few—and punish those who still intimidate and even murder prospective Negro voters.

How can we celebrate the series of concessions that have been forced by white liberals and middle class Negroes (the main beneficiaries of the civil rights movement), when we know the lower class Negro—about two-thirds of all Negroes—remains without hope? We see the lower class Negro family disintegrating. We see the overwhelming majority of Negroes still relegated to mop, handle and broom occupations. We see the unemployment rate among Negroes still doubling that of whites. We see the income gap between Negroes and whites widening rather than narrowing. We see the Negro still shortchanged in education, housing and politics. Too much work remains undone.

You speak to me of the white liberal's guilt. I am sympathetic, but did you know I have to fight myself daily to keep from being a racist? Dammit, I know all whites aren't bastards. Experience tells me that. Logic tells me that. White liberals tell me that. And then a southern white jury mocks the justice we boast about by freeing a Klan murderer. Or Mayor Daley forces the U.S. Commissioner of Education to withdraw his order withholding $30 million in federal funds from Chicago schools, accused by the CCCO of violating the 1964 Civil Rights Act. Isn't it painfully true, after all, that the many flagrant forms of racial injustice North and South could not exist without the acquiescence of liberals? In the face of that ugly reality, compassion for liberals—and I really shouldn't lump them all together—doesn't come easy.

I tell you, Bob, given our country's long and dishonorable history of racism, the overpowering urge is for revenge, for blood even. Hasn't America, like the Germans, committed racial genocide on a less-publicized scale? Haven't Negroes been gang-raped by whites then accused of promiscuity? How, then, can you remain civilized and sane while being a Negro in America? I suppose the good intentions of white liberals plus a tenacious clinging to hope has stayed our hand, otherwise the nation might long ago have had the Los Angeles riots multiplied a thousand-fold. And there would be no Negro problem, because by now Negroes would have been wiped out like the Indians. But also by now there might have been no country. You are caught in a cruel dilemma: somehow, in spite of everything, you love your country—it's the only one you have—and at the same time you entertain frightening thoughts like "burn baby burn!"

I suppose my own special bag is the need to act out on paper the aggressions that I'm too cowardly–and too educated—to act out in person. But I'm sure my blast furnace shows sometimes . . .

Well, buddy, that's the mood of the moment. Let's keep the dialogue going. We may not solve the race problem, but we may be able to strengthen whatever it is we have between us.

I have kept in touch with Alex, and in 1998 I invited him to participate in a *festschrift* in my honor at MIT. I noted that the agenda—while it covered my research interests—did not highlight my main passion and commitment over the years, namely, working in a variety of ways to improve race relations. Tom Kochan, organizer of the conference, agreed that we should find a way to do this, and I organized a panel discussion.

The first person I thought to invite was Alex; I also invited Malcolm Lovell to be on the panel. Malcolm had been a protégé of George Romney and considers himself a progressive—for example, he spearheaded a study of race relations under the auspices of the National Policy Association (NPA) where he had served as executive director for many years.

During the panel, Alex offered these thoughts on the topic of American race relations:

> During the civil rights movement in the 1960s, "racial integration" was sought by many African and European Americans. But integration was cultural suicide. African Americans could enter society's mainstream provided they were willing to accept its narcissistic stress on Western thought and institutions that embodied a myopic and limited view of the world and perpetuated the myth of civilization as a European monopoly. Meanwhile, despite the Supreme Court's momentous 1954 school desegregation decision, African Americans remained unwelcome in the U.S. mainstream. This was graphically illustrated, for example, by the turtle-slow pace of school, housing, and job desegregation. "You're not welcome" was illustrated by the mass beatings and jailing of black students who bravely staged lunch-counter sit-ins and freedom rides in the South, or risked their lives for so-called "integrated education" or for voter registration. Author James Baldwin was so angered by these and other spectacles of moral degeneracy, he asked, "Who wants to be integrated into a burning house?"

Alex's presentation generated wide-ranging reaction. A number of people said it was the best part of the two-day conference. Malcolm did not agree with the views expressed by Alex, so I asked him to put his thoughts on paper. Here is what he wrote:

> While it is certainly true that Black Americans have been trespassed against over the past several hundred years to a disgraceful degree, forgiveness is just as necessary for dreadful sins as it is an important ingredient for dealing with lesser indiscretions. And this is particularly

important because those who cannot forgive, in the long run, arguably suffer more than those who are not forgiven.

Clearly the majority of Black citizens in America today are less well off than the majority of people of European and perhaps Asian background. Certainly, however, the last 50 years have shown remarkable and dramatic improvement in the opportunities available to our Black citizens into a way of life, which they are in large numbers embracing.

Malcolm then referred to the study NPA had commissioned:

New Directions in Thinking about Race in America: African Americans in a Diversifying Nation concluded with the following recommendations:

1. Vigorous enforcement of racial and ethnic antidiscrimination laws in education, employment, housing, politics, health services, and criminal justice.
2. Development of a comprehensive private sector plan that addresses the long history of unequal racial treatment.
3. Rebuilding of neighborhoods and central cities.
4. Creation of programs that strengthen family formation and maintenance.
5. Implementation of educational and work opportunities for all.
6. Provision of transportation systems that permit access to good jobs and decent living conditions.

It is these positive actions that will move us as a nation toward our goals of economic and social equity. We must look to the future, not to the past. Sometimes slowly sometimes more vigorously, the black population in the United States is now clearly experiencing an ever increasing standard of living and great progress in building for the future.[12]

Alex and Malcolm enter the arena of race relations from very different starting points. Alex, early on, suffered the indignity of being treated as a second-class citizen, and he sees so many systems still in place that lock the black person into the status quo. Malcolm, a progressive Republican is, by nature, an optimist and celebrates the increasing prosperity that African Americans have experienced.

During the 2008 presidential election, which placed an African American in a contest with a European American, this juxtaposition of views held by Poinsett and Lovell mirrored the discussion that took place on the campaign trail as well as in bars and talk shows across the country. Can these viewpoints be reconciled? Is there common ground? On one point both Poinsett and Lovell agree: the disparity in outcomes for blacks, when measured against other members of society, is troubling. This gap needs to be recognized, highlighted, and addressed.

Just how the disadvantage should be addressed is the question to which many different answers have been offered. Some activists advocate reparations and quotas to close the gap. Poinsett does not support remediation, and certainly Lovell would oppose such steps except where discrimination has clearly occurred; in those cases, remedies should be mandated for those who have been denied equal opportunity. Tracking economic outcomes can be a yardstick for gauging how well we are doing as a nation, but it is not a sufficient guideline for how individuals in specific situations are treated. At the micro level, the operative concept should be focused on equal opportunity. Of course, public policy needs to recognize persistent deficits in education and social conditions that make it difficult for minorities to pursue the opportunities that could produce improved outcomes. In this connection, the types of programs mentioned by Lovell, such as upgrading educational and infrastructure systems, are necessary to put disadvantaged citizens into the "ballgame."

Where Poinsett and Lovell part company is on the question of integration as a policy goal. Poinsett sees integration as leading to a loss of identity for the African American community, what he refers to as "cultural suicide." Lovell endorses integration, as would most whites who call themselves progressive or liberal, for the expected benefit to society when any group leaves its "neighborhood" and mixes with others in the larger society.

Would the black youngsters from the streets of Philadelphia who spent ten days of their summer vacation at University Camp have been as well served if the leaders of the camp had permitted the separation of the races by camp periods to continue? I doubt it, and this point could be amplified many times by the experience of our armed forces, organizations that dramatize the powerful social gains realized when soldiers of all colors serve side by side in integrated units. An example closer to home that needs no further elaboration: Deval Patrick, a youngster growing up in a single-parent household in the inner city of Chicago, is given a scholarship to attend Milton Academy (Massachusetts) and, as they say, the rest is history. Patrick became governor of the Commonwealth of Massachusetts in 2006.

Reconciling different views about integration is not easy. Certainly, the leaders of the civil rights movement during the 1960s saw the integration of all the classrooms in the Chicago school system as *the* important objective. Data demonstrated that predominantly black schools lagged behind those of their white counterparts in funding and in teacher experience. So integration was seen as a means to achieving a better educational experience for all blacks. The leadership of the CCCO knew that the premise of the Supreme Court decision contained in *Brown v. Board of Education*, that separate is not equal, was validated by the situation facing the black community: the use of makeshift trailers to handle the overflow of crowded classrooms on the South Side and West Side of the city was terribly shortsighted.

Integration also became a major theme on the employment front, especially for occupations that had previously excluded blacks, such as those in the construction trades and skilled manufacturing (e.g., soldering work at Motorola). But integration was not a goal mandated by legislation in the 1960s. Rather, the public policy standard was framed in terms of equal opportunity: Blacks should not be discriminated against because of their skin color. This emphasis on equal opportunity and not integration also characterized the SCLC campaign for open housing during the summer of 1966 in Chicago. The task of achieving housing integration—even if, for the sake of argument, it were accepted as a worthwhile goal—presents a number of dilemmas. There are very few examples in the United States of what could be described as stable, integrated neighborhoods. Hyde Park in Chicago meets this test, but its uniqueness is attributable to the stabilizing influence of the University of Chicago. Elsewhere in Chicago, integration in housing describes the brief period between the arrival of the first black family and the time when the neighborhood—previously all white—turns all black.

This is not to say that in 2012 a black who wants to live in an upscale community, such as the North Side of Chicago, would face the same barriers to owning a home as was the case in 1966, at the time of the marches for open occupancy. Milt Davis, an African American who worked for a time in computer support at the Graduate School of Business before joining South Shore Bank, where he played a key role in the bank's initiative to foster urban redevelopment, commented, in the same vein as William Julius Wilson, on Magic Johnson's ability to live on the "tony" North Side of Chicago, implying that class has become more important than race in understanding how residential patterns are formed.[13]

How can the reality of Chicago as one of the most segregated cities in the country in terms of housing be reconciled with Milt Davis's observation that the opportunity for blacks to live where they want has increased significantly over the last forty years? As Poinsett points out, a shift has occurred in the thinking of many blacks as to whether they want to live in white neighborhoods. And while more needs to be done to make equal housing opportunity a reality, and while it is important to have the option to live in the same communities as whites and to have this guaranteed by law and enforced by government, nevertheless these may be options *not* exercised.

Why is this? It would be presumptuous for me to speak from the perspective of an African American. However, in my conversations with Alex Poinsett, he spoke to this issue. While Alex respected Martin Luther King's goal of integration, for Alex it was not possible "to integrate elephants and gophers because of the unequal power relationship and the unlevel playing field." For Alex, integration was a one-way street of movement of black to white and an assimilation process in which African Americans—instead of affirming their unique gifts—were becoming carbon copies of whites.

Alex maintains that the educational goals of the civil rights movement during the 1960s were misguided. Instead, he believes that the demand of the civil rights movement should have been to make the black schools as good as the white schools. Recall Bob Moore, speaking at a meeting in the Unitarian Church back in the 1960s, arguing in favor of improving education in the schools and not focusing on busing and integration. Similarly, many African Americans are embracing the notion that "black children do not need to sit next to white children to learn."

Many whites do not understand why blacks have pulled back from social integration. Why are they not interested in assimilation now that the barriers have (to some extent) been taken down? Other ethnic groups in the past and now new immigrant groups arriving on the scene, especially those from Asia, have demonstrated that the American melting pot is still working. Why have some blacks been reluctant to become Americans without any prefix? The answer must come from blacks.

Significantly, the emphasis on diversity and the celebration of the distinctiveness of the many racial and ethnic groups that now constitute the United States population has taken some focus away from African Americans. To the extent that schools support programs that honor cultural diversity, blacks can take pride in their own uniqueness and refuse to be homogenized. But the emphasis on diversity contains a major downside. This point is poignantly articulated by Norma Poinsett: "If you erase me out of a key role, and I become subsumed in the catch-all of diversity, and a member of another ethnic group takes the lead, that person is not going to represent me. For me, if I am not there, then nothing of value happens to me."[14]

While integration in housing and education may not be embraced in all quarters, the attitudes and behavior in the employment and business sectors have changed significantly. Commitment to inclusion and affirmative action is very evident within the American business community. Whether for reasons of high principle or good business ("our customers like to be served by a workforce that mirrors the larger population"), the racial makeup of business continues to evince increasing diversity. Even if this means less focus on hiring blacks per se, the emphasis on diversity in employment cannot but help benefit blacks along with Hispanic and Native American groups.

As I was writing an early draft of the final chapter of this story—part memoir, part chronicle, and part commentary—the campaign for the 2008 presidential election was in high gear. The subject of race, which emerged only briefly during the early days of the campaign, moved front and center when the Democratic candidate, Senator Barack Obama, found himself backed into a corner as a result of the fiery rhetoric of his minister, Rev. Jeremiah Wright. The episode culminated in a speech by Obama (appropriately, in Philadelphia) in which he called for an honest dialogue on race—something that John Hope Franklin, the chair of President Clinton's task force on race relations, had also urged on all Americans in 1997.[15]

Why has it been so difficult for blacks and whites to have a serious conversation about race? It is not due to the fact that thoughts about race

Dr. Norma Poinsett, a retired teacher, a member of First Unitarian Church, and the holder of key national leadership positions in the denomination, as well as an honorary doctorate from Meadville Theological School, Chicago. Courtesy Norma Poinsett

are absent from the minds of most Americans. On the contrary, they are often present, but articulating them opens the door to many traps and dilemmas. The first hurdle is that blacks, as individuals, find it uncomfortable to talk about racial issues every time they are in conversation with whites. It is one thing for whites to be concerned about the conditions facing an important segment of our population—poverty, inferior education, poor housing—all disparities that the civil rights movement attempted to redress. But this should not require individual blacks to always serve as interpreters of the problems facing their race. Taylor Branch makes the point this way: "In the years since [the March on Washington], the search for common ground has not gotten any easier."[16]

I am reminded of the reaction of a black whom I was anxious to recruit to my staff early in my tenure as a dean at Cornell. Certainly, considerations of affirmative action were on my mind, but I was wise enough not to mention this subject in our early conversations. But the candidate spoke to the issue: "I hope I am not being hired because I am black." He certainly was highly qualified, but there may have been some whites who were even more suited for the position. I responded disingenuously that affirmative action was not involved. Would the discourse on race have been better served if I had been more forthright? At the time I did not know how to formulate an answer that would have met his desire to be judged without reference to the color of his skin and my desire to bring a qualified *black* person onto my team.

In his Philadelphia speech, Obama acknowledged the resentment that is often generated by affirmative action, especially among whites who witness well-intentioned efforts to advance blacks who are not ready for the move. Don Perkins, former CEO of Jewel Tea, commented on this danger: "Because we had our older stores in the inner city, we needed to hire a black workforce, which reminds me of the mistake we made. We really did try to bring blacks into management. I finally learned that when we pushed people into jobs they weren't ready for, they failed. We didn't do what we should have done, and we ruined some careers in the process."[17]

Whites sometimes make the mistake that since blacks often talk about race when they are together—and this is especially true for black ministers preaching to their black congregations (to wit, the comments made by Reverend Wright)—then it must be equally appropriate for whites to raise race-related topics with blacks when in their company. From time to time, I have to catch myself from falling into this trap. At some point in 2010, a black family moved into the house across the street—a first for our neighborhood. On Memorial Day each year, a group of black Masons from a Boston Masonic Chapter hold services at a cemetery in our community to honor their founder. The fact that the cemetery is not in Boston but was established in what at the time was farmland west of Cambridge speaks to the lamentable attitude prevalent over a century ago: "We do not want your [black] dead buried near us."

So on the morning of the service, I crossed the street to have a friendly conversation with our black neighbors. At some point after we had talked about dealing with winter burn on our lawns and the nocturnal activities of the raccoon that lived in the nearby sewer, I decided to review the events that would be taking place in our town. I mentioned that the annual Memorial Day parade was about to take place on nearby Massachusetts Avenue. Then in passing I described another commemoration that would be taking place in town, this one sponsored by black Masons. I added that my father had been a Mason, and my grandfather had served as grand master. Then, as coincidence would have it, my neighbor mentioned that his father was also a Mason. He did not ask for directions to the cemetery, and he spent the remainder of the day doing what most Americans do on summer holidays—working in the yard, barbequing and relaxing.

This interaction came off better than many of my conversations with blacks during the 1960s. Then, most of my conversations with African Americans in some way addressed the "black condition" and overlooked the interests and richness of the individuals with whom I was interacting. I often think back to the comment made to me by a staff member from *Ebony*, at a party at Alex Poinsett's home: "I did not come to this party to talk only about civil rights. If I had known this, I would have stayed at the office." By persisting in asking questions about race relations, I did not relate to him as a person but solely as another resource for gathering data. No one likes to be treated in such a clinical (perhaps exploitive) way.

Is it possible to associate with blacks without race intruding into the relationship? It has to be attempted. I tried to discuss this issue in a letter to Alex in November 1965. I wrote: "Let me apologize for raising the question of race relations so explicitly in our correspondence. When I told Nancy the gist of what I had sent off to you several weeks ago she exclaimed: "You are obsessed—can't you talk with Alex about other things?" In a way she is right, but in a way there is more to the issue. People develop reasons for a dialogue. And when a white man and black man start interacting, race is bound to color everything."

While working with the NALC, CCCO, and Operation Breadbasket, all of the talk in meetings, as well as before and after the sessions, focused on the "black condition." Such dialogue placed whites in the position of "looking in" at the situation and experience of a disadvantaged element of our society. Most blacks on the receiving end of concern and willingness by whites to "help right the wrongs" see such concerns as helpful; others see such offers of assistance as demeaning and continuing a "plantation mentality" where the white folks "do good works" and the blacks are expected to show gratitude.[18]

As the civil rights movement evolved in the direction of Black Power and the oft-stated desire by black leaders to be in charge and for whites to stay in the deep background, most of us who were on the scene understood this newly voiced need for self-determination; yet at the same time, we felt a loss at no longer being needed. Blacks were pulling back, and this proved unsettling.

Achieving the right balance between involvement and respect for the leadership potential of blacks is not easy, but it is possible. Black leaders held key positions in the CCCO and Operation Breadbasket, at the same time whites were encouraged to play supporting roles. By contrast, the NALC and Sullivan's Operation Breadbasket in Philadelphia tended to exclude white participation. Al Pitcher illustrated how a white person could be for "all seasons": he stayed in the background, playing a very complementary role, as black leaders emerged and acquired credibility in the civil rights movement of Chicago.

Both blacks and whites face the same reality: they cannot change their skin color. But whites do not have their skin color regularly used as a descriptor. We do not resort to language with such labels as "*white* soccer moms," or "*white* lunch-bucket workers." But this is not the case for blacks. They are constantly reminded that their skin color is salient—and they will be described often as black truck drivers, black athletes, and black musicians.

The American dream of "making it"—of succeeding and having one's children fare even better—is alive and well, at least as an aspiration if not a realization, in the black community today. Middle-class blacks have embraced values that place them closer in outlook to their white counterparts than to fellow blacks who have not been as successful, at least in economic terms.

Barack Obama must have hoped he would not be seen as a black candidate for president. Many other descriptors could be mentioned in his case: lawyer, community organizer, Chicagoan, author, legislator, to name the obvious roles that all Americans are free to pursue. But as the campaign progressed, he was seen as a black candidate. Ironically, the white voting population cannot help coming to this conclusion when it was reported that 80 percent of blacks voted for Obama. Try as he might, Obama cannot escape his blackness.

Why did I become so involved in the civil rights movement during the 1960s? I am sure many motives were involved. Earlier, I mentioned several seminal influences that preconditioned me to be responsive to the opportunities that presented themselves; in fact, to seek connections so that I could "jump on board." In many respects, the civil rights movement of the 1960s was made to order. I was a young faculty member studying the labor movement, and here in the developing civil rights scene was another movement with many of the same characteristics. By getting involved, I could become a participant-observer in the best tradition of "Chicago School," which believed that good theory must be informed by good data.

I found my role positioned somewhere between the pure activism of Al Pitcher (a minister performing service to a congregation not defined by the walls of a church) and the policy work of social scientists such as Robert Havighurst and Philip Hauser. My research interests focused on understanding the process by which disadvantaged groups mobilized power, negotiated breakthrough agreements, and effected fundamental change. Many were the moments when I wondered whether I had gone too far on the activist side of the ledger. As a marcher, I was just another head to add to the head count. Would it have been better to have devoted all of my attention to research and efforts to influence the course of events from my academic post? Indeed, several of my colleagues intimated that redirecting my priorities toward more scholarly activities would have enhanced my career.

Fortunately, I gained tenure, in part because I used the "data" gained from first-hand exposure to the strategy and tactics of the civil rights movement to author several articles. At times I felt guilty because I was using my work in the civil rights movement to bolster my own interest in garnering material for publication and my quest for tenure. This has been an issue throughout my career. For example, union leaders often have asked me what union I belonged to and what have I been doing to organize academic colleagues?

So this same issue surfaced with my involvement in the civil rights movement, with an additional complication. In this case, was I exploiting black colleagues? Life is filled with mixed-motive situations, and my hope is that I delivered some value to the civil rights movement at the same time I was deriving insights and information that I could package into articles and publications. Derrick Bell, in *Silent Covenants*,[19] captures the essence of that mixed-motive situation with the phrase "interest convergence." His premise is that whites only work in behalf of blacks when doing so serves their own interests.

I am at a stage in life where publications do not carry the same weight as they once did. Of much higher value to me now are the friendships and associations that were fostered as a result of joining the civil rights movement. Hopefully this book demonstrates this priority.

Appendixes

Notes

Bibliography

Index

Appendix A: Acronyms

ABA   American Bar Association
AFL-CIO American Federation of Labor–Congress of Industrial
        Organizations
AFSCME American Federation of State, County, and Municipal
        Employees
BAC   Black Affairs Council
BAWA   Black and White Action
BUUC   Black Unitarian Universalist Caucus
CCCO   Coordinating Council of Community Organizations
CFM   Chicago Freedom Movement (merger of CCCO and SCLC in
        1966)
CNM   Careers for Negroes in Management
CORE   Congress of Racial Equality
CTS   Chicago Theological Seminary
EEOC   Equal Employment Opportunity Commission
FEPC   Fair Employment Practices Commission
GSB   Graduate School of Business, University of Chicago
MBA   Master of Business Administration
NALC   Negro American Labor Council
NLRA   National Labor Relations Act
OB   Operation Breadbasket
OFCCP   Office of Federal Contract Compliance and Programs
OMBE   Office of Minority Business Enterprise
PUSH   People United to Save Humanity
SBA   Small Business Administration
SCLC   Southern Christian Leadership Conference
SMSA   Standard Metropolitan Statistical Area

SNCC   Student Nonviolent Coordinating Committee
SRC   Social Responsibility Commission
TWO   The Woodlawn Organization (originally "Temporary Woodlawn Organization")
UAW   United Auto Workers
UUA   Unitarian Universalist Association

Appendix B: Chicago Geography
(including maps locating major events)

Within the general area referred to as Hyde Park and Woodlawn-Kenwood are several institutions that serve as markers (see map 1). The former KAM Temple, now the headquarters of Operation Push, sits at the corner of Drexel Boulevard and 50th Street. The First Unitarian Church, with its classic Gothic architecture, dominates the intersection of 57th Street and Woodlawn Avenue. As the crow flies, these two institutions are about 1.5 miles apart, a manageable distance for most people to traverse on foot.

Hyde Park's anchoring institution is the University of Chicago. With 10,000 students and a faculty in excess of 1,000 scholars, the university in many ways *is* Hyde Park. A number of other educational institutions and professional centers are located nearby, illustrating the magnetic quality of an internationally renowned university.

The Chicago Theological Seminary (CTS) sits at the edge of the University of Chicago campus. It was here, in 1964, that Jesse Jackson enrolled in pursuit of a divinity degree.

The First Unitarian Church, located just a block from the edge of the University of Chicago campus, served as my gateway to the civil rights movement.

The national headquarters for the American Bar Association (ABA) in the 1960s sat just south of the Midway Plaisance on East 60th Street. It was here in 1963 that I transitioned from researcher-observer to active participant in the civil rights movement. Technically, the ABA's address placed it in Woodlawn, in another community distinct from Hyde Park. The parklike Midway, which separates Hyde Park and Woodlawn, carries historical significance, since it and the nearby Museum of Science and Industry were preserved from the Colombian Exposition of 1893. It also serves as a several-blocks-wide border that enabled the university, for much of its history, to ignore this adjacent community to its south.

App B

Hyde Park (1965) The Geography of Sites
Referenced in the Text

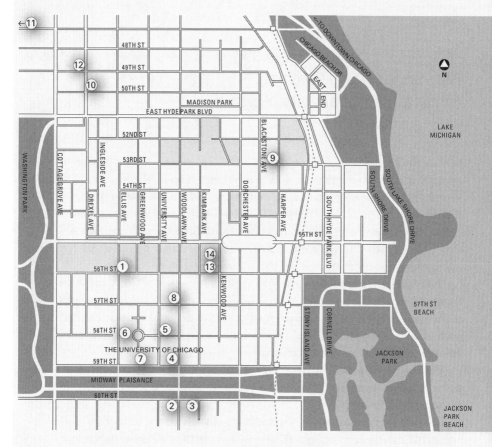

① Home for Incurables
② American Bar Association HQ
③ Industrial Relations Ctr (IRC)
④ Rockefeller Chapel
⑤ Chicago Theological Seminary dorm
and café (CTS)
⑥ University of Chicago Admin Bldg
⑦ University of Chicago Business School

⑧ Unitarian Church
⑨ Valois Restaurant
⑩ KAM Temple
⑪ Breadbasket HQ
(off map at 47th and South Park)
⑫ Tim Black apt
⑬ McKersie home
⑭ Patner home

Map 1. Hyde Park sites involved in the Chicago civil rights movement of the 1960s.
Chicago Creative Communications, University of Chicago.

During the 1960s, while many Hyde Parkers viewed Woodlawn as "off limits," others, including our family, visited this community regularly. The elevated (a rapid-transit line) ran above 63rd Street, and below, a wide variety of shops and restaurants made this strip an interesting place to visit on a Saturday afternoon. For instance, the best Chinese food our family ate came from Tai Sam Yon, and locals knew the regular chef's schedule; they also knew to avoid ordering his specialty, eggrolls, on his days off.

The emergence of a militant community organization called the Temporary Woodlawn Organization (TWO, which later dropped "Temporary" from its name but retained the "T") provided the impetus for the formation of the Coordinating Council of Community Organizations (CCCO), making Woodlawn one of the key nerve centers of the civil rights movement for much of the 1960s. How the University of Chicago chose to relate to Woodlawn, and how its strategy changed over time, is of considerable interest to the story.

To the north of Hyde Park, the demarcation cannot be as sharply drawn. While technically the dividing line is Hyde Park Boulevard (51st Street), Hyde Park blends into Kenwood, and for many purposes the two communities are joined. To further illustrate the linkage, the local civic organization is called the Hyde Park–Kenwood Community Conference.

Important demographic differences characterize the communities. Whites have been the majority racial group in Hyde Park, while African Americans represent the majority in Kenwood. When a group of black teenagers led a civil rights march to north Kenwood in July 1965, this black neighborhood reacted with ambivalence about being confronted by the reality that the civil rights movement was under way in Chicago.

Turning to map 2 for a broader view of the city of Chicago, several other landmarks are of interest. Most visitors know that the downtown area of Chicago is referred to as "the Loop," harking back to the early days of the first elevated railway, traversing a loop around the core of the city. In this chronicle of the 1960s, the Loop figures prominently. During the summer of 1965, daily marches to City Hall started from the gathering point at Buckingham Fountain in Grant Park. The park, named for President Ulysses S. Grant and planned by Daniel Burnham, offers the city a pleasant and unobstructed view of Lake Michigan.

But not all marches setting forth from the fountain headed for the Loop during the summer of 1965. Under the leadership of comedian Dick Gregory, nightly marches visited an all-white neighborhood to the southwest of the Loop referred to as Bridgeport, home of Mayor Daley.

Heading farther away from downtown Chicago in a southwesterly direction brings us to the predominantly white communities of Chicago Lawn,

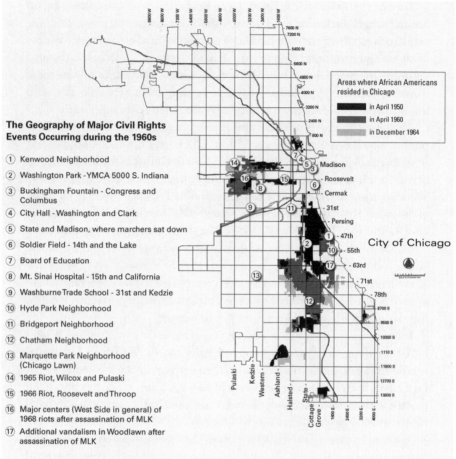

The Geography of Major Civil Rights
Events Occurring during the 1960s

Areas where African Americans
resided in Chicago

▇ in April 1950
▇ in April 1960
▒ in December 1964

① Kenwood Neighborhood

② Washington Park - YMCA 5000 S. Indiana

③ Buckingham Fountain - Congress and
Columbus

④ City Hall - Washington and Clark

⑤ State and Madison, where marchers sat down

⑥ Soldier Field - 14th and the Lake

⑦ Board of Education

⑧ Mt. Sinai Hospital - 15th and California

⑨ Washburne Trade School - 31st and Kedzie

⑩ Hyde Park Neighborhood

⑪ Bridgeport Neighborhood

⑫ Chatham Neighborhood

⑬ Marquette Park Neighborhood
(Chicago Lawn)

⑭ 1965 Riot, Wilcox and Pulaski

⑮ 1966 Riot, Roosevelt and Throop

⑯ Major centers (West Side in general) of
1968 riots after assassination of MLK

⑰ Additional vandalism in Woodlawn after
assassination of MLK

City of Chicago

MAP COURTESY OF CHICAGO URBAN LEAGUE

Map 2. Other Chicago sites important to the civil rights movement of the 1960s. From
the Chicago Urban League research report titled "Commentary on 'Areas of Negro Residence' Map": 1950,
1960, and 1964. Chicago Urban League records, series III, box 22, folder 276, CULR_03_0022_0276_001.
University of Illinois at Chicago Library, Special Collections.

Gage Park, and Marquette Park. These areas were the scene of several marches
during the summer of 1966 as part of the campaign for open occupancy in
housing. One of the marches, in which I participated, turned vicious. These
communities in the 1960s represented the dividing line between what was
then called the "Negro ghetto" and these adjoining white communities, for
the most part occupied by working-class whites.

The term "Negro ghetto" affirmed the fact that the racial pattern of housing was, from the start, highly segregated in Chicago. Unlike other sections

of the country, especially the South, where the racial profile of housing often resembled a checkerboard, in Chicago such a pattern only existed in a neighborhood for a short period of time—between the arrival of the first black family and the departure of the last white family.

While many blacks could find only substandard housing—and the story of Woodlawn during the 1960s and the decades thereafter amply illustrate this reality—many neighborhoods within the so-called ghetto looked very suburban, with single-family homes, well-tended lawns, and up-to-date cars parked in the driveways.

Alex Poinsett, a central player in this story, lived in such an area called Chatham. Housing would have been available to the Poinsetts in Hyde Park but at a price much higher than in Chatham. Chatham illustrated the broader patterns of race and housing in the city. Alex explains:

> I remember a discussion at the First Unitarian Church in Chicago about efforts to integrate Hyde Park housing back in the 1960s. "We want to integrate," claimed the wife of one of our associate ministers, "but we just can't find any Negroes (we weren't African Americans yet) willing to move in." I could not resist replying, "We want to integrate Chatham, but we just can't find whites willing to move in." In fact, by the time Norma and I bought our home in Chatham in 1961, most of our white neighbors had fled. Within two years, the last two white families still living on our block had broken their earlier promises to stay put.

A frequent epitaph, uttered ruefully by Hyde Parkers about the sociology of the community, was "We do not discriminate against blacks. It is black and white, shoulder to shoulder against the lower class." Meaning, of course, that racial discrimination had been replaced by economic discrimination.

Appendix C: Civil Rights Timeline—Major Events for Chicago and the Nation

1954

May   Supreme Court hands down decision in *Brown v. Board of Education*

1955

Apr   Richard J. Daley elected for his first term as mayor of Chicago.

Aug   Emmett Till, a youth from Chicago visiting relatives in the South, lynched in Jackson, Mississippi, for whistling at a white woman.

Dec   Rosa Parks's refusal to yield her seat and move to the back of the bus signals the start of the Montgomery bus boycott that continued through March 1956.

1956

Mar   Making the connection to the Montgomery bus boycott, blacks in Chicago throw a picket line around the headquarters for the bus owner, National City Lines.

1957

Sep   President Eisenhower sends federal troops to Little Rock, Arkansas, as violence erupts when the high school is integrated.

1959

Apr   Mayor Daley reelected for a second term as mayor.

1960–62

The Woodlawn Organization is formed.

1960

Feb   Lunch counter sit-ins begin in Greensboro, North Carolina, and Nashville, Tennessee.

1961

May   Freedom Rides aboard busses begin in the South and encounter violent attacks at several places.

1962

Jan   CORE conducts sit-in at University of Chicago's rental and administrative offices.

Apr   The Coordinating Council of Community Organizations (CCCO) is formed.

Sep   Operation Breadbasket, modeled after a program started in Philadelphia by Rev. Leon Sullivan, is formed nationally under the auspices of the SCLC.

Sep   James Meredith, with the aid of federal marshals, becomes first black student admitted to Ole Miss.

1963

Apr   Mayor Daley reelected to third term as mayor.

Apr   M. L. King is incarcerated and writes his "Letter from Birmingham Jail."

May   Riots break out in Birmingham, Alabama.

May   Jesse Jackson leads a march in Greensboro, North Carolina.

              Warren Bacon and James Clement, both supporters of the civil rights movement, join the Chicago Board of Education.

Jun   Activist Medgar Evers is assassinated.

Aug 28   M. L. King leads the March on Washington and delivers the "I have a dream" oration.

Sep 15   A black church in Birmingham is bombed, killing four young black girls.

Oct 22   The first Chicago school boycott is organized by the CCCO.

Nov 22   President John F. Kennedy is assassinated.

1964

Feb   The second school boycott is organized by the CCCO.

Feb   The school board issues a statement on integration.

Apr   Al Raby leads a Good Friday march on City Hall.

Jun   Among the many young people traveling from the North to the South to help with voter registration in the Freedom Summer campaign, three students, Michael Schwerner, James Chaney, and Andrew Goodman, are abducted and murdered on June 21.

Jun   M. L. King speaks at Soldier Field rally.

Jul   Civil Rights Act is passed by Congress and signed by President Johnson.

1965

Mar 7   Marchers attempt to march over the Edmond Pettus Bridge in Selma, Alabama, in what comes to be called "Bloody Sunday."

Mar 9   During a second attempt to march from Selma to Birmingham, Rev. James Reeb is fatally injured.

Mar 21   With National Guard troops present, the third march from Selma to Montgomery commences, with participation of members of the First Unitarian Church.

April   Elementary and Secondary School Act is signed into law authorizing the government to withhold federal money from segregated schools.

May   Despite protests and boycotts aiming at his removal, Benjamin Willis is reappointed as Chicago school superintendent.

Summer   The battle over Willis's reappointment intensifies, with daily marches, many led by Dick Gregory (40 in total).

Jul 26   M. L. King leads a march from Buckingham Fountain to City Hall.

Aug 6   The Voting Rights Act is signed into law.

Aug 11   Riots break out in the Watts section of Los Angeles.

Aug 12   A fire truck kills a black woman on Chicago's West Side, and riots break out.

Oct   Chicago school board announces it will take steps to address segregation at Washburne Trade School.

Sept   M. L. King announces that Chicago has been chosen as the northern site for an open housing campaign by SCLC.

1966

Feb	The Chicago branch of Operation Breadbasket, led by Jesse Jackson, commences.
Apr	Superintendent Benjamin Willis announces he will step down before the end of the year.
Jun 7	James Meredith, in a solo march from Memphis to Jackson, is wounded by a sniper.
Summer	Open housing marches are conducted to various white neighborhoods in Chicago.
Jul 10	After addressing a crowd of between 23,000 (City Hall's estimate) and 60,000 (civil rights movement's estimate) at Soldier Field, M. L. King affixes a list of demands to the door of City Hall.
Jul 12	Riots break out on Chicago's West Side, triggered by an argument over shutting off water from a fire hydrant on a hot summer day.
Jul 31	A march from Marquette Park to the Chicago Lawn neighborhood is marred by considerable violence.
Aug 26	Summit agreement is signed between civil rights movement, the City of Chicago, and real estate leaders.
Nov	Charles Percy unseats incumbent senator Paul Douglas.

1967

Apr	M. L. King voices his strongest opposition to the Vietnam War to date.
Apr	Mayor Daley is reelected to a fourth term with a plurality of half a million votes.
Sept	Al Raby steps down as the chairman of the CCCO, which ceases to function.

1968

Mar	The Kerner Commission report is issued.
Apr 4	M. L. King is assassinated and riots break out in several locations in Chicago.
Jun 5	Robert Kennedy is assassinated.

1971

Apr	Mayor Daley is returned to office with 78 percent support.
Dec	Jesse Jackson pulls out of the SCLC and forms Operation Push.

Notes

Foreword

1. "Beyond Dixie: The Black Freedom Struggle outside of the South," Special issue, *Magazine of History* 26 (January 2012). For other important, suggestive conceptualizations of recent writing on the black freedom struggle, see Jacquelyn Dowd Hall, "The Long Civil Rights Movement and the Political Uses of the Past," *Journal of American History* 91 (March 2005): 1233–63, and Sundiata Keita Cha-Jua and Clarence Lang, "The Long Civil Rights Movement as Vampire: Temporal and Spatial Fallacies in Recent Black Freedom Studies," *Journal of African-American History* 92 (Spring 2007): 265–88.

2. Patrick D. Jones, "Coming of Age in Cleveland," in "Beyond Dixie," 8.

3. The important works on black Chicago and race relations in Chicago are too numerous to list. Two books deserve particular attention. For a classic study of a mid-twentieth-century black urban community, see St. Clair Drake and Horace R. Cayton, *Black Metropolis: A Study of Negro Life in a Northern City* (New York: Harcourt, Brace & World, 1970). For a pioneering analysis of the construction of black ghettos after World War II, see Arnold R. Hirsch, *Making the Second Ghetto: Race and Housing in Chicago, 1940–1960* (New York: Cambridge University Press, 1983).

4. Alan Anderson and George Pickering, *Confronting the Color Line: The Broken Promise of the Civil Rights Movement in Chicago* (Athens: University of Georgia Press, 1986).

5. For more on the early years of Operation Breadbasket in Chicago, see Gary Massoni, "Perspectives on Operation Breadbasket," in *Chicago 1966: Open Housing Marches, Summit Negotiations, and Operation Breadbasket,* edited by David J. Garrow (Brooklyn: Carlson Publishing, 1989), Given the nature of his study, McKersie does not address protest efforts in Chicago before 1960.

6. Jeanne Theoharis, Introduction to *Freedom North: Black Freedom Struggles outside the South, 1940–1980,* edited by Theoharis and Komozi Woodard (New York: Palgrave Macmillan, 2003), 2.

7. Komozi Woodard, *A Nation within a Nation: Amiri Baraka (LeRoi Jones) and Black Power Politics* (Chapel Hill: University of North Carolina Press, 1999); Matthew Countryman, *Up South: Civil Rights and Black Power in Philadelphia* (Philadelphia: University of Pennsylvania Press, 2005). On Black Power, see the new synthesis presented by Peniel E. Joseph, ed., *Waiting 'til the Midnight Hour: A Narrative History of Black Power in America* (New York: Henry Holt, 2006).

8. August Meier and Elliot Rudwick, *CORE: A Study in the Civil Rights Movement* (Urbana: University of Illinois Press, 1973).

9. Thomas J. Sugrue, *Sweet Land of Liberty: The Forgotten Struggle for Civil Rights in the North* (New York: Random House, 2008).

10. The fight for access to public accommodations by Chicago blacks was essentially won by the early 1960s.

11. See, e.g., Countryman, *Up South*; Patrick D. Jones, *Selma of the North: Civil Rights Insurgency in Milwaukee* (Cambridge: Harvard University Press, 2009); Clarence Lang, *Grassroots at the Gateway: Class Politics and Black Freedom Struggle in St. Louis, 1936–1975* (Ann Arbor: University of Michigan Press, 2009); Gretchen Cassel Eick, *Dissent in Wichita: The Civil Rights Movement in the Midwest, 1954–1972* (Urbana: University of Illinois Press, 2001); Joan Singler et al., eds., *Seattle in Black and White: The Congress of Racial Equality and the Fight for Equal Opportunity* (Seattle: University of Washington Press, 2011).

12. See the comments by Theoharis in Theoharis and Woodard, *Freedom North*, 3–4.

13. See, e.g., David J. Garrow, *Bearing the Cross: Martin Luther King Jr. and the Southern Christian Leadership Conference* (New York: William Morrow, 1986), 431–526; Taylor Branch, *At Canaan's Edge: America in the King Years, 1965–68* (New York: Simon & Schuster, 2006), 501–36; Adam Fairclough, *To Redeem the Soul of America: The Southern Christian Leadership Conference and Martin Luther King Jr.* (Athens: University of Georgia Press, 1987), 279–308; James R. Ralph Jr., *Northern Protest: Martin Luther King Jr., Chicago, and the Civil Rights Movement* (Cambridge: Harvard University Press, 1993).

14. See Ralph, *Northern Protest*, and "Assessing the Chicago Freedom Movement," *Poverty and Race*, May/June 2006, 1–2, 7. Adam Fairclough also stresses the significance of the Chicago Freedom Movement in *Better Day Coming: Blacks and Equality, 1890–2000* (New York: Viking, 2001), 301–4.

15. Ralph David Abernathy, *And the Walls Came Tumbling Down: An Autobiography* (New York: Harper & Row, 1989); Andrew Young, *An Easy Burden: The Civil Rights Movement and the Transformation of America* (New York: HarperCollins, 1996); John Lewis, with Michael D'Orso, *Walking with the Wind: A Memoir of the Movement* (New York: Simon & Schuster, 1998); Stokely Carmichael, with Ekwueme Michael Thelwell, *Ready for Revolution: The Life and Struggles of Stokely Carmichael (Kwame Ture)* (New York: Scribner, 2003); James Forman, *The Making of Black Revolutionaries* (Washington: Open Hand, 1985); Cleveland Sellers, *The River of No Return: The Autobiography of a Black Militant and the Life and Death of SNCC* (New York: William Morrow, 1973); Mary E. King, *Freedom Song: A Personal Story of the 1960s Civil Rights Movement* (New York: William Morrow, 1987); James L. Farmer Jr., *Lay Bare the Heart: An Autobiography of the Civil Rights Movement* (New York: Arbor House, 1985). For an insightful analysis of the role and value of autobiographies, see Kathryn L. Nasstrom, "Between Memory and History: Autobiographies of the Civil Rights Movement and the Writing of Civil Rights History," *Journal of Southern History* 74 (May 2008): 325–64.

16. A number of members of the Black Panther Party, which was largely based in the North, have written autobiographical accounts. Initially, see Eldridge Cleaver, *Soul on Ice* (New York: Dell Books, 1968). For first-person accounts with more historical perspective, see, for instance, Elaine Brown, *A Taste of Power: A Black Woman's*

Story (New York: Pantheon Books, 1992); and David Hilliard and Lewis Cole, *This Side of Glory: The Autobiography of David Hilliard and the Story of the Black Panther Party* (New York: Little, Brown, 1993).

17. Arthur M. Brazier, *Black Self-Determination: The Story of the Woodlawn Organization* (Grand Rapids: Eerdmans, 1969).

18. Dempsey J. Travis, *An Autobiography of Black Chicago* (Chicago: Urban Research Institute, 1981) and *An Autobiography of Black Politics* (Chicago: Urban Research Press, 1987).

19. Don Benedict, *Born Again Radical* (New York: Pilgrim Press, 1982).

20. For an example of a published assessment by Al Pitcher, see "The Chicago Freedom Movement: What Is It?" in Garrow, *Chicago 1966*, 155–78.

21. "America's Gandhi: Rev. Martin Luther King, Jr.," *Time*, January 3, 1964. For King's view on the role of white liberals, see King, *Where Do We Go from Here: Chaos or Community?* (Boston: Beacon Press, 1967), 88–101. For a telling assessment of the response of intellectuals to the black freedom movement, many of whom were liberals, see Carol Polsgrove, *Divided Minds: Intellectuals and the Civil Rights Movement* (New York: W. W. Norton, 2001).

22. See, for example, Stokely Carmichael and Charles Hamilton, *Black Power: The Politics of Liberation in America* (New York: Vintage, 1967), 58–66.

23. For an interesting analysis of the biographical profiles of applicants for the Mississippi Freedom Summer Project, which shows the importance of religious orientation, see Doug McAdam, *Freedom Summer* (New York: Oxford University Press, 1988), 50–65. James F. Findlay covers the mobilization of white Protestants during the 1960s in *Church People in the Struggle: The National Council on Churches and the Black Freedom Movement, 1950–1970* (New York: Oxford University Press, 1993). Anderson and Pickering show the prevalence of religiously minded individuals in the CCCO in a survey they conducted of CCCO delegates in 1968. Anderson and Pickering, *Confronting the Color Line: The Broken Promise of the Civil Rights Movement in Chicago* (Athens: University of Georgia Press, 1987), 455–57.

24. The theme of interracial friendship in the civil rights era is one that deserves more scholarly attention. John Stauffer is a leading analyst of the theme in the nineteenth century. See, for example, *Giants: The Parallel Lives of Frederick Douglass and Abraham Lincoln* (New York: Twelve, 2008). Gayle Sayers's friendship in the late 1960s with his white teammate on the Chicago Bears, Brian Piccolo, became the source of a remarkably popular book and then television movie. Gayle Sayers with Al Silverman, *I Am Third* (New York: Viking Press, 1970) and *Brian's Song* (1971).

25. Social scientists have developed a wealth of insight into the efficacy of protests and social movements. Marco Giugni provides a useful overview in "How Social Movements Matter: Past Research, Present Problems, and Future Developments," in *How Social Movements Matter*, edited by Giugni, Doug McAdam, and Charles Tilly (St. Paul: University of Minnesota Press, 1999), xiii–xxxiii.

26. Thomas J. Sugrue, *Not Even Past: Barack Obama and the Burden of Race* (Princeton, NJ: Princeton University Press, 2010).

Preface

1. For an account of sit-ins at lunch counters in Nashville, Tennessee, see David Halberstam, *The Children* (New York: Fawcett Books, 1999).

2. Thomas Sugrue, *Sweet Land of Liberty: The Forgotten Struggle for Civil Rights in the North* (New York: Random House, 2008).

3. Jeanne Theoharis and Komozi Woodard, *Freedom North: Black Freedom Struggles outside the South, 1940–1980* (New York: Palgrave Macmillan, 2003).

4. Martha Biondi, *To Stand and Fight: The Struggle for Civil Rights in Postwar New York City* (Cambridge, MA: Harvard University Press, 2003), 278.

5. Matthew J. Countryman, *Up South: Civil Rights and Black Power in Philadelphia* (Philadelphia: University of Pennsylvania Press, 2005).

6. Patrick Jones, *The Selma of the North: Civil Rights Insurgency in Milwaukee* (Cambridge, MA: Harvard University Press, 2009).

7. Mary King, *Freedom Song: A Personal Story of the 1960s Civil Rights Movement* (New York: William Morrow, 1987). See also Douglas McAdam, *Freedom Summer* (New York: Oxford University Press, 1988).

8. James R. Ralph Jr., *Northern Protests: Martin Luther King Jr., Chicago, and the Civil Rights Movement* (Cambridge, MA: Harvard University Press, 1993).

9. Alan Anderson and George Pickering, *Confronting the Color Line: The Broken Promise of the Civil Rights Movement in Chicago* (Athens: University of Georgia Press, 1987).

10. See Appendix A for a list of the major civil rights organizations and their acronyms.

11. Readers not familiar with the geography of Chicago should consult Appendix B, Chicago Geography, which has maps designating the main venues of the story.

Prologue: Starting an Academic Career

1. Ray Marshall, "Unions and the Negro Community," *Industrial and Labor Relations Review* 17 (1964): 49.

2. Julius Jacobson, ed., *The Negro and the American Labor Movement* (New York: Doubleday, 1968), 1.

3. Lillian Roberts, interviewed by the author, May 2009.

4. Our findings appeared in Robert B. McKersie and Montague Brown, "Nonprofessional Hospital Workers and a Union Organizing Drive," *Quarterly Journal of Economics* 77, no. 3 (1963): 372–404.

1. The First Unitarian Church of Chicago: My Gateway to the Civil Rights Movement and to Alex Poinsett

1. Alicia McNary Forsey, ed., *In Their Own Words: A Conversation with Participants in the Black Empowerment Movement* (Berkeley, CA: Starr King School for the Ministry, 2001).

2. Speech by Alderman Leon (Len) Despres, at open meeting held January 30, 1962, to discuss CORE sit-in.

3. Arnold R. Hirsch, *Making the Second Ghetto: Race and Housing in Chicago, 1940–1960* (New York: Cambridge University Press, 1983), 145.

4. Martin Luther King Jr., "Letter From Birmingham Jail," *Christian Century*, April 16, 1963; reprinted as "Reporting Civil Rights, Part One," *American Journalism, 1941–1963* (New York: Library of America, 2003), 777–94.

2. Campaigns on the Employment Front

1. Paula F. Pfeffer, *A. Philip Randolph, Pioneer of the Civil Rights Movement* (Baton Rouge: Louisiana State University Press, 1990).
2. Ray Marshall, *The Negro and Organized Labor* (New York: John Wiley, 1965), 309.
3. Robert C. Weaver, *Negro Labor: A National Problem* (New York: Harcourt Brace, 1946), 184–85.
4. Ray Marshall, "Unions and the Negro Community," *Industrial and Labor Relations Review* 17 (1964): 179–202.
5. George Strauss and Sidney Ingerman, "Public Policy and Discrimination in Apprenticeship," *Hastings Law Journal* 16 (February 1965): 285–331.
6. These percentages are taken from a study I conducted for EEOC using data supplied by employers with more than 50 employees as of 1966. See Robert B. McKersie, *Minority Employment Patterns in an Urban Labor Market: The Chicago Experience* (Washington: EEOC, 1969).
7. Strauss and Ingerman, 304.
8. Timuel Black, interviewed by the author, May 1998.

3. Tim Black and the Motorola Campaign

1. Tim Black, interviewed by the author, May 1998.
2. While the Motorola campaign unfolded a few years prior to my research work for the EEOC, the percentages derived from the EEO-1 reports most likely reflected the situation that existed throughout the 1950s and early 1960s. See McKersie, *Minority Employment*.
3. The history of the various efforts by the federal government to promote voluntary cooperation by business to practice fair employment is covered in the following: John P. Davis, *The American Negro Reference Book* (New York: Prentice-Hall, 1969); S. Prakash Sethi, *Business Corporations and the Black Man* (Scranton, PA: Chandler Press, 1970); and Thomas Sugrue, *Sweet Land of Liberty: The Forgotten Struggle for Civil Rights in the North* (New York: Random House, 2008).
4. Motorola statement that appeared in an ad in the *New York Times*, July 24, 1963.
5. As it turned out, nothing was ever done about this item since having an office where many African Americans could apply would have placed the company in an embarrassing position, given the reality that many applicants would have been turned away for lack of qualifications.
6. George Yoxall, interviewed by the author, February 2001 and August 2002.
7. George Shultz, correspondence with the author, November 2002.
8. Sethi reported on Kodak's joining Plans for Progress. Interestingly, Motorola is not mentioned. S. Prakash Sethi, *Business Corporations and the Black Man* (Scranton, PA: Chandler Press, 1970), 24.
9. Richard E. Walton, Robert B. McKersie, and Joel E. Cutcher-Gershenfeld, *Strategic Negotiations* (Boston, MA: Harvard Business School Press, 1994).

4. Campaigns on the Education Front

1. Margery Frisbie, *An Alley in Chicago: The Life and Legacy of Monsignor John Egan* (Chicago: Sheed & Ward, 2003).

2. James R. Ralph Jr., *Northern Protests: Martin Luther King Jr., Chicago, and the Civil Rights Movement* (Cambridge, MA: Harvard University Press, 1993), 17.

3. Jacobson, 275.

4. Ralph, 14.

5. Ibid., 15.

6. James Bryant Conant, *Slums and Suburbs: A Commentary on Schools in Metropolitan Areas* (New York: McGraw-Hill, 1961).

7. Ralph, 19.

8. Dan Lortie, personal communication, November 2003.

9. Alan B. Anderson and George W. Pickering, *Confronting the Color Line: The Broken Promise of the Civil Rights Movement in Chicago* (Athens: University of Georgia Press, 1987), 125.

10. Document circulated to CCCO members, December 1963.

11. Anderson and Pickering, 65.

12. Kim Clement, interviewed by the author, April 2004.

13. Special Urban League Collection, University of Illinois–Chicago Archives.

14. Larry Cuban, *The Urban School Superintendency: A Century and a Half of Change* (Bloomington, IN: Phi Delta Kappan, 1976), 28.

15. Anderson and Pickering, 125.

5. The Movement Marks Time while the University Plays Catch-Up

1. Ralph, 23.

2. Philip M. Hauser, *Report of the Advisory Panel on Integration of the Public Schools, Chicago* (Chicago: Board of Education, 1964).

3. Robert J. Havighurst, *The Public Schools of Chicago: A Survey for the Board of Education of the City of Chicago* (Chicago: Board of Education, November 1964).

4. From a copy of a speech by Robert Havighurst in the archives of the University of Illinois at Chicago.

5. Benjamin C. Willis, interviewed on school segregation by R. Bruce McPherson, *Phi Delta Kappan* 48, no. 1 (September 1966): 11–15.

6. George Shultz, correspondence with the author, November 2002.

7. Hassell McClelland, personal communication, January 2003.

6. Spring and Summer 1965: Marches, More Marches, and Al Pitcher

1. Kay Clement, interviewed by the author, April 2004.

2. Anderson and Pickering, 153.

3. Dan Lortie, interviewed by the author, June 2004.

7. A Peaceful March in Kenwood and a Not-So-Peaceful March led by Dick Gregory

1. Patrick Jones, *The Selma of the North: Civil Rights Insurgency in Milwaukee* (Cambridge, MA: Harvard University Press, 2009), 255.

2. Justice House, writing the majority opinion in *City of Chicago v. Dick Gregory*, Case 233 N.E.2d 422. See http://web.lexis-nexis.com. Retrieved 12/13/02.

3. Paul Goldstein, interviewed by the author, December 2003.

4. *City of Chicago v. Dick Gregory*. 39 Ill. 2d 47, 60, 233 N.E. 2d, 422 (1968).

5. Justice Hugo Black, writing for the Concurring Opinion in: *Gregory et al. v*

City of Chicago, #60, USSC 394 U.S. 111. See http://web.lexis-nexis.com. Retrieved 12/12/02.

6. Irene Patner, interviewed by the author, April 2004.

7. Harry Kalven Jr., *A Worthy Tradition: Freedom of Speech in America* (New York: Harper & Row, 1988), 99.

8. Father William DuBay publicly requested, in 1964, that Pope Paul VI remove Father James Francis McIntyre, Cardinal of Los Angeles, from office for his failure to support civil rights for black people. DuBay stated, "His Eminence has condemned direct action demonstrations on the grounds that they incite violence." See http://en.wikipedia.og/wiki/ william_dubay.

9. The Campaign for Open Housing, Summer 1966

1. Thomas Sugrue, *Sweet Land of Liberty: The Forgotten Struggle for Civil Rights in the North* (New York: Random House, 2008), 271.

2. Ibid.

3. Mary King, 524.

4. Jon Rice, "The World of the Illinois Panthers." In Theoharis and Woodard, 41–64.

5. See Anderson and Pickering; and David Garrow, *Bearing the Cross: Martin Luther King, Jr. and the Southern Christian Leadership Conference* (New York: Harper, 1999).

6. Garrow, *Bearing the Cross,* 512–13.

7. Ralph, 196.

8. Sara Pitcher, interviewed by the author, July 2003.

9. Barbara Reynolds, *Jesse Jackson: America's David* (Washington, DC: JFJ Associates, 1985), 74.

10. Ralph, 223.

10. Jesse Jackson, Operation Breadbasket, and Minority Enterprise

1. St. Clair Drake and Horace Cayton, *Black Metropolis: A Study of Negro Life in a Northern City* (1945; reprint, Chicago: University of Chicago Press, 1993).

2. Rev. Calvin Morris, interviewed by the author, May 2004.

3. Countryman, 118.

4. Donald Perkins, interviewed by the author, July 2003.

5. Don Benedict, *Born Again Radical* (New York: Pilgrim Press, 1982), 185.

6. Gary Massoni. interviewed by the author, September 2004.

7. Morris interview.

8. Sugrue xxv.

9. Countryman, 118.

10. Garrow, *Bearing the Cross,* 232.

11. Reynolds, 142.

12. William Brackett, interviewed by the author, October 2002.

13. Reynolds, 143.

11. The Movement and the Decade Wind Down

1. Martha Biondi, *To Stand and Fight: The Struggle for Civil Rights in Postwar New York City* (Cambridge, MA: Harvard University Press, 2003).

2. Jones.

3. Sugrue, 495.

4. Countryman, 328.

5. Pfeffer, 216, 234.

6. Jones, 64.

7. Mary King, 533.

8. Jones, 65, 76, 202; Biondi, 278.

9. David Halberstam, *The Children* (New York: Fawcett Books, 1999).

10. Doug McAdam, *Freedom Summer* (New York: Oxford University Press, 1988).

11. Anderson and Pickering, 2.

12. Davis, 459.

13. Otto J. Kerner, *Report of the National Advisory Commission on Civil Disorders* (New York: Bantam Books, 1968).

14. Kerner, 203.

15. Ibid., viii.

16. Adam Cohen and Elizabeth Taylor, *American Pharaoh: Mayor Richard J. Daley—His Battle for Chicago and the Nation* (Boston: Little, Brown, 2001), 387, 389.

17. Donald Perkins, interviewed by the author, July 2003.18. Kerner, 206.

18. Kerner, 206.

19. Anderson and Pickering, 433.

12. Initiatives Continue within the University and the Unitarian Church

1. *New York Times Book Review*, September 12, 2010, 14.

2. Alex Poinsett reiterated these points in a 2001 conference at Starr King School for the Ministry, convened to review the history of BUUC. See Alicia Forsey, *In Their Own Words: A Conversation with Participants in the Black Empowerment Movement* (Berkeley, CA: Starr King School for the Ministry, 2001).

3. Leon (Len) Despres, interviewed by the author, April 2003.

4. The Woodlawn Organization, *Woodlawn's Model Cities Plan* (Northbrook, IL: Whitehall, 1970), 13.

5. Pierre de Vise, *Chicago's Widening Color Gap* (N.p.: Inter-university Social Research Committee, 1969), 60.

6. The Woodlawn Organization, 15.

7. Ibid., 22.

8. Donald C. Reitzes and Dietrich C. Reitzes, *The Alinsky Legacy: Alive and Kicking* (Greenwich, CT: JAI Press, 1987).

9. Eugene P. Foley, *The Achieving Ghetto* (Washington, DC: National Press, 1968); Harold M. Baron, "The Demand for Black Labor: Historical Notes on the Political Economy of Racism," *Radical America* 5 (March–April 1971), 30. See also Robert Weems and Lewis Randolph, "The Ideological Origins of Richard M. Nixon's 'Black Capitalism Initiative,'" *Review of Black Political Economy* 29 (June 2001): 49–61.

10. Robert Weems and Lewis Randolph, "The National Response to Richard M. Nixon's 'Black Capitalism Initiative': The Success of Domestic Détente," *Journal of Black Studies* 32 (2001): 58.

11. William F. Haddad and G. Douglas Pugh, eds., *Black Economic Development* (Englewood Cliffs, NJ: Prentice Hall, 1969); Laird Durham, *Black Capitalism: Critical Issues in Urban Management* (Washington, DC: Arthur D. Little, 1970); Theodore Cross, *Black Capitalism: Strategy for Business in the Ghetto* (New York: Athenaeum, 1969).

12. Robert B. McKersie, "Vitalize Black Enterprise," *Harvard Business Review* (September–October 1968): 88–99.

13. Gerald David Jaynes and Robin Murphy Williams, eds., *A Common Destiny: Blacks and American Society* (Washington, DC: National Academies Press, 1989), 318.

14. *Mississippi Power & Light Co. v. Mississippi ex rel. Moore*, 487 U.S. 354, No. 86-1970 1988.

13. Race Relations and the Personal Equation

1. Daniel Thompson, *The Negro Leadership Class* (Englewood Cliffs, NJ: Prentice Hall, 1963).

2. *University of Chicago Record*, February 1997.

3. Pfeffer, 216.

4. Mary King, 499.

5. Mitchell Duneier, *Slim's Table: Race, Respectability, and Masculinity* (University of Chicago Press, 1994).

6. Timuel D. Black Jr., *Bridges of Memory: Chicago's First Wave of Black Migration* (Evanston, IL: Northwestern University Press, 2003) and *Bridges of Memory, Chicago's Second Generation of Black Migration*. (Evanston, IL: Northwestern University Press, 2007).

7. Timuel D. Black Jr., interviewed by Lorene Richardson, Veterans History Project (Washington, DC: Library of Congress, 2001).

8. Harold Baron, interviewed by the author, March 2003.

9. Jack Mendelsohn, interviewed by the author, June 2008.

10. Surveys of black elites showed a decline from 18 percent to 7 percent in the number of civil rights leaders between 1963 and 1980—and the decline has no doubt continued. See Jaynes and Williams, 87, 88.

11. Alex Poinsett, *Black Power: Gary Style* (Chicago: Johnson Publishing, 1970); Alex Poinsett, *Walking with Presidents: Louis Martin and the Rise of Black Political Power* (Lanham, MD: Rowman & Littlefield, 2000).

12. James S. Jackson and Nicholas A. Jones, *New Directions in Thinking about Race in America: African Americans in a Diversifying Nation* (Washington, DC: National Policy Association, 1998).

13. Black, *Bridges of Memory: Chicago's Second Generation*; William J. Wilson, *The Truly Disadvantaged: The Inner City, the Underclass, and Public Policy* (Chicago: University of Chicago Press, 1987).

14. Norma Poinsett, interviewed by the author, October 2007.

15. *One America in the 21st Century: Forging a New Future*. Final Report, Presidential Commission on Race Relations (Washington, DC: GAO, 1998).

16. Taylor Branch, "Dr. King's Newest Marcher," *New York Times*, September 5, 2010.

17. Donald S. Perkins, interviewed by the author, July 2003.

18. Edgar Schein makes the point that in many situations, it is better to wait for the request rather than "barge in" with an offer of assistance. See *Helping: How to Offer, Give, and Receive Help* (San Francisco: Berrett-Koehler Publications, 2009).

19. Derrick Bell, *Silent Covenants: Brown v. Board of Education and the Unfulfilled Hopes for Racial Reform* (New York: Oxford University Press, 2004).

Bibliography

Anderson, Alan B., and George W. Pickering. *Confronting the Color Line: The Broken Promise of the Civil Rights Movement in Chicago.* Athens: University of Georgia Press, 1987.

Baron, Harold M. "The Demand for Black Labor: Historical Notes on the Political Economy of Racism." *Radical America* 5 (March–April 1971): 30.

———. Interviewed by R. B. McKersie. March 2003.

Bell, Derrick. *Silent Covenants: Brown v. Board of Education and the Unfulfilled Hopes for Racial Reform.* Oxford: Oxford University Press, 2004.

Biondi, Martha. *To Stand and Fight: The Struggle for Civil Rights in Postwar New York City.* Cambridge, MA: Harvard University Press, 2003.

Black, Timuel D., Jr. *Bridges of Memory: Chicago's First Wave of Black Migration.* Evanston, IL: Northwestern University Press, 2003.

———. *Bridges of Memory: Chicago's Second Generation of Black Migration.* Evanston, IL: Northwestern University Press, 2007.

———. Interviewed by R. B. McKersie. May 1998.

———. Interviewed by Lorene Richardson. Veterans History Project. Washington, DC: Library of Congress, 2001.

Brackett, William. Interviewed by R. B. McKersie. October 2002.

Branch, Taylor. "Dr. King's Newest Marcher." *New York Times,* September 5, 2010.

Brown, Harold, and Bennett Hymer. "The Negro Worker in the Chicago Labor Market." In *The Negro and the American Labor Movement,* edited by Julius Jacobson. New York: Doubleday, 1968.

City of Chicago v. Dick Gregory, 39 Ill. 2d 47, 60, 233 N.E. 2d, 422 (1968).

Clement, Kay. Interviewed by R. B. McKersie. April 2004.

Clement, Kim. Interviewed by R. B. McKersie. March 2004.

Cohen, Adam, and Elizabeth Taylor. *American Pharaoh: Mayor Richard J. Daley—His Battle for Chicago and the Nation.* Boston: Little, Brown, 2001.

Conant, James Bryant. *Slums and Suburbs.* New York: Signet, 1968.

Countryman, Matthew J. *Up South: Civil Rights and Black Power in Philadelphia.* Philadelphia: University of Pennsylvania Press, 2005.

Cross, Theodore. *Black Capitalism: Strategy for Business in the Ghetto.* New York: Athenaeum, 1969.

Cuban, Larry. *The Urban School Superintendency: A Century and a Half of Change.* Bloomington, IN: Phi Delta Kappa Educational Foundation, 1976.

Davis, John P., ed. *The American Negro Reference Book.* New York: Prentice-Hall, 1969.

Despres, Leon. Interviewed by R. B. McKersie. April 2003.

De Vise, Pierre. "Chicago's Widening Color Gap." Report no. 2 of the Inter-university Social Research Committee. N.p., December 1967.

Drake, St. Clair, and Horace R. Cayton. *Black Metropolis: The Study of Negro Life in a Northern City,* 1945. Reprinted, New York: Harcourt, Brace, 1993.

Duneier, Mitchell. *Slim's Table: Race, Respectability, and Masculinity.* Chicago: University of Chicago Press, 1992.

Durham, Laird. *Black Capitalism: Critical Issues in Urban Management.* Washington, DC: Arthur D. Little, 1970.

Foley, Eugene P. *The Achieving Ghetto.* Washington, DC: National Press, 1968.

Forsey, Alicia McNary, ed. *In Their Own Words: A Conversation with Participants in the Black Empowerment Movement.* Berkeley, CA: Starr King School for the Ministry, 2001.

Frisbie, Margery. *An Alley in Chicago: The Life and Legacy of Monsignor John Egan* (1991). Chicago: Sheed & Ward, 2003.

Garrow, David. *Bearing the Cross: Martin Luther King, Jr. and the Southern Christian Leadership Conference.* New York: Harper, 1999.

———, ed. *Chicago 1966: Open Housing Marches, Summit Negotiations, and Operation Breadbasket.* Brooklyn: Carlson Publishing, 1989.

Goldstein, Paul. Interviewed by R. B. McKersie. September 2002.

Gregory et al. v. City of Chicago, #60, USSC 394 U.S. 111. See http://web.lexis-nexis.com. Retrieved 12/12/02.

Haddad, William F., and G. Douglas Pugh, eds. *Black Economic Development.* Englewood Cliffs, NJ: Prentice Hall, 1969.

Halberstam, David. *The Children.* New York: Fawcett Books, 1999.

Haley, Alex, with Malcolm X. *The Autobiography of Malcolm X.* New York: Ballantine, 1965.

Hauser, Philip M. *Report of the Advisory Panel on Integration of the Public Schools, Chicago.* Chicago: Board of Education, March 31, 1964.

Havighurst, Robert J. *The Public Schools of Chicago: A Survey for the Board of Education of the City of Chicago.* Chicago: Board of Education, November 1964.

Hill, Herbert. *NAACP Labor Manual.* New York: NAACP, 1968.

Hirsch, Arnold R. *Making the Second Ghetto: Race and Housing in Chicago, 1940–1960.* New York: Cambridge University Press, 1983.

Jackson, James S., and Nicholas A. Jones. *New Directions in Thinking about Race in America: African Americans in a Diversifying Nation.* Washington, DC: National Policy Association, 1998.

Jacobson, Julius, ed. *The Negro and the American Labor Movement.* New York: Doubleday, 1968.

Jaynes, Gerald David, and Robin Murphy Williams, eds. *A Common Destiny: Blacks and American Society.* Washington, DC: National Academies Press, 1989.

Jones, Patrick. *The Selma of the North: Civil Rights Insurgency in Milwaukee.* Cambridge, MA: Harvard University Press, 2009.

Kalven, Harry, Jr. *A Worthy Tradition: Freedom of Speech in America.* New York: Harper & Row, 1988.

Kerner, Otto J. *Report of the National Advisory Commission on Civil Disorders*. New York: Bantam Books, 1968.

King, Martin Luther, Jr. "Letter from Birmingham Jail." *Christian Century*, April 16, 1963. Reprinted in *Reporting Civil Rights*, Vol. 1, *American Journalism, 1941–1963*. New York: Library of America, 2003: 777–94.

King, Mary. *Freedom Song: A Personal Story of the 1960s Civil Rights Movement*. New York: William Morrow, 1987.

Lawrence, Curtis. "Saving Memories of Black Chicago." *Chicago Sun Times*, October 27, 2003.

Lortie, Daniel. Interviewed by R. B. McKersie. June 2004.

Marshall, Ray. *The Negro and Organized Labor*. New York: John Wiley, 1965.

———. "Unions and the Negro Community." *Industrial and Labor Relations Review* 17 (1964): 179–202.

Massoni, Gary. Interviewed by R. B. McKersie. September 2004.

McAdam, Doug. *Freedom Summer*. New York: Oxford University Press, 1988.

McKersie, Robert B. *Minority Employment Patterns in an Urban Labor Market: The Chicago Experience*. Washington, DC: EEOC, 1969.

———. "Vitalize Black Enterprise." *Harvard Business Review* (September–October 1968): 88–99.

McKersie, Robert B., and Montague Brown. "Nonprofessional Hospital Workers and a Union Organizing Drive." *Quarterly Journal of Economics* 77 (1963): 372–404.

Mendelsohn, Jack. Interviewed by R. B. McKersie. June 2008.

Mississippi Power & Light Co. v. Mississippi ex rel. Moore, 487 U.S. 354, No. 86–1970 1988.

Morris, Calvin. Interviewed by R. B. McKersie. May 2004.

One America in the 21st Century: Forging a New Future. Final Report, Presidential Commission on Race Relations. Washington, DC: General Accounting Office, September 18, 1998.

Patner, Irene. Interviewed by R. B. McKersie. May 2004.

Perkins, Donald S. Interviewed by R. B. McKersie. July 2003.

Pfeffer, Paula F. *A. Philip Randolph, Pioneer of the Civil Rights Movement*. Baton Rouge: Louisiana State University Press, 1990.

Pitcher, Sara. Interviewed by R. B. McKersie. July 2003.

Poinsett, Alex. *Black Power: Gary Style*. Chicago: Johnson Publishing, 1970.

———. *Walking with Presidents: Louis Martin and the Rise of Black Political Power*. Lanham, MD: Rowman & Littlefield, 2000.

Poinsett, Norma. Interviewed by R. B. McKersie. October 2007.

Ralph, James R., Jr. *Northern Protests: Martin Luther King Jr., Chicago, and the Civil Rights Movement*. Cambridge, MA: Harvard University Press, 1993.

Reitzes, Donald C., and Dietrich C. Reitzes. *The Alinsky Legacy: Alive and Kicking*. Greenwich, CT: JAI Press, 1987.

Reynolds, Barbara. *Jesse Jackson: America's David*. JFJ Associates, 1985.

Rice, Jon. "The World of the Illinois Panthers." In Theoharis and Woodard, 41–64.

Roberts, Lillian. Interviewed by R. B. McKersie. May 2009.

Royko, Mike. *Boss: Richard J. Daley of Chicago*. Boston: Dutton, 1971.

Schein, Edgar. *Helping: How to Offer, Give, and Receive Help*. San Francisco: Berrett-Koehler Publications, 2009.

Sethi, S. Prakash. *Business Corporations and the Black Man.* Scranton, PA: Chandler Press, 1970.

Strauss, George, and Sidney Ingerman. "Public Policy and Discrimination in Apprenticeship." *Hastings Law Journal* 16 (February 1965): 285–331.

Strickland, Arvarh E. *History of the Chicago Urban League.* Columbia: University of Missouri Press, 2001.

Sugrue, Thomas. *Sweet Land of Liberty: The Forgotten Struggle for Civil Rights in the North.* New York: Random House, 2008.

Taylor, David P., and Edwin C. Berry, *The Unskilled Negro Worker in the Chicago Labor Market.* Chicago: Urban League, 1963.

Theoharis, Jeanne, and Komozi Woodard, eds. *Freedom North: Black Freedom Struggles outside the South, 1940–1980.* New York: Palgrave Macmillan, 2003.

Thompson, Daniel. *The Negro Leadership Class.* Englewood Cliffs, NJ: Prentice Hall, 1963.

Timmerman, Ken. *Shakedown: Exposing the Real Jesse Jackson.* Washington, DC: Regnery Publishing, 2002.

Walton, Richard E., and Robert B. McKersie. *A Behavioral Theory of Labor Negotiations.* New York: McGraw Hill, 1965. Reprinted, Ithaca, NY: ILR Press, 1993.

Walton, Richard E., Robert B. McKersie, and Joel E. Cutcher-Gershenfeld. *Strategic Negotiations.* Boston: Harvard Business School Press, 1994.

Weaver, Robert C. *Negro Labor: A National Problem.* New York: Harcourt Brace, 1946.

Weems, Robert, and Lewis Randolph. "The Ideological Origins of Richard M. Nixon's 'Black Capitalism Initiative.'" *Review of Black Political Economy* 29 (June 2001): 49–61.

———. "The National Response to Richard M. Nixon's Black Capitalism Initiative: The Success of Domestic Detente." *Journal of Black Studies* 32 (2001): 66–83.

Willis, Benjamin C. Interview on school segregation, by R. Bruce McPherson. *Phi Delta Kappan* 48, no. 1 (September 1966): 11–15.

Wilson, William J. *The Truly Disadvantaged: The Inner City, the Underclass, and Public Policy.* Chicago: University of Chicago Press, 1987.

Woodlawn Organization. *Woodlawn's Model Cities Plan.* Northbrook, IL: Whitehall, 1970.

Yoxall, George. Interviewed by R. B. McKersie. February 2001, August 2002.

Index

ABA. *See* American Bar Association
Abernathy, Ralph, xiv, 166
academic freedom, 43
activist(s), xii–xix, xxi–xxiv, 6, 15,
36, 39, 43, 47, 49, 59–60, 70, 123,
178, 211; approach, 111; and Dick
Gregory, 115; opposition, 73
Adult Discussion Group, xv–xvi, 8,
10, 13–15, 18, 59, 88, 136, 199
affirmative action, 195, 197, 213, 215
AFSCME. *See* American Federation
of State, County, and Municipal
Employees
Alinsky, Saul, xiv, 44, 47–48
American Bar Association (ABA), 21,
23–26, 45–46, 111, 179, 221, 223
American Federation of State,
County, and Municipal Employees
(AFSCME), 3, 5
Anderson, Alan B., xii, xxi, 56, 64,
184, 233, 235–36, 238–40
Anderson, Doug, 89
apprenticeship program, 4, 19–20, 27,
144, 156
Ashenhurst, Julie, 96, 100
Attunement Committee, 160–67, 189,
203

BAC (Black Affairs Council), 187
backlash: faculty, 78, business, 79
Bacon, Warren, 64, 94, 229

banks, 88, 158, 189; black-owned, 165;
white-owned, 156, 190
Baron, Harold M., 204, 240–41
BAWA (Black and White Action),
187, 221
Bell, Derrick, 218
Bell & Howell, 33–34, 37–39, 41
Benedict, Donald, xiv, 159, 235, 239
Berry, Edwin C. (Bill), 91–92, 151;
and black MBA program, 76; and
CCCO, 151; leadership style of, 177,
200; and Motorola, 27; and school
boycotts, 58
Biondi, Martha, xxi, 236, 239–40
Birmingham Jail, 14, 59
Black, Justice Hugo, 127, 238
Black, Timuel (Tim), vii, xvi, 24–46,
49, 69–72, 94, 99–100, 120, 144,
181, 237, 241; Adult Discussion
Group, 8; alderman campaign, 61;
Charles Gray confirmation, 38; and
Jeff Fort, 171–72; Kenwood rally,
111; leadership style, xxiii, 17–21, 61,
72, 201–2; March on Washington,
34; Motorola, 27, 33, 35; NALC, 17;
Washburne Project, 20; Writing
Project, 202
Black Affairs Council (BAC), 187
black aldermen, 61, 112, 200
Black and White Action (BAWA),
187, 221

247

Robert B. McKersie is a professor emeritus at the MIT Sloan School of Management. Previously he served as dean of the New York State School of Industrial and Labor Relations at Cornell University and, prior to that, during the 1960s, was a member of the faculty of the Graduate School of Business of the University of Chicago. The recipient of awards for his scholarship in the fields of industrial relations and negotiations, he continues to teach at MIT and Harvard, using literature as a basis for exploring the subject of leadership.